The
Making
and
Un-making
of
a
Marine

Bob
Thanks for the support
Peace / semper Fi
Jerry

The Making and Un-Making of A Marine is a superbly written, engaging book. A must read for anyone who has been to any war, loved someone who has been to war and even those of us who have never been to war. Winters' story is full of anger, grief, rage, hope and healing. I couldn't put it down.

John Lee
Author of *The Flying Boy, Growing Yourself Back Up*, and *THE MISSING PEACE: Solving The Anger Problem For Alcoholics/Addicts and Those Who Love Them*

The Making and Un-making of a Marine would be a must read if it was just about the deeply personal pathways a young man takes to war. But Larry Winters also brings us home and en route shows us an invaluable and compelling roadmap to redemption.

Steven Lewis
Author of *Zen and the Art of Fatherhood, The ABCs of Real Family Values, The Complete Guide for the Anxious Groom, Fear and Loathing of Boca Raton: A Hippies Guide to the Second Sixties*

Many go. Not as many return. Those who return are changed, often wounded in soul as well as in body. How does one heal from the wounds of war? An eternal question, from Troy to Baghdad, via Gettysburg, Flanders, Iwo Jima, and Pleiku. Here is one man's heart-rending account of his journey out and back, about the making and unmaking of a Marine.

Peter Pitzele Ph.D.
Author of *Our Fathers' Wells: A personal encounter with the myths of Genesis.*
(Harper 1997)

The Making and Un-making of a Marine

One Man's Struggle for Forgiveness

By

Lawrence J. Winters

Millrock Writers Collective
PO Box 563
New Paltz, New York 12561-0563

Millrock Writers Collective
PO Box 563
New Paltz, New York 12561-0563
http://www.milrockwriters.com

Cover Design by Jeff Vreeland

ISBN-13: 978-0-9792293-0-5

ISBN-10: 0-9792293-0-8

Library of Congress Control Number: 2007922108

Printed in the United States of America

This book is dedicated
to my son Jamie,
no stranger to war.

Appreciation

I want to thank the many who have supported me during the writing of this book. First, there are my parents. Although as you read this you may not believe they were supportive, I have grown to appreciate that, as the phrase goes, "they did the best they could." Next on the list is Steven Lewis who has been my writing mentor for years. Without his gentle and consistent support, this book would have lain fallow somewhere in my depths. There is also the writing group of which I have been a member for almost ten years. There have been various members over those years, but currently we have a special group: Tom Nolan, Stephanie Padovani, Mihai Grunfeld, Helise Winters, Steve Lewis, Dahlia Bartz Cabe and Tracy Leavitt. All of these folks have supported, critiqued, cajoled, and loved me into finishing this work. I must mention my good friend Peter who has read many renditions and been a spiritual brother to me. I thank my best friend, Dave Deyo, who signed up with me: you remain a steadfast friend who understands like no one else.

Others who have been invaluable are: Tom Davison, a fellow Marine whose insights and friendship over the years have guided me. Sam Klagsbrun, my boss, my friend, and my mentor and his most generous act of giving me the money that allowed me to go back to Vietnam in 1994. Barbara Carroll, who has copy-edited this work with careful and loving attention. Jeff Vreeland, whose care, attention and artistry has gone into making the cover, and whose support at more than ten years of lunches has been invaluable. My brothers, Paul (Pete) and John, as well as my sister Sharon, who have been along for the ride in our family. No one but you know the terror and joy of that ride.

I also want to thank Ron Robbins, a past therapist who shared his love with me. There is my current therapist, Richard Bachrach, who from his mountain in Woodstock has shown me new vistas in myself. Dan Jones, another loving man, who led the men's retreat in Las Vegas, NM. John Lee, a friend, author and teacher whose support was invaluable.

There is a long list of friends whose support and comments have fed me over the years: Jean Tupper, Abbe Ravins, Larry Summer, JoAnne Denne, Bruce DuBois, Bobbie McKenna, Susan Pitzele—who came up with the title of the book—and Sandy Mills.

I thank my stepdaughter, Elizabeth Benjamin, for her love and support though out this process. Thank you, Liz, for the newspaper article about me when you first started in journalism. And I thank you for your continued inquisitiveness about my experiences in the War without being judgmental.

I thank my son Jamie for his existence, and I dedicate this book to you. I only hope this manual of my struggle can be of help.

Finally, my wife, friend and teacher, Helise Winters, who has, above all else, tolerated my obsession with this book. She has allowed me the room to create it, as well as provided the loving arms to comfort me for what it has stirred up. Without her as my anchor--and my love-- these words would have spun out into a cosmic nowhere. I thank her from my heart.

Some names in this book have been changed, and some names I have been unable to remember.

Men:
When a ship is sinking and they lower the lifeboats
And hand out the life jackets, the men keep on their coats
The women and the children are the ones who must go first
And the men who try to save their skins are cowards and are cursed

Every man's a captain, men know how to drown
Man the lifeboats if there's room, otherwise go down

And it's the same when there's a war on: it's the men who go to fight
Women and children are civilians, when they're killed it's not right
Men kill men in uniform, it's the way war goes
When they run they're cowards, when they stay they are heroes

Every man's a general, men go off to war
The battlefield's a man's world, cannon fodder's what they're for

It's the men who have the power, it's the men who have the might
And the world's a place of horror because each man thinks he's right
A man's home is his castle so the family let him in
But what's important in that kingdom is the women and the children

A husband and a father, every man's a king
But he's really just a drone, gathers no honey, has no sting
Have pity on the general, the king, and the captain
They know they're expendable, after all they're men

Prologue

I tell the following story about my father's family to illustrate the genesis of one Marine. The story is constructed of fragments that I gathered from my childhood. I never met my grandparents and what I learned came from my uncle Hub and Dad. Neither of them ever told the entire story. My imagination supplied the connective tissue between the facts.

No Legs to Stand On

Alford Winters leaned back in his lion chair, the horsehair cushion squeaking under his weight. He slurped his heavily sweetened coffee, savoring what he knew would be the only quiet of his day. Soon he'd go to the train yard where the hulking engines and railroad cars clanked and rumbled. Sometimes he'd waken at night because the piercing squeals of steel against steel crept into his dreams.

Outside a breeze made the maple branches tick against the window like an out of control clock stealing seconds from his morning ritual. Orange light was brightening the east windows. Fine lines of frost crept like a spider web over the glass. "Two, three, four, five," he counted out loud the chimes of his repeater pocket watch. Only a half hour left for him to put on his work-boots and jacket and walk the half-mile to the train yard.

His wife Maude was still asleep, so he moved deliberately around the kitchen so as not to wake her. This was the first morning she wasn't awake before him. Since Elizabeth's difficult birth and then death before she was a month old, Maude had not really slept more than a few hours a day, although she'd not get out of bed.

Alford turned the crank on the cook stove to settle the ashes, then lifted the steel lid and placed a thick piece of oak in the firebox, turning down the damper as low as he dared. He knew Maude wouldn't be getting out of bed and it would be cold in the house when the kids came home from school. He'd made several attempts to get her out of bed but she'd refused even talk to him. She just stared at the wall.

Alford knew Hub, his oldest son, would make little John-Donald breakfast and get him off to school once he finished his chores of feeding the chickens and milking the Guernsey. Hub was 16 and little John-Donald was six. Hub had told Alford that yesterday he'd picked his little brother up and carried him out of the house because he wouldn't leave his mother alone. In Alford's mind he could see little John-Donald holding his mother's housedress and sucking his thumb.

Alford was at a loss about what to do for Maude, so he did what he knew best, he chopped wood and fed the animals. He was filled with guilt because he'd insisted the wailing baby be put out in the hallway. For three weeks Elizabeth screamed drawing her little knees to her chest. Her wailing kept them all on edge and awake at night. Alford needed his sleep desperately so he begged Maude to take the child out of their bedroom and put her in the hallway. She had refused until he told her he couldn't work safely around the big trains if he didn't have some rest. Maude grudgingly agreed to do it for one night. That night Elizabeth died.

Alford lowered his foot into his stiff new work boots. He hooked his fingers through the laces pulling them loose so his foot could slip in. These new boots cost a week's wages at Wager's store. He couldn't afford them. The doctor's bill for Maude and Elizabeth had taken all their savings. He had no choice but to buy the boots on credit.

Alford closed the front door softly and stepped out on to Route 32 and turned right. Walking towards the train yard he noticed the lights were on in the two-story building overlooking the yard. The first freight wasn't in until 6 a.m.; he had enough time to go upstairs and warm his hands over the barrel stove. Once warm, he'd walk the length of the incoming train to check that each car was properly attached, that branches or debris hadn't fouled the couplers. He picked up the clipboard and checked the cars he needed to chalk mark so they could be disconnected and pulled on to sidetracks.

The 6:00 a.m. came and went. Now Alford was working with the Albany engineer connecting empty cars that would be leaving for Albany at 9:05 a.m. Two cars were left to hook-up when Alford placed his clipboard on the jaws of the coupler. A slight vibration caused the clipboard to slip off. As he lunged to catch it, his boot wedged between two railroad ties. Snapping his head up he gauged the distance of the car rolling toward him: it was about ten feet away. He shifted his weight to his free leg and pulled with all his strength, bending and jumping, trying to dislodge it. It didn't budge. Grabbing his thigh with his hands he yanked his leg desperately. He twisted it hard and heard his ankle snap, but the new boot stayed stuck. The connecting jaws were just a few feet away. No time to unlace the boot. At first it was a soft nudge. Then he was pinned between the couplers. The steel jaws squeezed. He let out a horrific scream as he watched both of his legs get pinched off.

A man in the caboose car heard Alford's screams and ran to him. Alford was losing consciousness fast. The caboose man and the engineer took off their belts and wrapped tourniquets around each of Alford's thighs.

Two weeks later, Alford opened his eyes in Poughkeepsie's Saint Francis Hospital. Maude was sitting at his bedside wringing a handkerchief in her hands. She was looking out the window when Alford touched her. She jerked, making a startled yelp.

"Alford, good God, you're back," she said, eyes darting at the doorway. "I'll be right back sweetheart. I have to let the nurse know you're back."

Alford looked at the flat sheets below his knees. Maude heard him from the hallway. "My legs! My God, where are my legs?"

For the Winters family 1935 seemed like the year the gray sky got caught in the treetops and the wind was never strong enough to clear them away. Hub fed the chickens, milked the cow, shoveled her stall and weeded the garden. Sometimes John-Donald would carry in firewood Hub had split. Since Alford couldn't work, Hub started an egg route after school. He pushed a cart around to neighbors selling their extra eggs. After Alford's accident he convinced his Mom to let him hatch some eggs to make the flock larger. On the weekends Hub worked for Mr. Franklin splitting wood, or worked out on the Coy Farm bringing in hay or corn. John-Donald was left to pick up Hub's chores.

Months passed, but Alford still could not get out of bed. Maude was so depressed from the loss of Elizabeth and her husband's accident that it was a struggle taking care of Alford. She moped around, never changing out of her bathrobe.

Hub was angry. If John-Donald hadn't finished his chores he'd scream at him, slap him if no one was around to see. He complained to Maude about John-Donald, but it seemed to get stuck in his mother's thick gaze. Hub had turned 17, and the hair on his chest stuck out the top of his tee shirt. In the morning John-Donald sometimes watched him shave before they went to school.

One day in the driveway on their way to school Hub growled, "Hey Momma's boy. If you don't stop running to her every time I tell you to do something, I'm gonna make you pay, you little shit. I'm sick of doing all the Goddamn work, you lazy brat. While you're brushing her hair a hundred strokes every night, I'm out there hauling in a hundred sticks of firewood to keep your little ass warm." Hub pushed at John-Donald's shoulder.

John-Donald spun away, looking down and scuffing his feet in the dirt. Alford kept telling Maude she needed to make little John-Donald help out more. "It's weighing on Hub. He's doing all the chores and he's the only one bringing in any money."

"You get five-dollars a week from the railroad," Maude said, squeezing the bridge of her nose with her thumb and forefinger.

"What the Hell's that got to do with anything, Alford said under his breath as he shrugged his shoulders.

When Alford had first come home from the hospital he couldn't get out of bed to go to the bathroom; Maude would put a dishpan under him. Now, five months later, he was able to lift himself with his arms and slide to the edge of the bed where he could lower himself onto a chair. Hub had fastened the wheels off John-Donald's wagon to the chair legs so Maude could roll him to the toilet.

A year passed, and gray sky was still caught in the trees. Alford had gotten a pair of wooden legs that fastened to his thighs with leather straps. John-Donald would help him to get the legs tied on. When Alford walked it sounded like someone was knocking at the door.

As soon as Maude saw Alford was able to take care of himself, she announced she was taking a trip to see her mother's older sister, Catherine, in New York City. Catherine was a clairvoyant, born with a veil around her. She explained the Irish used the word caul. Maude said that people born in a caul could see into the future, predict events. She claimed that Catherine could do this, telling Alford, "I got to know what's in front of us."

Alford was not happy she was going, but kept his mouth shut because she was at least speaking.

"The caul's like a net over the child's head and face. It's always brought her good luck," Maude continued, closing the lid of the valise. "It allows her to see into other worlds--I mean read the future. No one paid much attention until she was 16 when she dreamt of men on horses fighting. A few months later the Spanish American War broke out. That's when people started listening to her dreams; some of them even paid her."

Alford turned his head and rolled his eyes so she couldn't see. He'd heard all this before and knew there was no use in saying anything. It happened that a letter from Catherine had arrived a week after Alford's accident. In it Catherine had told Maude to keep Alford home from work because she'd dreamt of something bad happening.

Maude left on the train that afternoon. She told Hub before she left to keep an eye on his Dad and brother for her.

Hub had graduated high school three weeks before his mother left on her trip. He'd gotten a job in Poughkeepsie at the Delaval plant that made rubber bushings and gaskets. Hub's job was to fill bins from the assembly line and stack them in a railroad car. Delaval gave him as much overtime as he wanted. This left John-Donald and Alford with all the chores.

Alford's arms had grown strong. His wooden legs were still awkward and the skin was sore where the bone met the wood so he didn't use them often. John-Donald also had grown stronger and could now lift his dad and carry him.

"John-Donald, get me that sheepskin pad and carry me out to the wood pile."

John-Donald got the pad from the closet and the thick leather strap. Alford looped the strap under his arms. "Ok son, let her go."

John-Donald hoisted the strap over his own head and positioned it across the front of his shoulders. "OK, Dad, on the count of three."

Back to back, John-Donald lifted his father, bending under his weight as he staggered the 50 yards out to the woodpile. John-Donald tossed a sheepskin on the snow. "That's good, right there son, lower me down. Then go to the wood shed and get me the ax and the file. I want to put an edge on it before I get started."

Alford sat on the sheepskin at the edge of the woodpile. He wheeled the ax, boxing the logs apart. They flew from his ax head like the wings of geese. When he couldn't reach any more logs, he called to John-Donald to come out and carry him back to the house. "You're my legs, son," he said as John-Donald lifted him.

Hub stuffed his hands in his pockets as he waited for his mother's train to come in. He was surprised she'd even taken the train after his father's accident. He looked at the used 1923 Model T Ford he'd just bought and couldn't wait to surprise her. The train pulled in and he watched the few people getting off. He didn't recognize his mother at first, until he saw her beat-up leather suitcase. She had a black scarf wrapped around her head. He walked to meet her.

"Mom, what's the matter?"

Maude lifted her swollen face. "Nothing, Hub. Aunt Catherine sends her love. She dreamt about you, said you're going to do real good in your new job."

"Damn right. I already am. You just wait and see, Ma."

Taking his mother's arm, Hub walked her to his black coupe. Opening the door he asked, "How do you like my new car, Ma? I only got it two days ago. Get in. I'll give you a ride home. I already gave Daddy a ride to Wallkill yesterday."

"I think I'd better walk, Hub."

"Come on Ma. Let me take you for a ride."

Maude lowered her head and stepped away from the open door. "You take my bag. I'll meet you at the house. I need the air."

Hub slammed the door.

Maude faced him, but said nothing. She turned and shuffled in the loose stones towards the house.

Weeks fell into months into years.

In the two years since Maude had visited Catherine, her silence had grown thick. Her cheeks were puffy and pallid; her dull blue eyes floated above crescents of purple. Ceaselessly she twisted her dark brown hair around her finger.

The less Hub was around, the more questions John-Donald asked his father. Questions like "What's the matter with Mom?"

Alford shrugged as he hobbled on his stumps to the back door, leaving John-Donald to dogpaddle in the ever-deepening pool of silence.

During dinner one night John-Donald asked, "Dad, why don't your put on your wooden legs anymore?"

Alford's face turned red as he burst out, "He took my legs!" pointing his forefinger high up the wall as if he were jabbing it into a huge man's chest. Then, his voice thickening, "Wood's for splitting and burning, not walking on."

One Sunday in December, when John-Donald entered Wager's store he saw three men sitting at the counter. Tim Wager reached up and turned on the radio so loud the announcer's booming baritone shook the plate glass windows.

"The Japanese have attacked Pearl Harbor Hawaii by air, President Roosevelt has just announced. The attack also was made on all naval and military activities on the principal island of Oahu. We take you now to Washington. The details are not available. They will be in a few minutes. The White House is now giving out its statement. The attack apparently was made on all naval and military activities on the principal island of Oahu…"

John-Donald stood with a paper bag in his arms staring at the radio. After a while Tim turned off the radio.

"What you got under your arm boy?" Tim Wager made a mocking punch at John-Donald's shoulder. "It's a dark day for America. How old are you John-Donald?"

"Fourteen, Mr. Wager."

"Could be you're gonna have to kill Japs"

"If I got to go, I'll go," John-Donald said, looking in the mirror behind the counter to see if furrowing his forehead like his father made him look more serious.

"What do you need, John-Donald?"

Reaching into the brown paper sack, he pulled out his father's work boots and sat them on the counter. "Dad was wondering if you might take the boots back. He said they're just like new. He only had them on once."

Tim Wager picked up the boots and looked down into them.

"It's been a few years," he said softly. "Why not, they're a popular size. I should be able to sell them again. Listening to what we just heard on that radio, I bet lots of men are going to be wearing combat boots." Tim pulled out ten bucks from the register and handed it to John-Donald. "Tell your old man I was asking for him. He leave the house anymore?"

"He's getting around a lot better. He's had the shoemaker make him thick sheepskin pads that he laces to his stumps. Store's still a little too far, though. Today Hub took him and Mom over to Poughkeepsie. Dad's getting a check up and so is Mom."

After the trip to the doctor's, Maude's silence deepened into a tar thick depression. John-Donald was the only one she'd respond to, and the best he'd get was a faint smile when he came home from school. He'd often find her staring out the window, or slumped in the living room chair, her head in her hands. Her shaking legs made the dinner table vibrate. She'd try to steady them with her hands, but it didn't help.

Alford took Hub's cart to the train station where he sold vegetables and eggs to folks getting off the train. John-Donald knew it was charity: when they saw Alford's stumps, they had to buy his produce. He hated when his father asked him to work the cart on weekends. He'd stand there all day for the few people that scrambled off at the Modena train stop. The small number of coins he put in his father's hand at the end of the day didn't make him feel any better. Hub would give his father a roll of bills. Sometimes Alford tried to hand it back, but Hub said, "Take it. You need it, Dad."

Steam lifted off a large bowl of boiled potatoes; a loaf of bread lay on the cutting board. The black kettle sat on the stove with an aroma of cooking meat wafting from it. Green beans were piled in a cut glass bowl. Maude's hair was tied back away from her face. She wore an ironed flower print dress. She heard tires on the stones and turned to look out the window. Hub took the three front steps with one bound but didn't come in. He stayed on the porch until Maude grew impatient and went to the door. Hub sat on the rail smoking a pipe.

"Hub, come on in. I got dinner on the table."

Hub turned. "You made dinner?"

"I was feeling better today so I put something together. Your father's washing up and I can see John-Donald coming up the road. Please come in."

No one could take their eyes off Maude as she spooned the food onto their plates. She was radiant. Her white skin glowed. "Alford, would you please say grace," Maude asked.

Eyes wide, Alford folded his thick hands in front of his face and bowed his head.

"God, let us thank you for this bountiful meal you have provided us. Thank you for allowing our family to gather again in your presence. God, thank you for bringing Maude through these hard times. From my heart I am grateful that you have returned her to us. Amen."

When he lifted his head, he saw tears in the corners of Maude's eyes. Nodding, he smiled at her and forked a slice of pot-roast onto his plate. He couldn't remember the last time Maude had cooked anything other than oatmeal for John-Donald's breakfast. When John-Donald got up to get more gravy off the stove, he put his hand on his mother's shoulder. Maude touched his fingers.

"Hub, I have to go to the doctor's next Wednesday. Is there any way you could drive me?" Maude asked.

Hub looked up from his plate. "Yeah Ma, they'll let me off anytime I want. I got so much sick time coming, the boss said that I could take a month off and still get paid."

Steam rose from the teakettle sitting on the woodstove. "I'll do the dishes," John-Donald said.

"I'll dry," said Maude, reaching for her apron.

Two weeks later when John-Donald stepped into the schoolyard, he knew it was going to rain before he'd make it home. Dirty white clouds piled up like bed linen tossed into a corner. The first drops landed on his head, making a snapping sound like breaking the ends off green beans. The storm over the Mohonk Mountain looked like smoke from a locomotive. A few yards from the house he heard the sound of thunder but there was no lightening. A steady rain was at his heels as he leaped the steps and burst into the front door. There on the living room floor laid the shotgun. Stepping over it, he wondered why his father left it there. Had he been shooting a woodchuck in the garden? Another step and he saw her feet in the doorway to the kitchen. Trying to back-peddle, a rolling feeling rushed up from his stomach. The next step carved a picture of horror into his brain.

"Momma, no! Momma! No! No! No!"

PART I

Chapter 1

Setting of the Jaw

I watched my father filing the nail of his right index finger into a small round nub. He always tells a story about when he was 12 and fell off the back of a tractor driven by his older brother, Hub. The tractor was pulling a hay rake. Dad rolled to miss the rake but it caught his right hand under one of the tines, scraping off his fingertip. The tine also bit into his right knee, leaving a star-shaped scar. He said he was lucky the fingertip grew back. The nail was thick and couldn't be cut with a clipper, so he used a mechanic's file to plane it smooth.

"I don't want it to look like a claw," Dad said, blowing away the nail dust.

I was six in the spring of 1954. Sun shone through the kitchen windows; the leaf shadows of the large maples danced on the gray Formica kitchen table. I shoveled in Rice Krispies from a bowl my Mom had put in front of me. Draping a diaper over her shoulder she said, "I have to go and feed the baby." My brother John was crying in a crib in the living room. "If Pete comes down, tell him there's a bowl of cereal on the table for him." Pete was three years old.

"OK, Ma," I said, spooning on more sugar and listening for Dad's footsteps on the stairs. I knew if I didn't finish before he came down he'd put me to work. At six I already understood the difference between work and play. If he found me sitting at the table he'd make me go get something he needed, tools or nails, things I didn't know the names of.

Mom's Phillips radio was playing on top of the refrigerator. I listened to the deep voice of the newsman for WGHQ: "The New York State Thruway has just been completed from Newburgh to Harriman, a stretch of 15 miles. Work has started on the next leg, which will be from Harriman to Hillburn, 14 miles. The completion of this portion of the superhighway is scheduled for May 27, 1955. The final destination is the

Bronx, hopefully completed by August 31, 1956. At the finishing point what has been called the Main Street of New York will be a length of 426-miles. Joseph C. Ingraham of The New York Times said, 'The 600 million dollar trunk line will be the longest toll highway in the world.'"

Once when Dad was driving us out to Ohioville to get pizza at Pantoni's, he pointed to the bulldozers and trucks. "That, my boy, is going to be one Hell of a highway when it's done."

"What's the route number?" I asked.

"They're calling it the New York State Race Way," he said, cupping his chin in his hand.

"Stop telling him stuff like that," Mom said.

"It's going to be called the New York State Thruway, and we're going to have to pay to ride on it," Mom said.

"It's gonna be the road that will take you outta here someday, son," Dad said looking sideways at Mom.

I knew Dad would just come outside and find me anyway so I poured more Rice Krispies in my bowl and got the milk bottle from the refrigerator. While stuffing in more cereal I wondered what Dad was going to have us do today. Yesterday I picked rocks from the garden. Each time I filled the wheelbarrow I had to go find him to come and dump it. Two years ago we'd moved to this old two-story white frame house three miles out of New Paltz on DuBois Rd. Dad said, "There's enough work here for a lifetime. Not only mine, but my three sons as well."

There were three other houses and a farm on our mile and a half dirt road. Our house was in the middle. My best friend Bruce DuBois lived a quarter mile away.

My father spent most of his free time working on our house. During the day he worked at Central Hudson, the local electric company. He worked when he got home from work and worked on weekends. I remember once when he came in for lunch saying to Mom, "I've had to hack this house out of a jungle of overgrowth. That old man who owned this place before us just let it go to Hell."

4

Dad had an old gas-powered bulldozer he used to clear the land. When he sat on the ripped horsehair seat of that dozer and pulled back on the throttle, fire shot out of the straight pipe that poked up from the red metal hood. It sounded like firecrackers going off. I'd put my hands over my ears and watch the wind carry the belch of black smoke out into the trees. One day Dad said he needed my help to pull out the old apple tree stumps that filled the front yard. He screamed over the roar of the dozer, "Walk the cable back so I don't run over it." I had to loop the heavy steel cable around the stumps while Dad backed the dozer up. "Keep that cable tight so I don't run over it," he yelled. He didn't want it to get caught up in the dozer tracks. That happened once and it took him a whole day of swearing to hacksaw it out.

The heavy steel hook bumped my knees, and my hands kept slipping around inside the huge leatherwork gloves he made me wear. Little needle burrs were sticking out of the cable from when the dozer pulled so hard on the stumps the cable started to break.

"Double loop this one," Dad hollered. "Slip the hook back over the cable, and get back away, and stay away! If that cable snaps, it'll cut your head off!"

Black smoke shot up over Dad's head, and the cable bit into the wood, strangling little droplets of sap out of the bark. The roar of the dozer slowed as it strained; muffled thuds came from the roots popping under the earth.

I'd finished my Rice Krispies before he came down, so I put my bowl in the sink and tiptoed out the back door. I felt the cool spring air on my face. A small red ball glowed in the wet grass. I picked it up and wiped the dew on my shirt. I threw it. It smacked against the sidewall of the back stoop. Reaching high, I caught it with one hand. Then the back door opened. Dad stepped out. "Don't go anywhere!" he ordered, pointing his nubby fingernail at me. I saw he was headed to the woodshed. A few minutes later he came out with a shovel and pick.

I kept bouncing the ball off the wall, seeing how close to the edge of the roof I could get. The back stoop had a flat roof. I knew if the ball went up there it was gone. I saw Dad coming across the driveway so I made my last throw. The ball went high over the lip of the roof and was gone. Lowering my face, I said, "I lost the ball."

Dad dumped the tools on the grass. "I told you a hundred times not to throw stuff up there!"

"I slipped."

"I'm sick of your Goddamn game. Get it yourself. I was watching you. You threw it up there on purpose!"

"How can I get up there?" I whined.

He turned and went back behind the woodshed. He came out grumbling with a wooden ladder over his shoulder. "You pain in the ass," he said, leaning the ladder against the side of the back stoop. "Go ahead, climb up."

I'd never climbed a ladder before. I squealed on the second rung, my knees shaking, but I kept going. When I got to the top I yelled, "Dad there's a ton of stuff up here."

"Pick it all up and throw it on the ground so it doesn't make the roof leak-- the stones, too."

I couldn't believe all the things I'd thrown up there: a baseball, yellow rubber ball, lots of rocks and a few toy soldiers. I thought all this stuff had disappeared forever. I filled my pockets with the good stuff and threw down the rest. I felt so big looking out over the lawn and garden.

After I picked everything up, I went to where the ladder was, but it was gone. With my toes at the edge of the roof I looked for Dad. He was gone. He was there a minute ago holding the bottom of the ladder.

"Daaaaaaaaaaad!"

No answer. I waited and heard only the rattle of dead leaves being swept by the wind across the garden.

"Dad, don't leave me! Please, Dad, come back! Please don't leave me!" I shrieked.

I started crying. I kept thinking that I'd never get down. Maybe I'd disappear like the rocks and balls I'd thrown up here. I'd once heard Dad say that the back stoop was 15 feet off the ground. It felt like I couldn't breathe, but I inched my toes over the edge of the roof. Closing my eyes, I leaped, screaming, "Dad! Dad!" as I fell. I landed on my feet but my knees buckled, slamming my rear end into the ground. I lay crumpled and sobbing. The back door flew open and Dad came running out screaming, "What the Hell is the matter with you? Why'd you jump?"

"You left me!" I said between sobs.

Rubbing my stomach I watched Dad's jaw tightening. Speaking through his teeth he said, "I was just playing a game. I was coming back." Looking down at his hands, he said, "Are you hurt?"

Nodding my head up and down I followed his eyes to the window where I saw my mother holding my brother John and staring at us. Lowering his voice he said, "Don't ever do anything crazy like this again."

His face was blurry though my tears as I searched, trying to understand what crazy thing I'd done.

"I was trying to teach you a lesson, son."

"I'm sorry, Daddy."

Chapter 2

Swallow It

Larry, go into the bedroom with your father."

"Why?" I asked.

"He's going to check out what's hurting you."

Dad closed the bedroom door. "Take off your pants."

Wrinkling my lips I stammered, "No."

"I'm not gonna hurt you. Pull down your pants and underwear; I want to see where you're hurting. Come on, stop it and act like a big boy. We might have to take you to the doctor's."

"I don't want to go to the doctor."

"Pull'em down! Now!"

Slowly I wiggled my pants and underwear down. Dad knelt and gently prodded me with his fingertips.

"I'm going to touch around your penis and testicles."

"What's that?"

"That's what your mother calls you're tinkle-bottle."

I squirmed when he poked my soft places.

"Now cough."

I tried to cough but I didn't have to, so I made a noise. "How come Pete and John don't have to do this?" I said pulling away.

"Pete's not complaining all the time that he hurts."

Not only was there Pete and John, Mom kept saying she had another kid in her belly. "You're gonna get another brother or maybe a sister after I come home from the hospital."

I liked things just fine before Pete and John came along; now there was going to be another one. Dad used to read to me at night. He stopped when my brother came along. I'd used to go to Grandma's with my mother before they were born; now she spent all her time taking care of them.

"Ouch, stop Daddy."

"Pull up your pants."

Back in the kitchen Dad said, "I think we need to take him to Dr. Cook again; he's sensitive down there. Damn good thing we got my Central Hudson medical insurance; it won't cost anything if he needs another operation. The one when he was three didn't cost us a cent and neither will this one."

"Another hernia? It's because he jumped off the roof isn't it?"

Dad didn't answer and walked outside.

That evening we ate boiled potatoes, canned green beans from a Mason jar, and big hunks of chuck steak. I flattened my potatoes with my fork and scooped a dollop of butter onto the ridges. Dad's eyes were looking over my head and he pointed. "Look, there's a rabbit in the yard!"

Turning, I searched the lawn for the rabbit. "Where, where is it?"

"You missed it. It ran just as you turned."

Mom looked at Dad funny. The butter was liquid on my potatoes, just the way I liked it. I put a big forkful in my mouth; the salty butter swirled on my tongue. I chewed slowly. All of a sudden my nose began to sting and my eyes started watering. I reached for my glass of milk and took several gulps.

Dad laughed. "What's the matter, something wrong with those potatoes?"

"Don, leave him alone; he'll be afraid to eat anything if you keep it up."

Dad had forked horseradish into my potatoes again. I swallowed. "It's all right, Ma. I like it." Mom reached for my plate, but I scooped the rest of the potatoes into my mouth before she could take it away.

"See, Helen, he likes it." Pointing his clawed finger at his chest, he said, "It'll put hair on your chest, son."

I looked at the tufts of dark hair springing out from the neckline of his striped tee shirt. I looked down the neck of my tee shirt at my bony chest; no hair was sprouting yet.

"You're going to have to feed him next week when I go to the hospital, so stop teasing him. And I've been thinking we'd better wait to take him to Dr. Cook until I get back home. If he's got to go the hospital for a hernia operation, we're going to have problems."

Dad rubbed his callused hand on my crew cut. "We're gonna be fine."

Mom rolled her eyes. "I asked my mother to take Pete and John for the week, so you'll only have him to take care of."

"We'll be fine."

"Mom, can I go to the hospital with you?"

"No, remember, I told you I am going to have a baby. If you have to go, it will be for surgery, like you had when you were three."

I crossed my legs remembering how much that hurt.

"You went to the hospital to fix a hernia, and you might have to go again because you jumped off the roof."

Dad cut in. "That's enough. It's time to get ready for bed. Go get washed up and put your pajamas on."

I wasn't sure what to do because Dad never told me to go to bed; it was always Mom.

I woke up looking at the white ceiling. Something wasn't right. There was a thick feather quilt on top of me, and the window was in the wrong place. I looked for the bedroom doorway. It wasn't there. I started getting scared that I'd never be able to get out of the room. Then I screamed, "Mommy!" I turned to a noise behind me and my grandmother came in the door.

"Grandma, why are you here?"

She sat on the bed and put her arm around me. "Your Mom's in the hospital having the baby. Daddy brought you last night when you were asleep." I smelled the starch of her pressed apron.

Sitting on my Grandpa's Morris chair I watched Grandma take the silver teakettle off the coal stove and fill the plastic dishpan with steaming water.

"How can you put your hands in that water, Grandma?"

The ash of her cigarette was growing longer and longer.

"I'm old. I've done a lot of dishes. You get used to hot water."

Standing on the chair I dipped my finger in the soapy water. "Ouch!" I squealed. "That's really hot."

That night Daddy picked me up after work. I got in the front seat with him.

"You got a little sister. Her name's Sharon Lee."

"When's Mommy coming home?"

"She'll be home in two days with your new sister."

Standing on the front seat with my hands on the dashboard, I watched the stores and cars flash by. We were almost home when Dad pulled into the parking lot of the Log Rail Inn.

"Why are we stopping, Daddy?"

"I'll be right back. I want to tell Bill we had a girl."

He rubbed my head and grabbed his cigarettes off the dashboard. He closed the door and stuck his head back in the window. "Don't get out of the car!"

The sun came in through the windshield, warming the brown seats. I looked at the numbers on the speedometer and said them out loud. "10, 20, 30, 40, 50, 60, 70, 80." I had seen Daddy go 70. Then I found the rearview mirror. Standing on the seat, I tried to look up my nose. I couldn't get the right angle and kept turning my head from side to side to see what was up there. Suddenly the car darkened. The sun had dropped behind the roof of the bar and the air started getting cooler. With both hands I tried to crank up the window, but I couldn't get it to go the right way.

I heard a car door open and looked up, hoping it was Daddy. It was a big man, bigger than Dad, standing by the car next to ours. I shrank down in the seat. The big man's shadow came into our car as he fumbled in his pocket for his keys. For a second I thought I'd ask him to go get Daddy, but I was too afraid, and he drove away.

It was almost dark when I crawled into the back seat. I tried sinking down into the curves of the soft material to keep warm; then I pushed my face into the seat and cried. Suddenly the car door opened and I heard Daddy say, "Oh shit, where the Hell is he?"

"Back here Dad," I said, standing up.

"Christ, I thought I'd lost you, Old Toppie."

Dad's voice sounded funny. He reached over the front seat, grabbed me under my arm, and cart wheeled me over the front seat, dragging my feet against the car ceiling. I flopped down next to him, and he started the car. His big elbow poked me in the chest when he shifted. When we got on the road he put his arm over my shoulder and reached under my butt and snuggled me into his side. I pushed my head into the folds of his work shirt hoping it would absorb my tears. He was softly singing, "You are my sunshine, my only sunshine..." Then he stopped. "Old Toppie, you're my sunshine," he murmured.

That night when he put me to bed I asked, "Am I still you're sunshine, Daddy?"

"You are, and you'll always be."

He hugged me goodnight. His breath smelled funny and his eyes were drooping.

Chapter 3

Building the Callus

My new sister Sharon came home, and Mom spent a lot of time with her. Dad took me to Dr. Cook who said I need a hernia operation, and it was set up. They took me to the hospital, and I was put under with ether, and I saw the Easter Bunny spinning at the end of a long tunnel. For weeks after the operation I could not sneeze or cough without lots of pain. For a little while Mom took care of Sharon and me. She'd sit on the couch feeding Sharon and talking to me. I really liked this.

When I got better, Dad and I started spending more time working. "It's our job to get the house in shape for your mother and the kids. You took that operation like a man, and now you're my right hand man," he told me.

That made me feel good, but I quickly found out that a right hand man never got a chance to play or go visit his friends; a right hand man worked and that was it. I'd loved when Dad called me his sunshine; he said it once when I was in the hospital, and now I wondered if he forgot.

All I remember of the years between eight and 12 was working on the house or garden with Dad. Every weekend we had a project. Now it was a new bathroom. We'd been using an outhouse for years.

We were framing in the bathroom walls when Dad said, "It's about time we lived like humans. Go down to the basement and get me some number ten nails."

I went down the stairs wondering if he meant we'd been living like animals. When I came back, he snatched the can out of my hands.

"You took forever. What are you pouting about? Your lip looks like it's dragging on the ground." Looking into the can, he barked, "I wanted ten-pennies; these are eights. I told you, it's the distance between your thumb and your little finger. Go! I need'em now!"

This time I ran down the stairs two at a time. Ever since Sharon came home Dad seemed to be angry. When I reached the basement I found the nail cans and stretched out my hand to see which nails fit. I thought I found the right one and raced back.

"Let me see them. You got it right. Now I want you to go check on what the dog's doing. Your mother told me that she's digging the dirt up around the foundation. Run over there and take a look and let me know what's going on. Maybe she's gonna drop her litter."

"What's a litter?"

"It's when a dog has puppies."

I ran to the side of the house hoping to see Tuffy with puppies. She was lying in a shallow hole but no puppies. I ran back and told Dad. "Bring her down to the cellar."

She'd never been in the house before.

"Daddy, why do you want her in the cellar?"

"So she stops digging the foundation."

Tuffy was a black cocker spaniel my uncle Hub gave us. He was a breeder of cocker spaniels and said he couldn't sell Tuffy because something was wrong with her. He never told us what. I'd been begging Mom and Dad for a dog, and they kept saying no until uncle Hub told us he had one. I remember him shielding his eyes with his hand as he looked out at our garden and pointed. She'll keep that groundhog from eating your vegetables."

Dad said he'd take her.

Tuffy and I became friends instantly. Mom said I was the only one old enough to feed her, so after dinner every night I cleaned the dishes into her food bowl. All we ever fed her was table scraps.

When I got to the side of the house Tuffy was curled up in the yellow dirt. "Hey girl, I'm going to take you in the house." I put my hand under her collar and pulled; she stiffened. "Come on girl." I reached my arm under her belly, lifting her out of the hole. Pulling her by the collar I grabbed the back-door-knob with my free hand and slid her into the kitchen, her toenails scraping the linoleum floor. I pulled her to the cellar door wondering why she could come in now but not on those freezing winter nights. Dad had said, "The damn dog belongs outside with the other animals."

I knew other people had dogs in their houses, even uncle Hub kept his dog Sally in his house.

Tuffy stiffened before the cellar door and I had to use both hands to pull her down the stairs.

Reaching for the light pull I turned on the single light bulb. I saw a burlap coal sack draped over the edge of the coal bin and shook the coal dust out of it and made a soft place for Tuffy to lie down. She nosed the bag, circling several times until she curled up in a black ball, shoving her wet nose under her hind leg. When I petted her she lifted her head and looked at me with runny brown eyes.

Back upstairs I told Mom I'd made a nest for Tuffy, and she said, "Leave the dog alone, and go wash the coal dust off your hand before dinner. Don't go down there again."

That night I went to bed praying to find puppies in the morning. I got up before everybody, stepping on the outside edges of the stairs so they wouldn't squeak. I tiptoed down the stairs and through the living room to the cellar.

"How you doing girl?" I whispered. Tuffy's little two-inch cut-off tail wagged when she saw me. Uncle Hub told me he'd cropped her tail off when she was a pup. He said, "Cocker spaniels need their tails cropped off to make them look right." Then he showed me on his finger how he did it. "You push the skin back and put their tail on a chopping block. Then you take a meet cleaver and plop, it's off." Pulling on his finger he showed me how you pull the skin back and tie it with a string. "It doesn't hurt the dog much."

I wondered if he would chop the tails off Tuffy's pups for us.

I found a piece of cardboard and used it to sit on the floor next to Tuffy. Resting my back against the stone foundation, I looked for a litter. The bulb was at the other end of the cellar so it was hard to see. I ran my hand over her back and down under her hot belly: nothing.

My eye caught something moving by the washing machine, and I remembered Mom said she'd seen a snake crawl down the floor drain. "I think it's just a garter snake," she'd said. I was afraid of snakes, so I got up and took the broken ax handle leaning in the corner.

My eyes had grown accustomed to the dark. Some light was now coming through the coal bin window. Lefevre's coal truck poked their silver coal chute through that window. It was my job to put the removable boards back in place so the coal wouldn't spill onto the cellar floor. I loved the rattling noise of coal coming down the chute; it sounded like a river.

Back upstairs Mom gave me breakfast. "There aren't any pups yet, Ma." I said spooning in cereal.

"After you feed her, don't go back in the cellar again. You can check tomorrow morning."

The next morning was Saturday so Dad was home. I checked again and there were still no puppies. Dad said he needed his right hand man to help him stack wood from a tree he'd cut behind the tool shed. In the afternoon, he let me walk over to my friend Bruce's house. I told Bruce that Tuffy was trying to have a litter. Bruce asked his mother, who was cooking in the kitchen, if they could have a pup.

"We've got a dog you don't take care of now; we're not getting another one!"

Bruce looked like he was going to cry.

Sunday morning before I reached the bottom of the cellar stairs, I heard squeals. Tuffy was stretched out on her side. In the dim light I saw six black and white, greasy fur balls rooting her belly. I carefully picked up a pup that was almost all black; its eyes were closed. It squeaked in my hands. Tuffy looked at me as if she were saying, "Be careful!" The pup's face was all wrinkled. He began to fuss so I put him back, remembering what Mom told me about baby birds: "Don't ever

16

touch a baby bird if it falls out of the nest. If you touch it, the mother will never come back to it. She'll smell your scent and leave it to die." Afraid the pup was going to die, I ran upstairs.

"Mom, Tuffy's had her pups! I touched one; is it going to die?"

"No, that's just for birds. Puppies like to be touched."

Jumping down the stairs in front of Mom I ran back to Tuffy. Mom bent over and picked up a pup. "Isn't he cute?" she said, rubbing noses with it. She talked baby talk like she did with my sister Sharon. "Hey there, little guy; how you doing?" She handed it back to me and said, "You know, we're not keeping them."

"What?"

"Remember our agreement, one dog."

"What are we going to do with them?"

"Ask your father; it's up to him."

During the next couple of weeks, I spent hours in the basement with Tuffy and her pups. She licked and nursed them and kept them cuddled into her for warmth. If a pup wandered too far, she'd retrieve it by picking it up by the scruff of its neck and carrying it back to the burlap sack. I took some flat rocks down into the basement and covered the hole where the snake came out. Sometimes I'd lay for hours next to Tuffy, cuddling close to her in the dark.

Dad never came down to see the pups. Once when he was in the cellar looking for sheetrock nails he yelled, "Larry, what's all that dog shit doing on the floor down here?"

I ran to the cellar. "What's the matter, Daddy?"

"Looks like you're not doing your job. It's starting to stink down here. You'd better clean it up. That means big and small dog shit. And take those rocks off the drain hole so water can get down it."

One night after I went to bed I overheard Mom and Dad talking in the kitchen. There was a heating grate in my bedroom floor directly above the kitchen and I lay down on it with my ear on the cold steel.

17

"We can't afford to keep the pups anymore. They'll need dog food soon; there aren't enough table scraps," Dad said.

"We could buy some dog food down at Agway," Mom said.

"It's expensive. I'm not working my ass off to pay for dog food."

There was a long silence. "If you wanted to get rid of them why didn't you do it when they were born? Larry's spent every day after school down in the cellar. It's going to break his heart."

"Listen, Helen, you think about that for a minute. Who let him go down there everyday? Anyway, when I was a kid my father had ways of taking care of this kind of thing. Leave it to me. I'll deal with it tomorrow."

"What you gonna do?"

"Never mind, I'll take care of it. We can't afford to feed'em."

"I'm telling you, the kid's going to be upset."

"He'll get over it. It's a fact of life. He's 11 years old; that's old enough. I was carrying my old man on my back when I was his age."

Crawling back into my bed, I curled up under the covers and wondered: What was he going to do? Maybe he was going to give the pups to the DuBois farm, up the road.

I was sleeping when I felt the bed shake. Dad stood over me jiggling the bunk bed and whispering, "Get your clothes on. Don't wake up your brothers. I need your help with something."

When I got downstairs he told me to eat my breakfast, and then walked out of the house. I saw him through the kitchen window headed towards the old barn. I got the box of cereal from the cupboard. Mom was standing at the sink doing the breakfast dishes.

"Morning, Ma. What's Dad doing?"

"I don't know. He told me that he was going down to the river and wanted you to go with him."

"Is he going fishing?"

18

"I don't know."

I poured a large bowl of cereal, added milk and reached for the sugar bowl. I quickly dumped on five spoonfuls of sugar and spread it out before she turned around. Dad was walking back from the barn with a burlap sack over his shoulder. I saw him toss it into the back of the truck.

He yelled through the screen door, "When you're done eating go get the empty cardboard box in the garage, take it to the basement and put the puppies in it. Then bring it to the truck."

"What's he going to do with the pups, Mom?"

"He didn't tell me."

She wiped her wet hands on the dishtowel, threw it against the toaster and walked out of the kitchen. I put my empty bowl in the sink and went to the garage. The hood of the truck was up when I walked by. Dad stuck his head out. "You get the puppies?"

"Not yet. I'm going for the box. What are we going to do, Dad?"

"I'll tell you when you get in the truck."

I opened the garage door and located the empty box. A dirty rag hung from the back of an old chair. I picked it up and folded it into the bottom. In the cellar, I lifted the pups one at a time, rubbing noses with each one before putting them in. Tuffy was making squealing sounds. I'd spent so many hours handling the pups they didn't make any noise when I lifted them into the box. I carried it up the cellar stairs and out into the back yard. Tuffy followed behind me.

The weight shifted as the pups moved inside. I sat it on the tailgate. Tuffy was running up and down the lawn smelling everything. She came over to me and cocked her head. She could hear her pups squealing. She cocked her head back and sniffed the air.

Dad slammed the hood and came around to the tailgate. He was wiping his hands on a rag. "Push the box onto the truck bed, close the tailgate, and get in!"

The 1937 hand-painted silver Dodge pick-up cranked over when Dad turned the key. I climbed onto the running boards, gripped above the door, and swung into the passenger seat. I liked riding in the old Dodge. It sat higher than a car, and I could look down into other people's cars. My stomach felt funny as we started down the driveway. Dad looked in the side mirror and stopped. I turned to see that Tuffy was following us. Dad stuck his head out the window and yelled, "Go home!" but she came right up to the truck and stood on her hind legs with her paws against the tailgate. Dad pounded his fist on the steering wheel. "Get out, and take her back to the house and put her down in the cellar. Make sure the door is closed. Then come right back; we need to get going."

Tuffy didn't want to leave the truck. I had to drag her most of the way back to the house. As soon as I closed the cellar door, she started barking. The truck door squealed its metal-to-metal noise when I opened it; Dad shifted into first gear and we started down DuBois Rd. I wondered if I should ask him again where we were going. I decided not to and started to cry. Wiping my tears on my jacket sleeve, I looked out the window, hoping the wind would dry my eyes. Then I blurted out, "What are we going to do with the pups?"

"It's going to cost a lot of money to feed those dogs when they get older. We can't afford to feed seven dogs, son."

"What are we gonna do with them?"

He didn't answer.

When we crossed over the Wallkill River Bridge, I looked down at the muddy water. It was spring, and the high water had pulled the frost-loosened dirt off the upper banks making the river the color of hot chocolate. Dad parked in the pull-off and got out, slamming the truck door.

"Get the box."

I pulled the box toward me, cradling it in my arms, and walked around to the front of the truck. Dad tossed the burlap bag to me and started climbing down the riverbank.

"Can I come down?" I yelled.

"No, it's dangerous down here. I don't want you to fall in."

Opening the lid of the box, I peeked in at the mass of wet noses reaching for the light. I was whispering to them when I jumped at the thud… thud… of two cantaloupe-size rocks falling in front of me.

"Put the rocks in the bag."

With two hands I picked up a cold heavy rock. Balancing it with one hand against my chest, I shook the sack open and bent forward. The rock and my heart flopped into the burlap sack.

Chapter 4

The "Persuader"

The deep shadows of the woods called more often once Dad made me drop the puppies into the river. I'd gone to the woods with clippers and cut a tunnel through the dense thicket, and in the middle I'd made a small clearing where I could lie down. In there no one knew where I was, not my brothers or anyone. It was already two years since I'd dropped her puppies into the Wallkill River, but still every six months Tuffy went into heat. I prayed she wouldn't get pregnant. We'd started locking Tuffy up in the garage when she was in heat— as many as ten male dogs at a time could be stalking the perimeter of the garage, lifting their legs to pee on the siding. It was inevitable that at least once during the two weeks of her being in heat, someone would leave the garage door open when they'd gone in there to get something, or sometimes Tuffy would squeeze out the door when you opened it. If any one of the waiting male dogs got to her, she'd be sure to have a litter of pups and Dad would force me to be involved in getting rid of them.

The year before he'd taken me behind the garage and made me watch him shoot four pups with his 22 rifle. "If someone lets her out again, you'll be doing this job," he said, while I was digging a hole to bury them.

It did happen again.

I started spending as much time as I could away from our house. My only neighbor was Bruce— he and I were in the same class at school. One day at Bruce's house I picked up a long, black, half-inch thick solid rubber hose that was lying coiled in the weeds. "What's this for?" I asked Bruce.

Bruce shrugged. "I don't know. My Dad brought it home from the farm."

Bruce's Dad's father owned the DuBois' farm up the road. They had cows, chickens, and apple orchards. Bruce's Dad, Bob, drove a milk truck for the farm.

I handed Bruce one end of the rubber hose and we began to swing it like a jump rope. Thin ridges were embedded in the hose's surface. I gave the hose a strong jerk, pulling it out of Bruce's hands. I took off running across the lawn while trailing the hose behind me. Heading towards the tree I thrust my arm forward like a pitcher; the hose came over my shoulder and slapped like a bullwhip against the tree.

Bruce came running up. "Give it to me. I want to try that." I handed him the hose, and he whipped it sidearm against the maple. It made a satisfying thwack.

"I got to go home. Can I have the hose?"

Bruce looked at the black curl of rubber. "Take it. Dad said it's just a piece of junk. He yelled at me yesterday after he had to get off the lawn mower to move it."

"Cool, thanks." I left, dragging the hose behind me.

That hunk of hose lay in our yard for a long time. Every so often one of my brothers would pick it up and swing it against something just to hear it smack. Then my father spotted it and asked, "Where'd that hose come from?"

"Bruce gave it to me," I said. "It's a piece of junk Bob brought home from the farm."

"Go get it." I handed it to Dad and watched as he made two loops and then squeezed them together. "Go get me some friction tape from the garage."

I ran to the garage for the tape. When I came back he said, "Do you know your ass sticks out like a girl's?"

I hated when he said this and looked down at the ground when I handed him the tape. He'd said this to me before, and when I looked in the mirror I thought my ass looked like everyone else's, but I wasn't sure; maybe it was a girl's ass.

"Don't trip over your lip. Stop pouting and hold these loops. Squeeze them tight so they don't spring back and I'll tape them."

He picked at the tape end with his nubby fingernail. "Goddamn it! See if you can get the end for me." I handed him back the hose and picked at the tape end with my fingernail.

"Here."

He took the tape. "Hold those loops tight, now."

"What're you making?"

"We're going to call it the Persuader."

"What's that mean?"

"You'll find out."

The Persuader took its place on a hook behind the refrigerator. It eventually became like one of the carpentry tools hanging in the garage, and all of us got persuaded by it at some point. Most often it was me because I was the oldest. He'd say, "Bring me the persuader." At first I'd try running out of the house; then I realized if he had to chase after me I'd get beat worse, so I learned to bring him the Persuader and to take what he dished out. It got to the point that if he looked at the refrigerator during dinner we'd all cringe.

Chapter 5

Mind Bending

I was going on 13 and had already picked tons of rocks from our fields, walls, and garden. We'd been growing our own food since we moved there. Dad told us we could work the garden better if it had fewer rocks in it. Mom canned beets, corn, beans, pickles, carrots, tomatoes, and we put potatoes in the cold cellar. Every spring before we started planting we'd pick wheelbarrow loads of rocks, dumping them in an area Dad wanted to make into a circle driveway. Picking out the stones made sense to me because the handles of the new rototiller would jerk my arms out of my shoulder sockets each time the tines hit a rock. The rototiller meant less weeding, so we picked rocks. I never understood how, after picking up every rock larger than a golf ball, next spring a new crop of big stones was always waiting. I couldn't believe we had more rocks each year and I asked Dad where they came from.

"Rocks work their way up from deep in the soil," he answered.

"How many do you think are down there?" I asked, wiping my forehead with my sleeve.

"As many as God put there," he grunted lifting the wheelbarrow handles.

"You think we'll ever catch up?" I saw my brother Pete shake his head "no" as he tossed his rock at the moving wheelbarrow.

Harold DuBois pulled up the driveway in his pickup truck. Fingering the brim of his work hat he sat it back on his head and said, "You boys look like you're working hard."

"Hey, Harold how you doing? I've got my chain-gang on the job."

"Hey, Don, you ever tell the boys about the lost diamond stick pin?"

"I haven't, but I think you might have a good idea there."

"Just stopped to tell you I saw your son Larry's picture on the Boy Scout calendar that Augy Martin gave me. The boy's really growing." Harold pointed his finger at me. Then he winked at my father. "Tell'em the story," he said, backing out of the driveway. We all waved at him as he went up the road.

"What's he talking about?" I asked, dumping a watermelon size rock into the wheelbarrow. The rock flopped out of my arm into the wheelbarrow, knocking it off balance and tipping it over. The wheelbarrow full of stones spilled on the ground. "Shit!" I yelled.

"Leave it," Dad said.

"All of you, come sit on the front steps for a few minutes. I want to tell you the story of the lost diamond stick pin." He sat on the top step and we sat on the lower ones.

"Before we bought this house an old gentleman farmer owned it. He was a friend of Harold's; that's why I know the story." Dad pointed at the garden with his knobbed finger. "Right out there is where it all happened. It was on a hot Sunday in August, not too different than this one. The old gentleman had just gotten dressed for church, and his wife was still upstairs putting on the finishing touches. He was sitting right about there," Dad said, nodding his head sideways. "The morning air was still cool. He decided to step out into the garden for a few minutes while he waited. He thought he'd get a head start on pulling weeds. He was being real careful to move slowly so he didn't sweat through his clean white shirt."

I looked at my brothers sitting there with their mouths open. Dad wasn't a big storyteller, and it seemed almost like someone else was telling us the story. He went on, "He was weeding the beans with one ear tuned to the house. He knew he'd be able to hear his wife coming down the stairs because her high heels would clomp. He didn't want her to catch him out in the garden. She liked it when he got all dressed up and insisted that he wear his father's diamond stickpin. She'd say to him,

'Every time I see you with that stickpin you look like a millionaire.' He liked it when she said that.

"The stickpin had come down through the family, from his father's grandfather and the grandfather before that. The family was originally from England. It was said that the stickpin was a gift from the King of England. It was given to the great, great, grandfather for saving the King's son's life."

"What did he do to save the King's son, Daddy?" John asked, wiggling his butt on the steps.

"Let me see if I can remember," Dad said, bringing his hand to his chin.

"Oh yeah, he saved the King's son because he was a cook in the Royal Court, and he saw the boy choking on a chicken bone and slapped him on the back, dislodged the bone and saved his life. Now let me get back to the real story. Remember the old gentleman was weeding in the garden. Suddenly he heard the clump, clump of his wife's shoes on the steps and he ran back to the porch and sat in his chair.

"His wife came out, and they got in the car and went off to church. The old gentleman parked in the church parking lot. His wife got out of the car and told him to stand still in front of her so she could look him over. You know what I mean, like your mother does with you guys before you go off to Sunday school.

"The old woman picked some lint off his shoulder, brushed a little mud off the lower part of his pants leg, and asked him to stand up so she could straighten his tie.

"'Where's your stickpin?' she asked, putting her hand to her mouth.

"'I put it in,' the old gentleman said, looking down at his tie.

"'It's not there. For God's sake, that pin is the most valuable thing we own. What were you doing when I was upstairs?'

"'I did a little weeding in the garden,' he said, raising his eyebrows and looking out over the trees. 'Maybe I didn't put it in. We'll look in the box when we get home,' he said, getting back into the car.

"They left church without going in. When they got home he went right upstairs and turned the box upside down. There was a tangle of old cufflinks, and tie clasps but no diamond stickpin. He changed his clothes and went into the garden and spent the whole afternoon looking, without finding it. When his wife called him to dinner, he pretended not to hear her and kept looking.

"Harold said the old man never found the pin. He said that pin was supposed to buy their retirement home in Florida. Instead they lived right here until both of them died. What do you think boys? You want to help me pick up some rocks in the garden after we eat lunch? Instead of calling it rock-picking we could call it gardening for diamonds."

"How much is the pin worth?" I asked, eyeing the garden for where I might start looking.

"Harold, who'd seen the pin in church, said it had a big diamond in the center and was surrounded by seven smaller ones. He told me once the sun came in at just the right angle through the stained glass window to hit the old gentleman's stickpin so that it made a star on the ceiling. It was so bright that the preacher stopped and asked everyone to look at it. Then the old gentlemen adjusted his coat and it went away. That's what Harold said."

"How much is it worth?" Pete asked.

"Enough to buy us a camper to pull behind the car, maybe even more."

"If I find it, I'm keeping the money for myself," said John who was already kicking some stones at the edge of the garden.

"Whoever finds it can do what they want with the money. I'll give you guys a hint: a diamond is just a shiny rock and the fewer rocks in the garden, the more likely one of us is going to find it."

"When are you going to dump the wheelbarrow so we can start?" Pete squealed running into the garden.

I kept seeing all of us going up the road on vacation to the Saint Lawrence River pulling a big camper behind the car.

The garden was clean of rocks for another planting season, but no one had found the diamond stickpin. Dad used that stickpin story whenever he needed rocks picked or weeding done. He'd say, "Why don't you pull the weeds around the beans? And be careful when you shake the dirt off the roots; you might find the stickpin."

By the summer's end the stickpin held little interest for me. While weeding after school one day I just picked up a stone and heaved it with all my might at the garage. It thudded against the siding, leaving a black scar on the green asphalt shingles. I hadn't thought about doing it; it just happened. I could feel my face flush and the tingle of blood in my arm. No one was around and I screamed, "Bastard! There's no fucking stickpin!" It felt good.

Chapter 6

Hardening of the Head

Standing back to back, I could feel Bruce's shoulder blades against mine. We'd been throwing stones at frogs and baseballs at empty gloves for years so our arms were pretty strong. I rolled up the sleeve on my right arm so I could throw better. Each of us took a step and counted out loud, "one two, three, four," as we paced away from each other. We stopped at 15 steps, turned and faced off.

I'd picked the ground carefully for just the right rocks. I liked rocks the size of a silver dollar, with a little heft. Flat rocks were best. If you threw a flat rock side-armed it would curve, making it hard to duck.

The rules for a rock fight were: You could only take as many rocks as you could carry in one hand. Only one man was allowed to throw at a time. You could duck, but if you moved your feet, the thrower got a free throw. If you got hit, it was automatically your turn to throw. If we couldn't hit each other at 30 paces, we'd begin moving closer one step at a time. If one of us got hit hard enough to cry, we agreed to quit.

Bruce's head was my target and my head was his. Body blows counted, but it was the head we were aiming at. Bruce pumped his arm back and heaved with fury. He was angry I'd just hit him on the forehead with a flat rock. I could see the bump rising. Staring at the space between us I searched for the rock; I couldn't see it. Then he pumped again. I'd started to yell "cheater" when his stone hit bone. At first I didn't know where I was hit. The inside of my head felt like it was a bell that had just been rung. The ache centered on my left cheek. I realized too late that Bruce had faked the first throw, and the second one walloped me. Fighting back tears, I bit my lip. Looking at Bruce, I swallowed hard.

"I give." Giving up in this game wasn't so hard; there was a kind of honor in having your blood drawn.

I saw tears in Bruce's eyes. We tossed our remaining rocks to the side of the road, like gun-fighters un-loading their pistols.

"Man, that's one Hell of bump. What are we gonna say to explain that?" I said.

"You're bleeding on your shirt. Better wipe it."

I wanted to say I was sorry, but it wasn't part of the game. Bringing my hand up to my throbbing cheek, I glanced toward the back of the garage and said, "Let's go up in the woods before my Mom sees us." We worked our way back through the brush just behind the garage and then sat shoulder to shoulder against a large ash tree. I dabbed spit on my bleeding check.

"I don't know any kids in our class that have rock fights," I said, pulling my finger out of my mouth.

"Shit, they're all pussies. One good hit and they'd be crying to their old ladies."

"Yeah, I bet your right." We were in seventh grade and most of our friends lived in town. They spent their time picking up soda bottles for the five-cent deposits or swimming at the town pool. We lived in the woods, and swam in the Plattekill River and threw rocks at each other like gun fighters.

"Listen, I think that's your mother calling."

Bruce cupped his hand to his ear. "That's her. I got to go." He stood quickly and headed down the hill.

I reached into my pocket, pulled out flat stone and tossed easy at him. It hit the back of his leg and he turned.

"Hey, man! What's that about?"

"Just fooling around. I didn't throw it hard."

Chapter 7

Learning to Numb

A storm came over Mohonk Mountain around dinnertime. It swooped into the valley rattling the trees at the edge of our lawn. Mom told me, "Go upstairs and close the windows." Pete and John were playing under a blanket on the couch while Mom fed Sharon from a baby food jar. It was ten after five, and Dad wasn't home yet. She kept looking at the clock. "Go get your brothers and all of you sit down at the table."

We were eating our pork chops, potatoes and green beans in silence when a clap of thunder rattled the windows and rain started pelting the trees. Dad wasn't at dinner and Mom took his plate off the table. Her jaw was set. The storm made it dark out, and Mom said, "Go get your pajamas on and go up to bed." I knew it was only eight, but decided I'd better keep my mouth shut. I lay in bed listening to the wind bending the tree limbs and knew that later there'd was going to be another storm inside the house when Dad came home.

The dark bathroom suddenly lit up with headlights. Dad was coming home from the Log Rail. I knew it was late because earlier, when Mom had looked in my room, I woke up and asked her what time it was, and she said 11. I lowered the toilet seat as quietly as I could, and made my way through the dark hallway to my bedroom. When I passed their bedroom I looked in; no one was in bed. I wondered if Mom was sleeping on the couch. As I settled under the covers, the car door slammed. I listened for him to come in.

I must have fallen asleep because the yelling woke me. It was just one scream from Mom: "Get your hands off me."

When I came downstairs for breakfast in the morning, Dad had already left. Mom was smoking at the kitchen table. There were no breakfast dishes in the sink and our three cereal bowls sat on the table. Dad's lunchbox was sitting unopened on the counter.

I watched Mom smoke as I ate, the tip of her cigarette glowed. She just sat there saying nothing. I stared down into my cereal. There were little flecks of black floating in the milk in my bowl. I spooned deeper through the sugary cereal and a cigarette butt popped to the surface of the milk. I gagged and ran for the bathroom, spitting my mouthful of cereal into the toilet.

That afternoon when we got off the school bus at the bottom of the driveway my brother Pete ran ahead of me, hoping to get to the cookie jar first. John was still in the bus when I yelled, "You'd better wait."

Peter stopped so he must have heard something in my voice because he almost never listened. He walked back towards me. "Why?" he asked.

"She's really pissed. Dad didn't come home until late last night."

Pete squirmed putting his hand into his jeans pockets. "What are we gonna do?"

"Stay out of the house. I'm going over to Bruce's."

"You're not gonna change?"

"Stop looking at me like I'm crazy. If you think it's a better idea to go in, go right ahead."

"Let John go in; she'll never yell at him," Pete said.

"Good idea," I said, turning to John who was behind me.

"Hey, John, tell Mom that I went over to Bruce's to get my homework assignment," I said.

Pete, asked, "Can I come with you?"

"No. Make your own plan."

"John, tell Mom I went with Larry."

"You ain't coming with me."

Peter looked like he was going to cry. He turned at me. "I didn't say I was."

John went up the driveway nodding. She wouldn't bother him; he was her baby. I walked towards Bruce's, and Peter headed for the barn.

A few hours had passed when Bruce's mother--who we all called Kay-- shouted upstairs for Bruce to come to dinner. Together we clomped down the stairs. "You'd better be going home; it's dinner time at your house, too," Kay said.

I walked home through the woods instead of along DuBois Rd. I knew I could survey what was going on better from behind the barn instead of walking up the driveway in clear sight. Standing next to the barn, I could see Dad's car wasn't parked in the driveway. Something moved inside the barn when I opened the side door. Pete was sitting on an old apple crate in the corner tapping a stick on the stones on the floor.

"What happened?" I asked.

"Nothing. I didn't go in yet. I heard her yell at John."

"Doesn't look like Dad's home."

"I've been watching for the car."

"Man, when he gets home she's really gonna be pissed." I tipped over another apple crate and sat next to Pete.

It was almost dark. Light spilled out the kitchen window into the backyard. Pete and I kept wondering if we should go in or not. If we went in it was hard to know what she might do. She'd thrown a butcher knife at me once. It just missed my head, all because I was mouthing off. She might let it all pass, and blame it on Dad; it was just too hard to read. The darker it got the more it looked like he wasn't coming home. We'd just decided to go in when the car came slowly up the driveway. We watched him get out, trying to see if he was drunk. It was too dark to tell. He hesitated before going in, running his hand through his hair.

He was in the house about five minutes before the back door burst open. He came running out, with Mom right behind him.

"Get the Hell out of here you drunken bastard! You leave me with these kids while you go drinking, and you tell me we ain't got no Goddamn money for clothes!" she screamed.

Dad turned towards her before he opened the car door and said, "Better back off, Helen. I've had enough of your shit. I'm the one working my ass off everyday."

He slammed the car door and peeled out down the driveway. The tires kicked up stones that fell at Mom's feet. We watched her cock her arm back and throw something. It hit the back windshield and bounced off. It sounded like metal.

Pete and I pulled back into the dark of the barn. We could hear Mom crying.

"Holy shit!" I said. Then Pete started crying.

Between sobs, he asked, "You think he's gonna come back?"

"Christ! I don't know," I said.

Mom yelled for us a couple times, but we just sat silent, too afraid to answer. It was getting cold in the barn, so after the lights went out in the kitchen, we decided to go in. There was nothing left but to face it. As we approached the house I saw Pete bend over and pick something up from the driveway. It rattled. "It's Dad's bank," he said. Dad had a small metal bank shaped like a miniature cash register. He put his pocket change in it every night. When he pressed down the lever it would ring up how much money was in it. Pete handed it to me. It read $9.30. Dad said it would open automatically at ten dollars.

We could smell dinner when we entered the kitchen. There were two plates on the kitchen table. The bank rattled when I sat it on the counter. Pete was holding onto my shirttail as I walked quietly across the kitchen. I was hoping Mom was in bed. Then the overhead light came on.

"Where the Hell have you two been?" She stood in the living room doorway, in her turquoise bathrobe with her hair in curlers.

I bumped into Pete as I backed toward the door.

"Get back in here!" she sneered. "Sit down at the table."

She moved towards the refrigerator. I put both my hands on the table and looked at the back door. Pete was holding his breath. She opened the icebox and took out a dish of potatoes and some cooked hamburgers wrapped in wax paper while we both settled down in the chairs. She reheated our meal. Then, leaving the room, she said, "Put the dishes in the sink when you're done and go to bed."

Chapter 8

Furrowing the Brow

Night after night Dad came home for dinner on time, and we sat silently around the table forking in the food. Mom washed the dishes. John and Pete got out of the house as soon as we finished eating, and I'd stay to dry the dishes.

Dad shifted his chair to face me at the sink. "What's that note about we got from school?"

"I was put in a special reading class, to help me learn to read," I said, picking up the dishtowel.

"Seventh grade and you don't know how to read?"

"I can read."

"He can read; he's just getting some extra help," Mom said.

"OK, OK. I just wanted to understand what the letter was about."

This was the first thing she'd said to him in three weeks. I picked up a big pot and started to dry it.

Dad looked up at her. "For Christ sake, I'm sorry," he continued.

I kept drying the dishes while Mom dried her hands and sat at the table. She didn't look at Dad; they just sat there not saying anything. I quickly dried the last plate and ran out the backdoor. As I closed the door I saw Mom put her hand on Dad's knee under the table.

Running across the front lawn towards my brothers I yelled, "I think it's over!"

The next day when I got off the school bus, I figured things would be back to normal. Tossing my books on the chair in the living room I strolled into the kitchen. "Hey, Ma."

"Hello, Larry. When you're done with the cookies take a look at that list your father left on the table."

"Shit!" I said under my breath.

Squeezing her eyebrows, she said, "You'd better start on it before he gets home."

The only one thing on the list was, "LARRY, FILL IN THE DITCH." During the weeks of silence Dad and I dug a 50-foot ditch, four feet deep, ending at a drywell. We'd finished laying pipe just before dark Sunday night. It was my job to cover the pipe.

I finished my cookie and went upstairs to change my clothes. As I was shoveling I wondered why we had to hand-dig the ditch when Bruce's father got a guy with a backhoe to do it. The guy wasn't there a day.

Bruce always asked me before getting off the bus if I had to work. He wouldn't come over if Dad left work for me. He'd been put to work too many times by Dad.

The September sun was hot. I pushed the shovel into the soft dirt and the blade struck a rock. Scraping the dirt off the big rock I levered the shovel under it. It barely budged. "Goddamn rock." I pushed down harder on the shovel handle. The stone nosed towards the ditch, when the handle suddenly cracked. Slamming the shovel down, I pushed the stone into the ditch with my hands.

Mom must have been watching me through the kitchen window because when I flipped a baseball size stone against the side of the house, she came running out. With her hands on her hips she looked at the dirt mark on the cedar siding.

"I saw you do that."

"What?"

"You threw the stone against the house. On purpose."

"It slipped."

38

Glaring at me, she hissed, "What the Hell's the matter with you? Why can't you ever just do what you're told? Everything's got to become a pain in the ass. Then I have to listen to his bullshit every time he comes home."

"Right," I muttered, kicking the shovel.

She came at me, then stooped to pick up the shovel. "Get over here and start digging!"

I didn't move, but stared into her reddening face.

"Get over here right now and start digging!"

"You go in the house and I'll dig." I didn't move. Before I knew it she raised the shovel over her head. I stooped forward as she brought the shovel down over my back. The blow pushed me to my knees, and the handle broke in half.

Looking up at her I saw she was stunned and trembling. I stood, then went towards her. Inches from her face I laughed, "I guess you were trying to kill me, Ma."

I sensed fear rising in her. She raised her arms and made fists. I grabbed her wrists and squeezed with all my strength. Glaring into her scorching blue eyes, I gritted my teeth. "Don't ever hit me again!"

I let go of her wrists, and she turned away with tears on her cheeks. Over her shoulder she said, "Wait 'til he gets home."

Too low for her to hear, I mumbled, "You hit me; I didn't hit you."

Two hours later Dad sat at the far end of the table. Mom was to his left, John sat at his right, and Pete was next to me across from Dad. Dinner started as usual with Mom asking Dad how work had gone. He was in a good mood.

The arms of her sweater were pushed up, and I could see black and blue bands around her wrists.

"Looks like you got a good bunch done on the ditch," Dad said.

"Yeah, but I broke the shovel."

"There's another one in the garage. Your mother tells me you put your hands on her." He turned to Mom. My brothers were shoving in their food fast.

Dad dropped his fork on the plate. "Come here. I'm going to give you a tuning," he said.

I stepped back away from his hands. The screen door slammed behind my brothers.

"Why did you hit your mother?"

"I didn't. She broke the shovel over my back."

"Where'd those black and blue marks come from?"

I shook my head.

"Get over here!"

There was an opening between him and the kitchen counter. I tried to squeeze through it, but he tipped his chair back, trapping me. He grabbed my arm and yanked me in front of him.

"I didn't hit her!"

He looked at Mom. "Go into the bedroom."

She got up from the table and left. "Don't hurt him."

His hairy knuckles vice-gripped around my arm, and he flung me toward the living room door. "Get your ass in the living room." He followed, grabbing the persuader off its hook behind the refrigerator. I ran behind the overstuffed chairs.

"Get your ass out here and take down your pants. I'm gonna persuade you to keep your hands off your mother."

I stayed behind the chair.

"I'll say it one more time and if you don't get your ass over here I'm gonna wail you so hard you won't sit for a week."

"I didn't hit her."

His jaw muscles tightened. "She told me what you did, and that's enough."

My throat was closing with fear, but I willed my tears back. I didn't budge from the chair. The curtains puffed out in the evening breeze. I could feel his eyes stab at me. All of a sudden the huge stuffed chair tipped over. I jumped to avoid his lunge but he caught me under the arm and pulled me towards him. He lifted me off the floor with one arm and began kicking me in the ass. I bounced off his work boot as we rodeo'd around the living room. The steel toe pounded my ass, and spittle dribbled out of my mouth. Flinging me around to face him, he yelled, "Take down your pants, now!" His eyes were needles. I searched for something to hit him with. Following my eyes, he read my mind and slapped my face. "Don't be stupid."

Jerking my arm free, I turned my back to him, undid my belt and dropped my pants. Then I pulled down my underwear and bent over. We'd done this before, and I knew he wouldn't be happy until he saw the skin of my ass. I said to myself, "Hit me as hard as you want but I ain't gonna cry for you." The rubber hose smacked my behind and I bit my lip. He whaled me, and the harder he hit me the more I shoved my ass at him.

My sobs came breaking thorough the bindings I was using to hold back my tears.

He stopped. Naked from the waist down, I covered the sparse hair above my shriveled penis with my hand and pushed passed my mother, who was standing in the doorway. She grabbed at me. "Let me look."

I wrenched my shoulder free from her hand and limped out the back door headed towards the barn.

It felt like I was coming apart. I wasn't ever able to work hard enough for him. He called me a girl every time he saw my ass sticking out. He didn't even have an ass. His pants hug flat where his ass was supposed to be. I couldn't spell or read and they kept making a big deal about it in school. I wouldn't be able to play sports if I got put on the ineligible list. No girls were interested in me, and it felt like my mother was out to get me. I made a fist and pounded the barn siding until the skin on my hand was raw. Gritting my teeth, I hissed, "I hate you, you fuckin' bastard."

Chapter 9

Brothers' Keeper

No one was home but me. Mom and Dad took Sharon with them shopping. Pete and John were at Steven DuBois' birthday party. Steven was Bruce's younger brother. I lay on my Davy Crocket bedspread that was embroidered with muskets and coonskin hats. The distant sound of a lawnmower droned outside the window. This was more comfortable than lying in my secret place in the thicket.

I had at least an hour before the birthday party was over. I unfastened my belt and unzipped my jeans. Sitting up, I kicked the denim bundle off my feet, then took the lamp off the night table and slid it into the closet. Standing on the table, I reached up to the ceiling tiles and sprung the right one free. Groping, I searched for the Playboy magazine. I opened the March 1962 issue and there she was: Pamela Anne Gordon, on the centerfold. The magazine was two years old, but I didn't care. My new friend, Bobby McKenna, whose family had just built a house down the road, gave it to me. He had a stash of them and said he was tired of this one. I wasn't; I had almost no time to look at it.

Back on the bed I stared at the blonde's naked breasts; her white nightgown was draped over her shoulders.

I tried memorizing every bit of Pamela Anne Gordon's picture. I lay the centerfold over my face. A desperate scream stopped my rocking. Something was going on downstairs.

On the second burst of hysterical screaming I recognized the "Leave me alone!" as Pete's voice.

"What the fuck's going on?" I grunted as I leaped out of bed, pulling on my pants. I jumped onto the end table and tossed the Playboy back in the hole, leaving the ceiling tile for later.

"Leave me alone Goddamn it!" repeated as I hit the head of the stairs. Sliding both hands down the stair rails I swung from top to bottom without touching a step.

John's index finger pushed up his nose exposing his nostrils. He was pursing his lips and making a snorting sound like a pig. Then he squealed, "Hey pig! Come get me little piggy." He sounded just like my father: when Mom found banana peels under Pete's bed, Dad had started calling Pete, Pig.

Pete was a head taller than John and he was really getting pissed. His tone changed when he said, "Leave me the fuck alone, Alford!"

John hated "Alford." It was really his first name, but no one called him that unless they were teasing him.

"What's the matter, Al?" Pete bellowed as he picked up a butcher knife from the counter.

"Cut the shit!" I yelled too late.

John had squealed again and Pete made a stab at him--not really to stick him, just a warning, but John reached out and grabbed the knife blade. The yelling suddenly stopped. The three of us stared at John's hand.

Pete tossed the butcher knife onto the counter. John started bleeding and he held his wrist as if his hand belonged to someone else. His eyes bugged at the blood dripping on the floor.

Pete started moaning, "He's gonna kill me."

I took hold of John's hand and saw white globules of fat in the open wound, and all I could think was, "It's gonna be my ass on the line for this."

"Stop whimpering and throw me that dishtowel," I hollered at Pete.

The towel was red, and I knew we needed help. The only person I could think of to call was Bruce's mom. "I'm going to call Kay. When I get off the phone we've got to get our story straight. Pete, wipe your nose and stop crying. He's going to kill us if we don't have a good story. Clean up the floor and counter and wash the knife and I'll call Kay."

I knew Bruce's number by heart. Kay answered. I exhaled all the words in one long sentence ending with, "John cut himself and it looks pretty deep."

"Is that you, Larry?"

"Yeah, it's me."

"Does he need a doctor?"

"I don't know. Looks like it."

"I'll be right over. Bob can watch the kids."

Pete was still crying when I grabbed his arm and yanked him into my face, "Stop fucking squealing, Pig. You got us into this shit. Shut up, so I can think."

Pete swallowed, his chest convulsing.

If we don't have a story, we're dead," I yelled.

"What are we going to tell them?" John sniffled. He was handling it better than Pete.

"That you grabbed the fucking knife," Pete erupted.

I was still holding Pete's arm and I squeezed it as hard as I could. "Shut up! Kay's gonna be here in a few minutes. I got it. Here's what we're going to tell 'em: John was trying to open that can of cocoa with the butcher knife and it slipped." I took the can of cocoa off the counter and dug the knifepoint into the lid making scratches.

Taking the loose end of the towel I made another wrap around John's wrist and tied it. "Alright guys, what are we going to tell them?"

John's tear-stained face cleared for a moment and he said, "I was trying to open the cocoa with the butcher knife and it slipped."

"Good."

I pushed John's hair back out of his face. Peter was looking relieved. I put my arm over his shoulders, "What are you going to say, Peter?"

With snot still dribbling from his nose he said, "He cut himself trying to open the can of cocoa."

There was a knock on the back door.

"Larry?"

Chapter 10

Clenched Teeth

School was hard for me. Having to sit still drove me crazy. I was reading a lot better since Mr. Barker started pulling me out of class for one-on-one reading instruction. But, for most of my classes, I fidgeted in the seat, looked out the window, and made jokes under my breath. I'd been hoping ninth grade was going to be better since we had different teachers for each class, but it wasn't. What I liked was that school gave me a chance to play sports so I didn't have to go home after school. I tried out for everything: track, football and basketball. I made all the teams, so my father lost his right hand man.

During basketball season I was working in Mr. Van Valkenburgh's study hall, trying to get though a reading assignment for Mr. Bennett's freshmen history class. Out of the corner of my eye came a flash and suddenly a burning feeling on my left forearm. Tommy Power had just raked his ballpoint pen across my arm so hard that blood was coming out of the ink seam he'd made.

"What the fuck's the matter with you, asshole?" I said, staring at him.

He made another jab, and I pulled my arm away. Gripping my pen, I looked for an opening to attack him back when I saw Mr. Van Valkenburgh watching me. Mr. Van Valkenburgh's forearms were built like Popeye's; when he nodded at me I put my hands in front of me on the desk.

As soon as the bell rang Tommy bolted for the stairs. I got to about the third step and suddenly it went dark. Tommy had thrown his jacket over my head and was punching me through it. I ripped his jacket from my head and screamed, "Meet me after school, you asshole! I'll kick your fuckin' ass!"

"Don't be late, shithead!" he screamed back.

The whole school knew there was going to be a fight. It would be across the street from the school behind Western Auto. No teachers would be there to break it up because it was off school property. All day kids kept asking me if I was going to show.

Ted Smith said, "He's a punk. You'll kick his ass. You want me to back you up in case his friends step in?"

"Yeah, that'd be cool," I answered.

I couldn't think of anything all day but fighting Tommy Powers. He was a grade behind me, but he was a big kid. He bullied a lot of the kids in his class. I'd never been in a serious fight before. I knew this one was about really hurting the other guy. All I could think of was that Tommy had already out-smarted me on the stairs. I wasn't sure what I was supposed to do to get ready. I kept saying over and over to myself, "Just don't back down. Don't be afraid to hurt him, cause he sure as Hell wants to hurt you."

When I crossed the street the only thing I could see in the crowd was Tommy Power's head. There must have been a hundred kids milling around waiting. He was in the center of them. He'd taken off his shirt and was in his tee shirt. I took my shirt off to and tossed it to Teddy. A tight ring of boys, his friends and mine, formed around us.

"Kick his ass!"

"Give him one good one to the head!"

"Wipe the ground with him!"

"Look at him. He's a pussy!"

I couldn't tell if they were talking to Tommy or me. Tommy's eyes were wide, and he kept looking into the crowd. I followed his eye to see who he was looking at and that's when he lunged. His fist hit me in the cheek. A roar went up from the group. I brought my fists up to box. Tommy made another lunge, his fist flying at me. This time I was ready and moved to the left side. He lost his balance and I looped my right arm around his neck and joined my arms together in a headlock.

All the wheelbarrows full of rocks and the holes that I'd dug for my old man went into squeezing Tommy's head.

"Give up, bastard," I said through my teeth as I tried to crush his head.

"Fuck you!" came back at me, along with a punch in my stomach. It was as if blood had been squirted into my eyes. I brought my knee up, smashing Tommy's nose. Blood dripped on the ground, and I could feel his body slacken.

"Give up or I'm going to kill you, you fucking bastard."

Tommy whimpered, and I gave him another shot to the nose with my knee--not quite as hard. Then I felt a finger on the back of my neck. I still had Tommy's head tight in my arms. A deep voice yelled, "Stop right now!"

I didn't. I jerked my head away from the gripping fingers and twisted Tommy's head hard sideways until we fell to the ground. I lay on top of him.

"I said give up you little fucking bastard."

Then I saw the principal, Mr. Dippel, pulling at Tommy's feet trying to get him free of me. I squeezed harder and Tommy cried, "I give. You win. Let me go! I give!"

I let go. Before I knew it Mr. Dippel's big hand had vice-gripped around my bicep and his other hand around Tommy's. He dragged us both across the street to his office and pushed us down in opposite chairs.

"What the Hell is going on here?"

I looked at Tommy; the front of his tee shirt was covered with blood.

"That son of a bitch started it. He dug my arm with a pen this morning for no reason," I said, showing him my arm.

"Did you do that, Tommy?"

"No sir."

I jumped out of my chair and put Tommy in another headlock, squeezing as hard as I had before. Mr. Dippel struggled to get out from behind his desk.

"What the Hell's the matter with you? You're going to kill him. Stop it!" he said, digging his fingernails into the back of my neck until I let go. Slamming me into a chair he said, "Don't you touch this kid again or it's going to be me you're dealing with next."

"The fight was off school property; you had no right to stop it."

"Shut up and don't move from that seat. I'll be right back." He took Tommy by the arm and started leading him out of the room.

"I couldn't hear you; did you give, bastard?"

Tommy looked at me. Tears were coming down his cheeks as he shook his head yes.

"Then tell him you started it."

"I marked him with my pen," he whimpered as Mr. Dippel dragged him through the door.

When the principal came back I asked, "Where'd you take him?"

"I took him to the nurse's office. What the Hell is this about?"

"I told you."

"I've never had you in this office before. You could have killed him."

"He could have killed me."

"The nurse took a look at his nose and said it isn't broken. You're right; the fight was not on school grounds so there is nothing I can do. I can call your parents and tell them what's happened. How would you like that?"

"I wouldn't like that."

"I want a promise from you that this kind of thing isn't going to happen again."

"I can't make that promise. If he or someone else hurts me like he did, I'll get him back. I can promise you I won't do it on school grounds."

"You're a real hard head aren't you? Get the Hell out of my office."

Chapter 11

Steel Face

The 1964 New York World's Fair at Flushing Meadow in Queens, New York, had been open almost a year when my sophomore class made a trip down to see it. The fair's theme was "Man in a Shrinking Globe in an Expanding Universe." That felt like my house: not enough room in it for my father and me, and the Vietnam War was looking more and more like it was going to become part of my universe. I read in a local paper about a Captain Roger Donlon receiving the Medal of Honor. Captain Donlon was born in Saugerties, which was only a few miles north of New Paltz. I read how he fought the Viet Cong, and how he'd gotten wounded many times, but had still held his position. When the fight was over 54 Viet Cong were dead.

His citation ended:

His dynamic leadership, fortitude, and valiant efforts inspired not only the American personnel, but the friendly Vietnamese defenders as well and resulted in the successful defense of the camp. Capt. Donlon's extraordinary heroism, at the risk of his life above and beyond the call of duty, are in the highest traditions of the U.S. Army and reflect great credit upon himself and the Armed Forces of his country.

Every time I read this, it gave me the chills.

I was on the track team and had a job at JD's Dairy Bar at night. There was no time left to work with Dad, thank God. He wasn't happy about it, but couldn't stop me. The way I saw it, Pete and John could pick up the slack. They were 12 and 11 and could pick rocks and pull weeds just like I had.

One day after English class, Ted Smith handed me a note. He said a girl named Diana had asked him to give it to me:

Hi Larry, My name's Diana. I've been watching you play basketball. You're great! Would you like to go to Zup's for an egg cream after school?????

The handwriting was loopy and the ink was purple. I wondered how she knew that I loved egg creams. When I saw Ted later I asked him, "Who's this chick, Diana?"

"She's that blond chick, with nice pecs. She hangs out with Carol Corwin. You've seen her; I know you have," Ted said, with a big smile.

"Yeah, she's the one with the mole near her upper lip." I moved my palms up and down in front of my chest.

"That's her!" Ted said.

After our egg creams at Zup's, it only took a few weeks before Diana and I were going steady. She was moving up to ninth grade, and I was going into tenth. Our romance grew hotter along with the spring weather. By June I had the promise of a summer job from Diana's dad.

Mr. Astikanen was heavy in the shoulders with a potbelly and graying hair. His ruby nose blossomed with the aid of evening vodka. When he spoke, a thick Finnish accent drew out the O's. He was an electrician who worked for himself. I was to be his summer laborer. The arrangement was that he'd pick me up at 8 a.m. at my house and bring me home by 4 p.m. so I could eat and get ready for my second job at JD's.

"Yo'll be drilling lotso holes this summer, boy," he told me. He explained that most of the jobs we'd be working on didn't have an electrical supply, so I'd be using a brace and bit to drill through studs and floor joists.

All that summer Mr. Astikanen kept asking me if I was going into the service. I said I didn't know. When I heard on the transistor radio at work that on August 7 the Joint Resolution of Congress had passed, giving President Johnson permission to step up the war, Mr. Astikanen asked me again if I was going. I told him there were two years yet before I graduated, and the War would probably be over by then.

"Don't think so, son," was all he said. Maybe he was worried I wouldn't come back to marry his daughter. I never asked, but I think he'd seen some action in Finland during World War II.

One day, more than half way through the summer, after Mr. Astikanen had dropped me off at home. I jumped into the shower, changed my clothes and ate a quick dinner. Then I walked to my friend Bobby's house. Bobby had a license, and he used his mom's car to drive us to JD's where we both worked. Dave Jewett owned JD's, and he was ahead of everyone with soft ice cream. There wasn't another dairy bar within a 50-mile radius. On hot summer nights the lines at all three windows didn't slow down until long after dark. I filled hundreds of 15 and 25-cent cones. I made $1.25 an hour there and $1.50 from Mr. Astikanen.

It was my job to empty the cash from the register at 11 p.m. I put it into a cookie tin and walked it up to Dave's house on South Manheim St. where I stashed it in his garage and locked the door. Then I'd walk down North Manheim to John St., over to Route 32 North and out to Diana's. It took a half hour of fast walking to get there. I'd toss a pebble against her bedroom window screen. She'd sneak out, and we'd spread a blanket out on the lawn behind the empty bungalow and neck. After a few hours I'd walk the six miles home. I'd climb into bed around 3 a.m. only to wake at 7:30 to meet Mr. Astikanen outside my front door.

For the Fourth of July Dave Jewett took his wife and kids on vacation, so I had the next three days off. Diana's family was also on vacation. Dave Deyo called, asking if there was any way I could give him a ride up to Mohonk Mountain House where he was a busboy. "If I don't get there in time, I'm gonna lose my job. The maître d's been riding me. He said that one more time late and I could stop kissing his ass and kiss the job goodbye."

Dave knew I didn't have a license or a car, but I'd told him that morning when he walked over to the house that I'd found the keys to the Bostrup's Corvair station wagon. I was feeding their dog and cat while they were away for the week. "I took it for a few spins around the driveway," I'd bragged to Dave.

The only thing I'd driven before was a tractor at the DuBois farm, so I said, "If Bruce will come with me I might be willing to take you to work after dark."

"That would be great. It's a six mile walk from town," Dave said cheerfully.

At Bostrup's I fingered the keys on the hooks above the kitchen counter. I made sure I knew what hook the car key came off of. Then I fed the dog and cat.

Tommy Bostrup was a painter and he used this old car for his business. Paint can rings were all over the floor. It was an automatic transmission. The car started right up. I took a few trips around their circle driveway before getting on the road. We were to meet a hundred yards past Bruce's house, but when I got there, he wasn't there.

Bruce didn't have a driver's license either, but he'd been driving his father's old Packard around their long semicircle driveway every time his folks weren't home. Once we'd gotten the speedometer up to 50. I sat there thinking that now it was Bruce's turn to ride shotgun.

I kept looking for headlights in the rearview mirror, afraid someone might come by. Everyone knew Tommy Bostrup's Corvair. Suddenly the car started rocking. I grabbed the wheel and turned around; Bruce was standing on the bumper jumping up and down.

"Cut the shit and get in before somebody comes," I yelled out the window.

"Did I scare ya?"

"Fuck, no."

"Bullshit. I saw your face. I really didn't think you'd be able to get it down here."

"It was easy."

"How you gonna go?

"Plains Rd. The cops never patrol there."

"Good idea."

"Shit, look at the gas gauge? We ain't gonna make Mohonk without some gas, and I ain't got any money," I said.

Bruce fished into his front pocket and came up with a quarter. "This will get us a gallon. You think that's enough?"

"I don't know. If we get stuck somewhere we'll be dead. Let's go back to my house. I got a buck in my bedroom," I said.

I parked the car in the apple orchard, and we walked back to my house.

"We need a gas can," Bruce said.

"There's one in the garage."

Shaking it with both hands, I said, "It's empty."

Once in town, we parked on South Oakwood St., where we were supposed to meet Dave, and walked down to Reid & Donahue's Gas Station at the corner of Prospect and Main. Frank Donahue came out.

"Can you give us three gallons, Frank?" I asked.

"You boys ain't mowing any grass this time of night, are ya?"

"We're getting set up for tomorrow," Bruce said.

"You gonna carry that can the three miles out to DuBois Rd.?"

"Yep," I lied.

Frank shook his head. "You guys better be making some real money on that lawn."

"Yeah, we are," said Bruce.

We got back to the car ten minutes before Dave was supposed to show up. I hadn't taken the spout for the gas can, so when I tried to pour it into the car it ran down the side of the fender.

"I can't see. Is any going in?"

"I can't tell. I think so," Bruce said.

There was a little gas left in the can when I put it on the back seat. We got back in and started it up. The gas gauge had moved.

"I think we're good," I said.

We sat waiting with the lights off. We could see a figure turn at the corner.

"Is that Dave?"

"Can't tell," Bruce said, squinting.

"It's him."

We slid down in the seat. When he got next to the car, I turned on the lights and blew the horn. Dave froze--until he heard us laughing.

"Get in," I said.

"It smells like gas."

"Calm down. We had a hard time pouring the gas in the tank, and I got it all over my pants." I said.

"Shit. I didn't think you were really going to do it. What happens if we get caught?"

"Who's gonna get caught? Bostrups aren't coming home for three more days."

Bruce turned toward the back seat. "Do we have to take you all the way in, or can we leave you at the gate?"

"It's a mile and a half from the gate and there's no lights."

"It's up to Larry. It's his ass on the line," Bruce said.

"Do we have to stop at the gatehouse and talk to the guy?" I asked.

"What guy?"

"The gatekeeper, you know, the guy that lets you in."

Dave nodded at me.

"I don't want to chance that," I said.

"You chicken?" Dave asked, pulling on the back of my seat.

"Listen, Mr. Walker, you'd be walking your ass up the side of this mountain right now if it weren't for us, so shut up," I said.

We rolled over the Wallkill Bridge and turned right on Springtown Rd. When we reached Mountain Rest Rd., stones started rattling up under the fenders.

"It sounds like the road's just been paved," Bruce said.

"Yeah, it sounds like popcorn being made in the wheel-wells," I added.

The sound made me feel like I was really moving. I pushed on the gas pedal and we built up a little more speed.

"Come on, man! Show us what this baby can do," Bruce said, thumping the dashboard.

"Pedal to the metal!" Dave whooped.

The curve was long and sweeping. I couldn't see the end of it. Halfway through I felt the wheels slip. I slammed on the brakes, the back end spun around and we slid off the road into the ditch. I watched our headlights glance off large white rocks. We slammed to a stop, and one headlight shone into the trees. I'd been slammed against the steering wheel, hitting my head on the windshield. Bruce was crunched against the door moaning.

"You OK?" I mumbled.

"I think so. The door won't open."

I felt something on the back of my neck and reached up and wiped. It was wet. I didn't want to look back, figuring Dave was covered in blood. When I did look, he wasn't there; he was standing outside.

"You bleeding?" I asked through the window.

"No, the Goddamn gas can didn't have a cap on it and sprayed gas all over. Oh, man, look! Lights just came on in that house," Dave said.

I started the car and tried to rock it out of the ditch. It vibrated a little and the engine died.

"Are you alright?" a voice came through the trees.

"We're fine," I said in the deepest voice I could manage. "We just ran into the ditch."

The voice asked, "Need any help?"

"We're good. We're just stuck in the ditch. We'll be back in the morning to tow it out."

The three of us huddled at the side of the road.

"What the Hell we gonna do?" Bruce whimpered.

Sweat was dripping off my nose, and the bump on my head started to hurt.

"Dave, you got a watch?"

"No. There's a clock on the dash."

I put the key in the ignition, and when the lights came on I noticed I had on my wristwatch. It was 9:30.

"Aren't you going to try again to get it out?" Bruce asked.

"It won't move. I already tried."

"That's fucking great. How the fuck we gonna get home? It's got to be ten miles," Bruce sniffled. "What're we gonna do?"

"Shut the fuck up! Let's start with that. It's my ass," I said, shoving Bruce's shoulder.

"Dave, we're almost to Mohonk. Why don't you walk the rest of the way and we'll head home? By the time we get there we'll have a plan. We can leave you out of it. Your old man would kill you if he found out about this."

"And your old man won't?" Dave said.

"Better one dead man than three."

"Thanks man," Dave said, turning and walking up the hill. His voice came out of the dark. "Thanks man, really!"

The peepers along Mountain Rest were screaming as we walked towards New Paltz. The sky was speckled with stars, but there was no moon. We walked a long way before I couldn't stand it anymore.

"Sorry I pushed you."

"We're really in deep shit. And don't think it's just your ass. It's gonna be mine, too," Bruce said.

"You weren't driving."

"You think that's gonna make any difference? My old man knows I'm not home and it is gonna take about three seconds before he finds out from your old man where you've been."

"Tell him you were out with someone else."

"Right, who's that gonna be?"

"I mean it. Tell him you were hanging out with Bobby McKenna. It makes no sense for both of us to get into trouble. There ain't no way I can get out of it."

"The last time Bobby and I hung out was two years ago, so that ain't gonna work. What are you gonna tell'em?"

"Maybe I'll tell'em nothing. Let Bostrup come home and think his car's been stolen."

"Ain't nobody gonna buy that shit. You got to go up there and feed those animals for the next three days. You think they're gonna believe you didn't notice the car was gone? You better have a better story than that."

I suddenly felt the humidity close around me and I began to sweat.

"Wait a minute," I said, bending over in the road like a runner trying to catch his breath after a long race. "My old man's going to flip," I moaned.

Bruce put his hand on my back. "Come on, we got to get going."

When we came back across the Wallkill Bridge I tossed a handful of pebbles into the river. Then we turned right on Plains Rd., walked to its end where we crossed Route 208 and made it the rest of the way home. We got to Bruce's house at 1 a.m. I rolled around on his bedroom floor until dawn. As I lay there I decided I had no choice but to tell the truth. No other story I could think of would work. I'd leave Bruce and Dave out of it. I got up early and left Bruce's house knowing I'd have to tell my folks before the police found the car.

My hand shook as I opened the back door. The kitchen light was on. Dad sat at the kitchen table sipping coffee; Mom was across from him, smoking. Dad had his work clothes on; Mom was in her nightgown.

I stood for a minute and Dad asked, "Where you been?"

"I stayed at Bruce's last night. It was too late to call."

"Your mother's been worried."

"Sorry."

"You got to work today?" he asked.

"No."

"What's the matter with you; you're white?" Mom asked.

"Nothing. I mean …I don't feel good."

"You got a fever?" Putting her cigarette in her mouth she got up and put her hand to my head.

"You're not hot. How come you're shaking?"

"I got to go to the bathroom."

Walking past them I went into the bathroom. Sitting on the toilet lid I held my head in my hands. After ten minutes I flushed and looked into the mirror. Wiping my eyes I left the bathroom through the door to my parent's bedroom.

I sat on the corner of their bed. "Mom, come here a minute," I said in a loud voice.

She came right in. "What's the matter? Are you getting sick?"

"I'm not sick. I'm in trouble."

She took a deep drag on her cigarette and put it out in the ashtray on the bureau. Exhaling smoke through her nose, she inspected my face.

"Diana's pregnant?"

"No!" But I wondered to myself, "How'd she know we're having sex?"

"What's the matter then?"

"Dad's gonna kill me," I said, lowering my head.

She put her arm around me. "Stop crying. He's not going to kill you." Her tobacco breath mixed with the sweet shampoo smell of her still-wet hair.

Her closeness caused me to just blurt out, "I stole Bostrup's car and wracked it up."

The weight of her arm left my shoulders.

"You did what?" Then, looking towards the kitchen she said, "You have to tell your father right now."

"Ma, can't you tell him? He's going to hit me."

I got up and she grabbed my bare arm, digging in her fingernails. "Give me two minutes and then come in."

I wiped my tears on my forearm, and saw three red half-moons on my skin. When I came in she was leaning over him, whispering. When she heard me she sprung back.

"He's got something to tell you, Honey."

"What have you done this time? Get over here!"

His forehead held waves of wrinkles, and his jaw muscles stood out. "Stand over here!"

I moved towards him, staring into his glacier blue eyes.

"I borrowed Bostrup's car last night and ran it off the road up on Mountain Rest." When his shoulders tensed I took a half step back.

"How bad is it?"

"I don't know. I couldn't get it out."

"Get your ass in the car. We'll see what you did. Who was with you?

"Nobody!"

"Bullshit, you never do anything without one of your asshole friends. Which one was it, Bruce or Dave?"

"I was alone."

"Get away from me."

I sat in the back seat of his car. He came out and said, "Get in the front."

I squeezed against the passenger door and we drove in silence. We were climbing the mountain and I felt the car slow.

"Where is it?"

"Up a little further, in the middle of the curve at the top of this hill."

The only thing visible when we got there was the driver's side of the Corvair. It was almost all the way over on its side. Dad pulled off the road and got out. I watched him disappear in the ditch. A few minutes later he was back in the car.

"Looks totaled. You must have been going like a bat out of Hell; the back axle's bent. No way we're gonna get it out."

Fifteen minutes later we pulled into Smitty's Body Shop. I watched him talking to Smitty Ruger through the window. On the way home neither of us spoke until I opened the car door.

"Don't go anywhere! I've got something to keep you busy. If you leave this house you better keep going because if I get my hands on you I'll bust your ass," he hissed.

I clenched my teeth and screamed a silent, "Fuck you," making sure he couldn't see it.

"You're going to feed Bostrup's animals for the next three days and you're going to write a note and put it on their kitchen counter so they know to call you when they get home," Mom said.

Each time I walked up their driveway my knees shook.

It was in the afternoon on the third day after the accident that the phone rang. My mother picked it up.

"Hello, Tommy."

I walked into the back yard after I heard her say, "Wait a minute, I'll put Don on."

"Get in here!" Dad said ten minutes later, pointing his finger at me. "Tommy's waiting. Get your ass up there and don't give him any shit. He's thinking of calling the police. I told him it might not be a bad idea. Go!"

I stood in the doorway to Tommy Bostrup's house while he extracted every last detail of the accident from me. Tommy kept putting his finger in my face as if he were trying to drill his questions into my eyes. White spittle was collecting at the corners of his mouth.

"You're going to pay for this, you little son of a bitch! I used that car to make my living. Go home and tell your old man I'll let him know in a few days what I'm gonna do."

Shrugging, I turned to walk home. He yelled after me, "I hope you had fun, cause you're gonna be working your ass off to pay for that little joy ride."

A few days later Tommy pulled up the driveway in his family car. His hair was slicked straight back and his cigarettes were folded under the sleeve of his tee shirt. I was in the garage so I watched him through the window. He was in the house about a half hour before they called me. Mom was in the kitchen when I came in. She put her arm out to stop me.

"Keep your mouth shut. He's out to screw you, and if you give him lip he said he's going to call the cops."

Tommy was sitting in the chair my mother always sat in. When he saw me come in he said, "There's the thief."

I looked away from him.

"Stealing my car's gonna cost you, boy."

Dad sat steel-faced. Mom stood in the doorway of the kitchen. I walked over behind the couch.

"That little driving escapade's gonna run you 500 bucks. Oh, and by the way, I found out your buddy Bruce was part of the adventure. He's gonna pay four. Me and Bob already worked that out," Tommy grinned.

I stared at him and in a calm voice said, "Fuck you. Smitty said the most that car's worth is a hundred bucks."

Tommy's eyes widened.

"Listen you little son of a bitch. You keep using language like that with me and I'll call the police right now. What do you think about that?"

He was at the edge of the chair pointing his finger at my chest.

"Call the fucking police, asshole!" I hissed.

"Shut up!" Dad barked at me. "Don't say another word!" Then he looked at Tommy. "You're gonna do just what Tommy wants."

Tommy sat back in the chair, fingering the pack of cigarettes in his shirtsleeve.

"I gotta go."

He stood and came towards me. He was a few inches taller than me. He tapped me on the breastbone with his stiff finger. Through his tobacco-stained teeth he snarled, "I expect payment by the end of the week, crook."

I balled my fist up and looked at Dad. He widened his eyes. I wanted my father to grab Tommy and tell him to back off from his boy, but his blank face made me think he didn't even give a shit.

They walked into the kitchen, and I heard Dad say, "See ya, Tommy. I'll make sure he takes care of it."

They sounded like good friends. I took hold of the front door doorknob with both hands and pulled it with all my strength until the paint cracked and the door came free for the first time in years. Paint flakes were all over the floor, and the door vibrated with a loud hum. I bolted outside screaming, "Fuck you!"

Chapter 12

Leather Neck

Tenth grade had started, and by the end of September I found out I'd made the varsity basketball team. One night at practice, the lights in the gym went out. It was so dark you couldn't see. Coach Helhoski said, "All of you walk towards my voice. I'm standing by the stairs. Move slowly; I don't want any of you guys falling down the stairs."

When he got us down to the locker room he called roll from memory; then he found his office and came back with a flashlight. Coach shined his light on two different clocks; each had stopped at 5:17 p.m.

"Listen up. I want you guys to take quick showers and go home. I turned on the portable radio in my office and it's clear that something big has happened; they just don't know what yet. While you're taking showers I'll go back and listen some more."

He stood the flashlight on end in the showers. When we finished washing up, Coach told us the radio announcer said that most of New York State was in darkness. Reports coming in said that there was a massive power failure.

When I walked out the locker room door it was strange not seeing streetlights. I was used to walking home after dark, but the streets in town were always lit. Once I got out of town it was like it always was, except that there were no houses with outside lights on. Candles were burning in the windows of some homes.

An hour later when I got home Mom told me Dad was at work. She said that all Central Hudson employees had been asked to stay late. I was glad he wasn't home. Since my car accident we just grunted at each other.

The power failure was on November 9, 1965. Three weeks later to the day, I moved out of my family's house and into the cabin Bobby McKenna and I had just finished building behind his house. Bobby was a junior. He'd moved here when his parents bought one of the houses built in 1958. He lived only a quarter mile down the road, and we had quickly become friends playing on the same little league team together.

Bobby's dad had recently left his mom. When we asked her if we could build a cabin in the woods behind the house, she never really answered, just shook her head and rolled her eyes. We promised her it wouldn't cost her a penny. Truth was Mrs. McKenna was glad to give Bobby's room to one of her other two sons who'd been crammed into a small bedroom.

We'd started by cutting down ash trees for corner posts. We dug holes with a posthole digger and planted each post in cement. The materials for the cabin came from lumber we'd picked off the scrap piles from several new houses being built on DuBois Rd. Bobby also worked at JD's, so we both had some money to pitch in for shingles and plywood for the roof and floor. The two old windows we found lying in Bobby's basement gave us everything we needed.

I'd given up the job with Diana's dad before the summer ended so we could build the cabin. Anyway, Diana and I weren't getting along. She was upset that I was building the cabin with Bobby and not spending time with her. I was stretched thin with trying to work at JD's to pay off the car, going to school and basketball practices. Now my girlfriend was telling me I had her at the bottom of my list. "Maybe you need to look at who's making the list," I said when she told me. She didn't like my comment.

By late September, there was only one job left to finish on the cabin: digging a hundred yard trench from Bobby's mom's house to the cabin. Bobby's electrician uncle said he'd hook up the wiring. For a whole weekend we picked and shoveled across the back lawn. Then we laid the electric and phone cables in the ditch. Once Bobby's uncle screwed the wires into the panel box in the basement, we ran out to the cabin to turn our lights on.

The cabin became our home, no parents to deal with, come and go as we pleased. In December we bought a small electric heater at Western Auto and two rolls of foil faced, pink insulation, which we stapled between the studs. We slept in sleeping bags on top of our mattresses.

Midway into the basketball season I went to Coach Helhoski and told him I had to quit.

"What's the matter, son?" he asked.

"I got in this car accident over the summer and totaled the car. Now I have a loan payment. That's why I can't quit my JD's job."

"But Larry, you're one of the better players. Can't you work something out with your folks?"

"I'll see what I can do Coach," I said, but I never asked my father.

Every time Tommy Bostrup, in his brand new Chevy station wagon, passed me walking on the road, my swearing grew louder.

"Hope you enjoy the new car I bought you, son of a bitch!" I screamed at his taillights.

Tommy's driving past daily was getting to me. It wasn't enough just to swear. So one night when I was off from JD's I went over to Bruce's and asked him if he had an ashcan firecracker left over from the Fourth of July.

"Yeah, I lifted a whole box of them from the old-man."

"Let's wait until dark and sneak up to Bostrup's house. I stole a couple cigarettes from Mom, and we can use them as fuses. I saw a guy do it once; he stuck the ashcan fuse into the end of the cigarette, and it didn't go off for 20 minutes. We can stick one under his windows."

"We can hide in the apple orchard to see what happens. I got ten of 'em; we could set one off every couple of days. That would sure as Hell keep old Tommy on edge. I hate when that bastard goes up the road in a brand new car we bought him," Bruce said, scowling.

"Tomorrow I get home late from JD's. I'll come up to your house around one in the morning. In a few nights we'll do another one."

"Cool. We've got to be careful to not be predictable."

That summer we watched the lights come on in Tommy's house at all hours of the night. He had to know who was doing it. Bruce and I felt like commandos sneaking up to his house in the dark, waiting to see Tommy come out the front door with a shotgun.

It felt good to know that Tommy's new car wasn't completely free.

Chapter 13

Devil Dog

In eleventh grade history class Mr. Bennett asked, "Anyone know who Tu'i Malila is?"

Nothing but blank faces peered back at him.

"He or she's the oldest tortoise ever recorded. It died last year on May 19, 1965."

"Cool," said Harold O'Byrne, the class clown.

Looking around the class, I saw kids rolling their eyes and shrugging their shoulders, their body language saying, "What the Hell's he talking about?"

Mr. Bennett went on to say that the baby tortoise, Tu'i Malila, had come from the Galapagos Islands and was given as a gift to the Tongan royal family in 1777 by Captain Cook, a British explorer. "The 188 year life span of this animal is the time span in world history we are going to be learning about," he continued with a funny smile.

As I sat there thinking about this turtle, Tu'i Malila's, long life, I wondered what it must have been like for it to leave its family and live on some strange island for all those years. I'd just moved out of my family's house. I liked the freedom, but my relationship with my family felt like it was dying like the turtle did.

My mother begged me to come up to eat at the house a few times a week, which I had agreed to do. Meals were quiet. Nobody asked me any questions; we all just made believe that the Tommy Bostrup incident had never happened.

When Bobby wasn't in the cabin, I'd spend hours tucked into my sleeping bag talking on the phone to Diana. We'd been close for a year, but lately there'd been longer and longer silences during our conversations. When I started talking about how it wasn't working with us anymore, she said we needed more time together. I said I wanted to see my friends without feeling guilty. The arguing kept going until it ended during the first few weeks of school when we broke up. She gave me back my class ring along with a long letter about how I'd destroyed her life.

Breaking up was harder than I thought. We had broken the taboo of sex. There had been something deeper than just the excitement of exploring each other's bodies. The I-love-you's that we practiced saying to each other had somehow managed to wrap around my internal organs. It hurt not to have Diana in my life and having to try to avoid her in school. We'd fought because we didn't have much in common. I knew I'd stayed longer in the relationship than I should have because I liked her dad. Leaving your girlfriend wasn't easy.

Maybe the hurt I was feeling for leaving Diana was why, within the first month, I noticed a dark-haired, dark-eyed girl named Sandy Martino. We started flirting in Mrs. Sunshine's art class. It soon became evident that we knew each other from years earlier. When Sandy was in fifth grade, I was the crossing guard at the corner; I'd waved to her when it was safe to cross the street. We spoke of the coincidence as destiny. We'd sit in art class listening to anti-war songs by Peter, Paul and Mary and Bob Dylan.

Sandy had her life all planned out. She was going to go to New Paltz State Teachers College and become an art teacher. She said she'd be able to do this because she'd live with her parents and not have to pay for the dorms.

"What are you planning to do when you graduate?" she asked looking right into my eyes.

"Anything I want," I stammered, trying to make a joke out of not knowing what the Hell I was going to do.

"We're at war. You're going to have to make up your mind or the military's going to do it for you. Do you know a man named Hank Schulte?"

"Yeah, I know Hank. He graduated last year. We were in Boy Scouts together."

"He's dead, killed in Vietnam. My mother told me this morning."

"Shit, you're kidding."

"No, I heard Mrs. Sunshine talking with Mr. Stanley in the hall."

"Christ! Dead. I can't believe that. His dad's a stonemason. They built a lot of the brick houses in New Paltz."

"You've been thinking about going, haven't you?"

"What do you mean?"

"I can see how much Hank's death upsets you. And I know you haven't filled out your application to Dutchess Community College, have you?"

"I have to. In fact, I've been accepted."

"Why didn't you tell me?"

"I don't know. Let's just drop it for now, OK?"

I took her hand and drew her behind a standing screen and wrapped my arms around her. Her long black hair encircled both of us as we kissed.

It was April when I gave Sandy my class ring. She put the ring on a gold chain and wore it around her neck. I asked her to my Senior Prom, and we went with Dave and his new girlfriend, Donna Badami. What I was planning to do at the end of the school year came up in our conversations more and more.

My good friend, Tom Davison said, "I'm signing up before he kills me." Tom was talking about his dad who was a retired Air Force pilot who flew in World War II.

"He can't leave the military out of his house, so fuck him. I'll join the Marines and show him what the real military is about."

Tom wanted Dave and me to join with him. We said we would, but it didn't happen. Then Tom showed up one day saying he'd signed up. We'd gotten our wires crossed; he signed up, but Dave and I hadn't. I felt like I'd let him down.

Tom joining the Marines pushed Dave and me further into confusion. Tom's needing to get away from his old man was the same problem I was facing. If I went to college I'd have no choice but to ask my father for money. I was sure he'd be extracting a price for that. The more I thought about it the clearer it became: signing up would solve the problem for me, too. It would be something so outrageous everyone would think I was cool. I wasn't a good student anyway, and I had no real interest in anything except keeping away from my father.

In the summer of 1967 the body counts were on TV every night. It was in Mr. Bennett's history class that the War drilled into my consciousness. Until then I didn't know where Vietnam was on the world map. When Bennett's wooden pointer popped against the plastic map, I sat up in my seat.

"You boys better pay attention; some of you are going to call this place home. It's Vietnam."

It was hard to think of Dave as a Marine; he was overweight with a round pimply face. His mom had worked serving food in the school cafeteria. She died of cancer that year. After her death his dad got lost in whiskey. Dave started spending a lot of time with me. He wasn't sure of a meal at home anymore. He put his sleeping bag on the floor of the cabin.

Dave's older brother, John, had graduated a year earlier. He joined the Marines to get away from his mom's death and the old man's drinking. One day Dave showed me a letter from John. "I'll kill you if you join the Marines," it read. That Saturday Dave and I took the local bus to Kingston to talk with the Marine Corps recruiter.

"You boys are going to have the time of your lives!" said Gunny Claypool. The fluorescent lights above his desk glared off his clean-shaven head. His green uniform was pressed knife-blade sharp and the red insignias gleamed on his shoulders.

"If you guys sign up for a four year hitch you'll be eligible for the Buddy Plan. The Corps will guarantee that you'll stay together for your entire four-year tour. What do you think about that, men?" Gunny asked, pulling down his uniform sleeve. "Why don't you men step into the other room with me? I have a test that will determine if you can get into the Air Wing."

He pushed the door open and Dave and I walked in. I could smell his aftershave. We sat at a large round table, and Claypool handed us each a stack of papers.

"Give me one hour after you finish the test and I'll have the results. Can you stay for another hour?"

I looked at Dave and he nodded yes.

"Good, I'll give you a few bucks and you can have lunch on me while you wait. How's that sound, men?"

"Great, Gunny. Thanks."

"Gunny, is this going to require any spelling?"

"No it's a multiple choice test. Why do you ask?"

"I can't spell for shit and just needed a heads up. Thanks," I said, turning over the top page.

When Gunny had left, Dave said, "Seems like a nice guy."

"Yeah, he's paying for lunch."

"What happens if we pass?" Dave asked.

"Listen, you know if we don't go to college, we're going to have about a month before we're drafted. That means we'll go in and become ground-pounders, grunts. Those are the guys coming home in body bags. If we pass, we can see the War from an airplane. That's what I think."

Dave ran his hand through his long, dirty-blond hair. "I like the idea of being sent to school for a year before they send us to Nam. The War might be over by then and we'll come out with a skill. I'll do it if you do," he said.

"OK." I closed my eyes and thought about how I'd break the news to my parents and Sandy.

A few days later, sitting on Sandy's front porch, I decided to just blurt it out. "Saturday Dave and I signed up."

She looked at me, but didn't say anything. Then she bent her head and started to weep. After a long while she looked up at me.

"You've just put our lives on hold for four years, and you didn't even talk to me."

"I didn't feel I had any choice."

"You had a choice to tell me what you were doing, didn't you?"

"No, well you're right, I should've talked to you. When I started looking at going to college I knew it meant being under my father's rule. I couldn't take that. You know how he treats me."

"Maybe that's true, but I don't treat you like him. You should've talked to me. You might be killed over there. Did you think about that?"

"That's why I joined the Marine Air Wing. I won't be going over there as a grunt and they're giving me a year of education. Maybe the War will be over by then. Anyway my training on aircraft could mean a job when I get out." I put my arm around her shoulders. "San, if I don't go to school I'll go to Nam anyway. This way I get some kind of choice."

She looked at me, trying to absorb what I was saying. She folded into my arms and we squeezed each other, trying to form a bond that might survive my decision.

Chapter 14

Jarhead

The bait on the end of the Marine Corps hook was a poster of a young man with close-cropped hair in a dress blue uniform. His expression said, "I'm a nice guy, but don't fuck with me." My father's flinching when I asked him if he'd pay for college had set the hook for the USMC to reel me in.

When I told friends I'd joined the Marines, I'd see their eyes glaze over. I loved this. Only later did I realize it was sorrow in their eyes and not envy. Already in 1967 protesters and warmongers were showing their teeth to each other at New Paltz State Teachers College, which was only a block from my high school. College students paraded around with hand painted signs saying things like Stop The War Now! and Johnson's a killer. The warmongers were not as visible; they were men like John the barber, the guy who'd cut my hair since I was a kid. When I told him I was going, he put his scissors down, snapped his heels together and saluted me. "You kill as many of those Gook bastards as you can get your hands on."

Most of my father's friends belonged to the VFW. When I ran into my father's friend, Bill, he said, "We should be kicking more ass over there. Johnson should just drop the big one, kill the fuckin' Commies and get the Goddamn thing over with."

One night in the cabin I finally told Bobby I'd joined. He rolled his eyes.

"Good luck man. I'm going to college. The Marines are crazy. You're gonna get killed."

"Cut the shit, Bobby. I'm just doing what you're afraid to do."

"I'm telling you, man. People are getting killed over there. Look at Hank Schulte, and he was in the Army. Marines are always the first in and the last out, and not all of them come out. My Uncle Jim was a Marine."

"He came home, didn't he?"

"Yeah, but he never stops talking about killing Gooks."

"Isn't that what war is about: kill them before they kill you. Your trouble is that you think like a hippie. You think maybe we should go over there and plow the Gooks' rice paddy for them."

Bobby shrugged. "You're a Goddamn hardhead. That's just the kind of guy the Marines want."

"No shit. Thank God for hardheads. Somebody's got to protect your ass while you're expanding your brain. Did you ever notice your uncle doesn't take any shit from anyone?"

"Yeah, you're right; no one messes with him. My mother won't let him drink in our house anymore after he pinned my old man against the wall for saying Korea was a waste of time."

Towards the end of August, Bobby was getting ready to go off to college. He gave me his key to our padlock. "Keep this away from your brothers so they don't mess with our stuff."

I was working at a local apple farm, lugging 50 pound crates of Mackintosh, Red and Golden Delicious apples for 12 hours a day. I felt my body was ready for whatever the Marines had to dish out.

Everyone kept telling me how tough the Marines were on their recruits. But not everyone had an old man like mine. If the old man taught me anything, it was how to take a beating. He'd kicked me with his steel-toed work boots, whipped me with a rubber hose, slapped and punched me into line, and worked me like a man since I was old enough to pick up a shovel. The way I saw it, what could the Marines do that the old man hadn't already done?

Chapter 15

Gyrenes

Gunny Claypool smiled at the two new Gyrenes he was reeling in.

"In 30 days, men, you'll be going to Albany to get physicals; then you'll be off to Parris Island boot camp in South Carolina."

Gunny snapped his heels together and snapped his right arm up. I flinched, then relaxed when I saw that he was saluting us.

"Good luck, men."

We had September to do whatever we wanted. Sandy was busy taking AP courses in high school, already working towards her college degree. For a month Dave and I got up whenever we felt like it, ate whatever we wanted and tried to forget what we were waiting for. Dave's dad, who was a World War II vet, was feeling guilty that his son hadn't asked him for advice about joining the Marines, so he let us use his 1960 Chevy Bel Air. He didn't need the car anyway; the Ireland Corners bar was right across the street from their house.

On bright September days we drove the streets of New Paltz ogling the new shipment of college girls that had just arrived. The ratio at New Paltz College was ten women to one man. The sexual revolution was in full swing and many of these fine women weren't wearing bras.

Dave and I were puffing up with Marine pride and went around telling everyone we were going to Nam. We'd often have lunch at P&G's Bar where we'd drink beer and brag that we were going over to kill Viet Cong. No one paid much attention to us.

We spent the days of September as quickly as two boys could spend ten dollars at a carnival. Suddenly October 2 was upon us, the day before we were to leave. I was at Sandy's house until the wee hours of the morning. She waved when I left. I looked back and saw her standing in the doorway, the porch light shining on her long black hair. I turned and walked home.

In the morning Mom was sitting in the kitchen when I came down. It was the first time in two years that I'd slept in my bedroom. I could see Dad outside fiddling with the lawn mower. Mom was softly crying with a crumpled tissue in her hand. She shoved the tissue up the sleeve of her housecoat and stood.

"You want me to make you something?"

"I'm not hungry, Ma."

"You've got to eat."

"We'll get something at the bus station."

She went to the sink and looked out the window. I put my arm over her shoulders.

"Ma, I got to go."

"Yell for your father to come in first."

I opened the back door. "Dad, I got to go."

He left the mower and came in. The three of us stood in the kitchen looking at the floor. My two brothers and sister were still sleeping.

"I got to go."

Mom pulled me to her, pushing her face into my neck. Dad looked at his hands. Pulling away, I opened the back door.

"See ya, Ma. See ya, Dad."

"See ya, son," Dad whispered, taking a step towards me. He stuck out his hand and squeezed mine firmly. "How're you going?" he asked.

"Thruway to Albany, then we'll come back down the Thruway to the City."

"Remember once I told you that the Thruway would take you out of here."

"Yeah," I said, dropping his hand.

He put his arm around Mom. "It's OK, sweetheart; he'll be coming back."

Chapter 16

"Girl, Turd, Puke, Worm"

October 3, 1967, held the promise of a dazzling day: no clouds, and a keen breeze reddened our faces. The sun lit up Mohonk Mountain when Dave and I stepped on the Trailways bus. We were bound for Albany where we had a reservation in a hotel. It was the first time staying in a hotel for both of us.

After getting our room key we checked out the room; it smelled of urine. That afternoon, we both passed our military physicals. Afterwards we made jokes about the doctor with 60 men in their underwear standing in line waiting for him. One at a time he asked each one of us, "Drop 'em please." With his new rubber glove he inserted his index finger.

"You think being a Marine is a tough job. Nothing compares to what that doctor has to face everyday," I said, squeezing my nose with my thumb and forefinger.

That night we slept in our clothes.

In the morning we stood in a line waiting to board a Greyhound bus. Parris Island was on the marquee. Dave and I took a seat near the back. Looking towards the windshield we saw heads with hair of various lengths: some close cropped as if they'd been getting ready for what was to come, others shoulder length as if they'd come right from a rock concert. In a few hours all the hair in that bus would be heaped in a pile on the barber's floor in Parris Island.

The bus tunneled all the sounds. I heard New York City street talk with its punching nasal barks. Boston boys spoke with their R's in the back of their throats. We sped into the October night with a constant chattering. It reminded me of trips I'd taken in high school to basketball games. Instead of hearing the names of the opposing team members, the word Gook was repeated over and over again. Anyone overhearing this bus conversation might have thought we were a busload of vets returning from Vietnam, not a bunch of recruits headed there.

By the second hour into our 16-hour ride the chatter quieted. At a rest stop the guys sitting in front of us headed into a bar across the street. They came back with brown paper bags stuffed in their pockets, and sipped from them for the next hour. One guy with short hair started talking loudly.

"My brother's a Marine, and he's been to Nam. He told me that they shot anything with slant eyes."

Moans arose around him. Short Hair realized he'd captured some attention. Stammering a little, he went on.

"M-m-m-my brother said you can't tell the difference between Vietnamese and Viet Cong. So it doesn't matter. They're all Gooks. When his squad came into a village, they shot the dogs and cows."

Somebody in the dark said, "Like Sherman did in the Civil War. Kill and burn all the food sources."

Someone else yelled, "Did they kill women and children?"

Short Hair squinted to see who'd asked the question. "Not until they found one of their men dead with his cock and balls cut off and stuffed into his mouth. That's when the shit really broke loose."

From the front of the bus someone yelled, "Sounds like bullshit. Marines don't kill women and children. Any idiot knows that."

Short Hair looked in the direction of the new voice. "I'm just telling you guys what my brother said."

"This guy's full of shit," I whispered to Dave.

"My brother John's never told me anything like that and he's been in for six months now."

"Yeah, but he's stationed in DC, not Nam," I said.

After Short Hair's lecture we rode on for hours with no one saying much. A hum of voices rose when we passed a sign that read Parris Island Marine Corps Recruit Training Post. A few minutes later the bus tilted forward with a squeal of brakes. The door flew open and a man with a state trooper's hat on sprang up the steps. The interior lights were on and I could see his red face. Veins popped out on his neck. Then he roared, "You assholes got one minute to unload this fucking bus. Now! Goddamn it! Now!" It was as if he was jabbing his head at us trying to bludgeon us with it.

We stepped off the air-conditioned bus into what felt like a warm river. Mold and other strange smells filled my nostrils. I started to sweat, and in moments a swarm of bugs was hovering over my head. The bulging-eyed Drill Instructor was pacing like an enraged animal. White globs of saliva collected at the corners of his mouth. His body jerked like a junkyard dog at the end of its chain.

"All right girls. Keep your fucking mouths shut. Stand on the yellow footprints. Closer, Turds. I want you asshole to belly button. I don't want to see you move, talk, fart or think. You got that, girls?" The Drill Instructor spit his words. Then it became so still I could hear the men around me breathing.

"I said you got that, girls? If I don't hear a "Yes, Sir!" real quick, you girls will be standing at attention all night. Did you hear me, girls?"

"YES, SIR!" all 60 of us sang out.

There was a soft giggle. Every head in the formation turned to see the DI take two enormous steps, splitting our ranks. Standing in front of a still smiling recruit, he shoved his mug so close to the boy's face it looked like they were kissing. Then came the sound of clacking teeth. It looked like the DI was biting at the boy's nose. The boy brought his hands to his face.

"Drop those fucking hands!"

A whimpering, "Yes, Sir," came from the boy's mouth.

The DI turned and saw all of us looking at him. "Attention, assholes! Stop eye-fucking me."

The ranks stiffened and someone started laughing. Out of the corner of my eye I saw a man with long hair standing so rigid his clothes were shaking; I couldn't tell if he was giggling or speaking gibberish. The DI mustn't have heard it because he just screamed, "March!" We staggered off the yellow footprints, stumbling to a frog grunting song the DI was singing. Later I'd learn it was called cadence. "Hut, two, three, four! Girls, you look like a herd of fucking sheep."

I stepped on the heels of the man in front of me and slapped arms with the men on either side. "Right flank march!" The column awkwardly turned right, down an unlit street. Our line snaked its way forward, and the night settled in around us.

The air splintered with a shriek. "Platoon halt!" Men tripped and bumped into each other as the platoon attempted to stop. In front of us was a dimly lit sign that read, Receiving Barracks. Yellow light spilled out of a line of windows. We stood at attention, watching as the DI disappeared inside. After 15 minutes of waiting, whispers and low conversations started up. "What do we do next?" was repeated everywhere.

The man behind me slammed into me. I turned to see a running projectile hurl itself into the middle of the platoon. Men tumbled like bowling pins. With a flurry of grunts and slaps, the DI climbed back out of our ranks. Out in front of us, he stood with his hands on his hips baying like a dog.

"Who the Fuck gave you girls permission to talk?"

There was no reply.

"You've got one minute to get your lazy fucking asses into that Goddamn barn, now!"

We stampeded the entrance.

Inside, the DI boomed, "Attention! When I give you the word I want you fucking worms to take everything--I mean EVERYTHING-- out of your pockets and suitcases. If I find you've stashed something, you'll eat it. Do it. Now!"

Jackknives, wallets, and coins tumbled onto the green tables. Paraphernalia poured out as if someone had hit the jackpot at Vegas. Men left their pockets turned out. The DI walked up and down the lines inspecting.

"Are you some kind of faggot?" he said, holding up a man's colored briefs. My tongue was swelling as he moved towards me. He was in front of me, but he suddenly turned towards a crashing sound like a log being dropped off the back of a truck. At the far end of the barracks the man I'd seen shaking and speaking gibberish lay on his back convulsing. The DI rushed to the sick man. Stooping down on one knee he put his mouth to the man's ear and bellowed, "You fucking puke hippie! What the fuck are you doing to my floor?"

The man stiffened and vomited. He tried to cover his mouth with his hands, but his spasms made the vomit spew out between his fingers. The DI stood with his hands on his hips. Lifting his right, spit-shined combat boot, he placed it squarely on the squirming man's chest. Through clenched teeth he slurred, "Get your worthless fucking ass off my floor." The man slithered beneath the DI's foot, smearing his vomit. Vomit clung to his long hair as he struggled to his feet. In a calm voice the DI said, "Take off your shirt and clean up my fucking floor, you fucking puke hippie!"

Strolling over to one of the green tables, the DI fingered through a pile of junk until he found a bottle of Aqua Velva. He handed it to Longhair. "Drink it, you worthless piece of longhaired shit. Your breath stinks. I don't want any of my girls having puke breath."

The man's shaking hand brought the bottle to his lips. He tried to swallow the blue liquid but he couldn't seem to get it down.

"Swallow it, you stinking longhaired puke!"

Bubbles gurgled into the bottle. The recruit's Adam's apple bobbed, and then he doubled over and puked again. A synchronized groan came out of the platoon. I remembered Dave and looked for him. He was standing two tables away with his eyes showing more white than blue.

Taped on the wall behind the DI was the recruiting poster of the Marine in dress blues that had hooked me in high school.

Chapter 17

Assembling a Marine

I'd survived three weeks of boot camp. I never drank so much water in my life. The October sun in South Carolina and the Marine physical training (PT) pumped the water out of my pores. Sweating became like breathing. We had been issued a Marine Corps manual and were told to read the chapter about the M-1 rifle: The M-1 rifle is a gas-operated, clip-fed, air-cooled, semi-automatic shoulder weapon. We already knew that a Marine without a weapon was only a half a Marine. We'd just been issued M-1's, but all of us were disappointed that we got these old World War II weapons instead of the M-16's Marines were using in Nam. We wouldn't even be using the M-16 at the rifle range; we were told we'd be getting M-14's.

Marine training was about building physical strength, endurance and discipline and our rifle was central to all of it. We'd start with PT everyday, sometimes doing a thousand squat-thrusts before doing short order drill on the parade deck with our rifles for an hour and a half. We'd pound our heels into the parade deck trying to synchronize them all hitting at the same instant. We must have looked like a green caterpillar bristling with M-1 rifle barrels.

This morning we'd been awake only a few minutes and already I felt the humidity filming on my skin. A quick look at my wristwatch told me it was 5 a.m.

"All right girls, give me a hundred," Corporal White barked.

He wanted a hundred squat thrusts from each of us. After a few minutes the rhythm of our hands on the floor together, then our feet thrust back landing on our toes together, then the sliding of feet back to the position so we could stand became the heartbeat of the platoon. Each one of us was attuned to these sounds and tried to time them to happen at the same moment. In just a few minutes our skivvies were sweat-soaked. I'd never had a sports workout in high school that was anything like this.

At the mess hall I shoveled food like coal into a locomotive. I'd quickly learned that before I sat down to eat it was a good idea to gulp four or five glasses of milk standing at the machine just in case we got called out of the mess hall before we ate. This had happened several times already. I gulped milk, feeling the energy in it being sucked right into my blood stream.

Each drill instructor seemed to have his own way of Making a Marine. It was easy to see that the first task was to weed out the weak and insubordinate. Corporal White, the youngest of our three DI's, had this job well in hand. He had a finely tuned sense of where a man's breaking point was and pushed each of us right to the very edge of it. Several men disappeared in the first few days. Corporal White took a recruit named Savage and strapped his arms under his belt because he'd swing them out every time he did an about-face. White then marched Savage in the back of our platoon where every passing DI could laugh openly at the spectacle. I felt sorry for Savage, but it looked so outrageous I had to swallow hard not laugh.

Sergeant Montgomery was the DI that tested our basic Marine Corps education such as learning the chain of command. I watched him disassemble a bleached-face recruit named Calvin who stood in formation across from me.

"What's the color of Napoleon's white horse?" Corporal Montgomery asked Calvin.

Calvin's forehead wrinkled and his eyes rolled around. "Not sure, Sir." Calvin was gone that afternoon.

Heat, humiliation, physical exhaustion and loneliness were the DI's tools for separating possible Marines from the non-hackers. Gunny Webb, our senior drill instructor, had other more sophisticated psychological tools in his box. He was the only DI that handed out our mail. Before he'd hand the mail out we'd have to sit around him on the floor and listen to him tell us what a Marine was. "Leadership is what Marines are about. What you are learning today, right now in fact, is leadership. Years from now you'll remember me and the other DI's you met here in boot camp. Did you hear me?"

"Yes, Sir," we bellowed.

"I don't want any of you men to kid yourselves about why you are here. It's simple; you're here to learn to kill. To learn to kill you must first learn obedience and discipline. What two words did I just say?"

"Obedience and discipline, Sir."

"Good, that's very good. If you don't obey an order on the battlefield you will become dead or the other men you are with will become dead. I've seen many of you men slapping at the sand fleas biting your necks. The sand flea is one of our most important trainers here at Parris Island. When I tell you to stand at attention and sand fleas are biting you, it's your job to stand at attention and let them bite. On the battlefield if you slap at insects biting you, you could have a bullet hole in your forehead and so could the men around you. Are you with me men?"

"Yes, Sir."

"The last thing I'm going to talk about is tradition. The day before you graduate you'll be given the globe and anchor pin, this will connect you to every Marine, dead and alive. You will then become part of the brotherhood of Marines who have fought in the wars that have protected democracy and freedom in America. Did you hear me men?

"Yes, Sir!"

Stuffing our mail back into the pouch, he said, "That's enough for now. I'll hand the mail out tomorrow. Good night men!"

"Good Night, Sir."

Chapter 18

My New Best Friend

My platoon number was 2058 and we were in our seventh week of training, which meant we'd be going to the rifle range. We'd traded in our M-1 rifles in order to get used to the M-14's that we'd be firing at the range. They weren't M-16's, but were happy to get rid of the old M-1's; the M-14 had a lot more firepower. Gunny Webb told us that the range was the most important week of our training. "The range is the equalizer. If you weren't good at physical fitness or parade drill, you can redeem yourself by being a crack shot."

We all learned to recite The Marine's Code:

This is my Rifle.

There are many like it but this one is mine. My rifle is my best friend. It is my life. My rifle, without me is useless. Without my rifle, I am useless. I must fire my rifle true. I must shoot straighter than my enemy who is trying to kill me. I must shoot him before he shoots me. I will.

The late November South Carolina sun felt like July in New York. Every time the DI let us go to the head I'd wrap my lips around the end of the sink faucet and turn the cold on until it filled my stomach. There'd been some scuttlebutt whispered at night about the rifle range. It was said that the DI's eased up on pushing us. Dave had whispered to me once in the head, "They'll stop fucking with us when we get to the range; they want good target scores." I knew that the base Commanders watched each platoon carefully, judging everything from how fast, hard and long we could force march, to the precision we'd mastered in parade-drill. Every platoon in our battalion was in competition to be the best. The highest score meant a feather in the DI's Smokey Bear hat.

The scuttlebutt turned out to be true; the DI's backed off when we got to the range. Our only focus for the week was shooting. In the final days at the range our concentration was focused on qualifying. The lowest acceptable score earned you a Marksman badge, next the

Sharpshooter badge, and the highest was the two-crossed silver rifles, the Expert badge. The night before our final day on the range Corporal White sat us down and told us that anyone who didn't qualify would be crawling the three miles back to the barracks.

In the end three men didn't qualify. It was around midnight when they stumbled into the barracks. Gunny Webb turned on the lights, and standing there were three men covered in mud. Their red knees stuck out of the holes in their utility trousers. It felt good to climb back into my rack with its clean sheets.

That last day on the range I'd been firing my rifle from the prone position, the sun warm on my back. I was enjoying pulling the trigger, knowing I'd already qualified with a Marksman badge. Through the burst of rifle fire came the screeching of a siren. I hadn't heard a siren since I'd been in boot camp. When it stopped, an angry voice boomed over a bullhorn, "No one move! All recruits stand at attention. No one move. I repeat, no one. All shooters, put your safeties on, remove the clips from your rifles and check your chambers for rounds. Then stand at attention. Those lying prone, do not move."

Once I'd put the safety on and checked my chamber I lay still on my stomach. I heard the two DI's behind me whispering.

"Holy, shit! Some crazy fucking recruit's shot a DI down on Range Three."

Glancing sideways I saw the recruit laying a few yards to my left roll his head side to side when he heard this. The two DI's dropped on him like starving sled dogs on raw meat. One grabbed his rifle. The other screamed in his ear, "Are you fucking deaf asshole?" They jerked him to his feet, put the bullhorn over his nose and bellowed, "If you move as much as a fucking hair you'll be in the brig."

Slowly I checked to make sure I'd put the safety on. I had and I relaxed. For ten minutes I looked down range at the red and white flags fluttering on top of the target buildings. Crows landed in the trees at the edge of the range. It felt good to lie in the prone position. I couldn't remember the last time I lay on my stomach doing nothing. I imagined the recruits standing at attention, how their knees must be feeling.

I woke when I felt something between my legs. I was being squeezed. I couldn't figure out what was going on but the pain grew stronger. Then I realized my balls were being squashed. I'd fallen asleep waiting for the bullhorn. I turned my head slowly to see a Lance Corporal Range Instructor with his foot lodged between my legs. He pressed harder on my balls with the toe of his boot.

"Get your fucking foot off of me or I'll blow your mother-fucking head off," I whispered.

He lifted his boot and backed away silently. He wasn't a DI, but it was against orders to speak to anyone who held a higher rank. Nothing had happened, but somewhere deep inside I knew it could have. I couldn't get the term "hair-trigger" out of my head. It was a term the DI's used about different rifles. I heard Gunny telling Private Johnson, "Someone may have filed that rifle; watch it carefully; it's got a hair-trigger."

My own trigger had been filed to within a breath of exploding. Every time I got pushed, like the guy putting his foot on my balls, I could feel my ability to control myself lessen. A week before I'd seen a man snap. Our platoon was marching past another platoon standing at attention when Corporal White said, "Keep your eyes forward men." Out of the corner of my eye I saw a recruit being held down by two DI's. He screamed, "Leave me the fuck alone. I'll kill for you if you let me go." Before we got past them he began to weep uncontrollably.

"That ain't no Marine; it's just some punk kid who snapped," Corporal White said.

I wondered if I snapped would I kill someone or run. Then I remembered Parris Island was surrounded by swamp. I'd heard about men dying in that swamp; they said it was filled with gators and cottonmouth snakes.

Chapter 19

The Hymn

One early November afternoon, we'd finished the range and were sitting at the feet of Gunny Webb waiting for our mail. He was telling us about how he felt being a Marine. "Soon you'll call yourselves Marines. When I hear the Marine Corps Hymn the hair on the back of my neck stands up. There is no greater honor than to know you'll give your life for your country," he said, sitting up even straighter.

Like boys we sat at Gunny's feet listening. "Let me tell you about something that happened to me in Nam. That's where most of you are going. I had a squad of good men in the hills around Da Nang in 1965. Cramer, stop looking at the door and listen to what I'm telling you! We talk a lot about killing Gooks here in boot camp. But what you better know is that a Gook is a God forsaken bastard, but he's a Goddamn good fighter, especially if you piss him off. Did you hear what I said?"

"Yes, Sir," we all bellowed at once."

"They'll crawl through a mile of wire a night to cut your throat. I know. I lost three of my best men from perimeter guard that night. A Gook had cut his way through the wire and was struggling with Bates, my M-60 machinegunner. The Gook had one hand over Bates' mouth to keep him from yelling and was trying to hack him with the machete in his other hand. Bates bit his fingers and screamed, "We're being overrun." The Gook stepped back and swung the machete, hacking off Bates' arm at the elbow. Then a stream of Gook raced in through the wire. We killed 15 that night and lost three good men."

"What happened to Bates, Sir?" Private Savage asked from behind the hand that was covering his mouth. None of us expected an answer. I hadn't heard a DI answer a direct question since I'd been there.

"Silver Star," Gunny said, bringing his hand to his chin. "That was the good part. The bad part was that I had to tell the families about how I'd lost their sons." Slowly he looked around the room taking each one of us in.

Later that night the three men who didn't qualify at the rifle range all got GI showers. Gunny had called three of his best recruits into his office before lights out. He told the recruits who to get to help them on the shower detail and that they were never to tell anyone that he was involved.

An hour after lights out someone yanked on my bed sheets. "Cabresio's in the head. Gunny told me you have to help us. Let's go."

Four of us circled Cabresio, one man with a scrub brush in his hand, another one with a bar of soap in a sock. I grabbed Cabresio's arm and twisted it until he went down on his knees on the wet tile floor. Another man pulled out his legs, flattening him. The guy with the soap in a sock started pelting Cabresio with a fury. I could hear him grunting through his teeth, "If you open your fucking mouth, I'll hit you in the head." The guy holding his legs kept saying, "Sorry, man. I'm really sorry, man. Gunny Webb told us we had to do this cause you fucked up at the range."

I took my turn with the scrub brush on his back and became flushed with excitement--hating what I was doing...and loving it.

We left Cabresio curled up in his underwear on the shower room floor.

The GI shower worked. Cabresio, who had been lagging behind during forced marches, was now pulling his own weight. No longer did other Marines have to hold him under the arms and carry him to the end. He stood straighter and pushed himself a lot harder.

One afternoon Gunny Webb's voice boomed down the squad-bay. "I want you Marines, with full packs and rifles, standing at attention in front of the barracks in two minutes."

"Forward, march," Gunny said softly. We started easy; Gunny talked softly. "You girls been doing nothing but lying around on your asses on the range. It's time for a little motivation. Those rifle scores were shit, girls," he scoffed.

He ran next to us, gradually pushing the pace up to the point where we couldn't quite catch our breath. We ran on like this for a long time before he whispered, "Platoon, halt!" Only half of us heard him, so our formation fell into mayhem. We looked like we did the first night we came to boot camp, falling all over each other. By now we had perfected our marching so that we could perform a perfectly synchronized halt.

"You girls march like a herd of fucking sheep. Attention. Order arms. Port arms. Right shoulder arms. Inspection arms." He spat the commands in rapid succession.

For the past few weeks he'd become obsessed with drilling us in the manual of arms. No great guess that this was the next thing we'd be judged on. Every idle moment he was running us through a rifle drill. We did the manual of arms until our arms ached. I thought I could hear my muscles snapping over my bones.

"Girls, the object is to feel the weapon as if it were part of your body. It is pain that makes this happen. Stack arms!" he finally ordered. With his hands behind his back he walked up and down our ranks inspecting weapons stacked in tripods. He stopped and looked at my rifle. Slowly raising his head he stepped towards me, put his mouth to my ear and whispered, "Retrieve your weapon, Turd."

I broke formation and reached for my rifle. The two men adjacent to me were forced to break formation to retrieve their rifles so they wouldn't fall. The moment I had my rifle in my hands I saw that the safety was off.

Gunny stood back and smiled, then lowered his head so the broad brim of his hat hid his face. I was trying to figure out how to put the safety on when he jerked his head up and roared, "Present Arms!" I was so scared I didn't understand the command and made no response.

"Present arms, you fucking worm!"

Weeks of discipline took over, and my rifle snapped from my right shoulder to the position of Present Arms. My legs were shaking. Gunny's arm shot out like a rattlesnake, grabbing my rifle by the barrel and flinging it into the sand. I stared at my rifle lying in the dirt. It was sacrilege for a Marine's rifle to be dirty. It was drilled into me that a dirty weapon equaled death.

92

"Retrieve your rifle!"

When I picked it up, sand streamed out of the barrel.

"Attention, Turd! Port arms."

Gunny stood in front of me. I studied his face without moving my eyes. He was a short man who had to stand on his toes to reach my ear. He walked over to an ammo box and sat down.

"Give me your rifle, son," he said in an endearing voice.

I pushed the rifle out from my chest for him to take. He lay the rifle across his knees.

"Come here, son."

I stepped towards him.

Looking up into my eyes he said, "At ease. Pull back the operating rod."

I bent over the rifle and pulled back the operation rod. I heard the sand grinding against the steel as the bolt locked in place.

"Put your thumb in the chamber, son."

"Why is he making me do this?" I wondered to myself.

"Release the bolt."

I remembered reading in the Marine manual that 15 pounds of spring tension forced the M-14's steel bolt into the chamber. I wanted to ask Gunny why the Hell I would want to do such a stupid thing?

My fingers trembled as I released the bolt. The driving steel cylinder sank into my thumbnail. My arm muscles danced spasmodically causing the operating rod to push further home. Gunny Webb smiled. The 75-man platoon stood at attention a few yards away.

"Pull the trigger, son."

"I hate you," I thought to silently to myself. "What?" I snapped out loud, quickly adding, "Sir."

"Pull the trigger." He still spoke in a soft voice.

"But, Sir?"

"Pull the Goddamn trigger or the next thing you'll be doing is putting your cock in the chamber," he screeched in a falsetto.

Reaching across my body, I put my index finger in the trigger guard and pulled. A faint click sent the firing pin into my thumbnail. Pain raced up the bones of my arm as if I'd stuck my thumb into an electrical outlet.

I sank to my knees, my weapon still in Gunny's lap. Tears ran down my cheeks. I worried they'd drip on his trousers. With my lip between my teeth I tried to bite back the pain. When I closed my eyes all I could see was Gunny's thick red neck. It was happening. I could feel it coming. A few more seconds and I'd kill him. Not him or any man or group of men would be able to stop me. Swallowing lumps of pain, I forced myself away from the image of his neck.

"Stand up, son."

When I straightened, the rifle lifted off his lap. Searing pain ran up my forearm to my shoulder, then circled inside my skull.

"Attention, you fucking Turd! Forward march! Not that way, Turd. Out there, in front of my girls. Show them that filthy rifle, you worthless Shit!" Gunny's eyebrows scrunched; his nostrils flared. "Listen to me, Turd! Now sing the Marine Corps Hymn."

"Yes, Sir," I whimpered, thinking he must know me better than I do. He was still alive and I was doing what he told me. He knew just how far to push. I reached to support the rifle with my free hand. Blood was dripping from the barrel.

"Get your fucking hand off that weapon, Turd. You jeopardized the lives of my girls. Keep your fucking hand off that weapon or we're going to be here all night."

"Yes, Sir."

I staggered in front of the platoon, avoiding their eyes. Every one of them knew it could have been them. Today each one breathed easier; Winters was the Turd to teach the lesson.

I mouthed the hymn, the words sticking in my throat. "From the Halls of Montezuma to the shores of Tripoli."

"I can't hear you, Turd! Louder!"

"Yes, Sir." I raised my voice and it cracked with pain. "From...the H-h-h--halls of Montezuma, to the shores of Tripoli; we will f-f-fight our country's battles, in the air, on land, and sea..."

Tiptoeing, trying not to jounce the rifle, I sang. The brilliant pains strengthened my voice. Each throbbing spike infused me with unknown power. I bellowed out the verses louder with every drip of blood. I stopped tiptoeing, stood straighter and sang full-throated. Between breaths I could hear the platoon singing the hymn with me and the hair on the back of my neck stood up.

Chapter 20

Job's Done

My parents came to Parris Island for boot camp graduation. They seemed so unhappy about me joining the Marines that I couldn't believe they came. It was good to see them. I felt like something had changed when I was talking with my father. I saw something different in his eyes, and he seemed smaller. Spending the last 13 weeks learning the most advanced methods of how to kill, must have changed me. Dave's Dad didn't come, so he hung out with me and my parents.

A few days after graduation we went home on leave. It felt great getting off the bus in my hard-earned dress uniform. Dave's sister picked him up at the bus station, and I walked up to see Sandy a few blocks away. When she came to the door I stood proudly at attention. She crashed into me, wrapping me in her arms and sobbing.

After a few days home Dave and I decided to go over to the high school. Dave was looking for a new teacher named Gino Ventura. His girlfriend Donna had written him a Dear John letter in boot camp. Donna said in the letter that she had a new boyfriend. She didn't tell him that it was her teacher; he found that out from some friends he'd run into in town.

We had our uniforms on when we walked through the doors of the high school. It felt like we owned the place. We were pumped up and wild. We'd spent months singing songs about killing Viet Cong, and we were back to show everyone our War Dance.

With puffed out chests we dug our shoe heels into the asphalt tiles of the high school hallway, looking for this guy Ventura who was screwing Dave's girl.

We made enough noise to bring out a few teachers, but when they saw who it was, we got handshakes. Mr. Bennett, Mr. Fiori, Mrs. Moore, they all knew we were going Nam. Before we remembered why we'd come, we were leaving with a group of well wishers standing in the hall, waving good-bye and saying, "Good luck, men, and God bless."

It was hard being home after getting so keyed up by boot camp. We'd been trained to do the job like Gunny said: "To kill." Now we were home on vacation. Sure I was afraid I might be killed in Nam, but still, the waiting was murder. It was hard knowing that death loomed somewhere in my future. There was no escape from it. The War was on the news every day. Every person I spoke with asked me if I was going. It was becoming sickening to see the fear in people's eyes. I wanted the focus of boot camp to come back, where I felt proud and strong. It had already faded with the falling of fresh January snow in New York. My thin uniform was not enough for the cold.

We left New Paltz a few days later, taking the bus to Camp Geiger, North Carolina, where we'd start infantry training.

Chapter 21

Freedom's Fall

It was freezing in North Carolina but nothing like what we'd left in New York. There was no snow on the ground and the green field jacket they issued me was warm enough. Infantry training at Camp Geiger was to teach us things like how to throw grenades and all the nomenclature and operation of the Marine ground weapons. We would also "bivouac," the military term for camping out, and do several ten-mile forced marches in full gear.

I got stuck on mess duty for the first 30 days. One day I spent the afternoon opening cans of potatoes dated 1945; we were eating food prepared for Marines who fought in World War II.

After three month of infantry training, Dave and I got sent to Memphis Navel Base to train at metal smith school to give us the skills to repair airplanes and helicopters. On April 4, 1968, Martin Luther King was assassinated in Memphis, only 20 miles from our base. The base commander ordered Marines to be issued riot gear and to begin training in riot control. As the tension built we practiced being spit on and pushing protective shields into each other's faces. Nothing ever happened, and after a week, we went back to learning how to rivet metal patches on aircraft.

Dave and I graduated metal smith school in the fall of 1968. We both got orders for New River, North Carolina, where we joined the helicopter squadron HMH 361. There we learned the nomenclature and mechanical operation of a CH-53 helicopter. After eight more months we left New River knowing how to patch bullet holes on helicopters, and not much more.

Early summer of 1969 our squadron received orders to deploy to Vietnam. But first, Dave and I got 30 days of leave back in New Paltz. The unease of the War before us penetrated our days. The daily newscasts from Vietnam and the long nights at Sandy's house made the leave feel like it lasted forever.

We found out after we came back from leave that half the squadron would fly to Vietnam on commercial planes, and the other half would go with the choppers to San Diego, California, to board the USS New Orleans, a small Naval aircraft carrier called an LPH--Landing Platform for Helicopters. We sailed from San Diego via Hawaii to Okinawa, then the final leg ending off the coast of Vietnam.

I got orders to go with the choppers. Dave flew over with the squadron. In San Diego I spent a week in a barracks while our birds were being loaded onto the ship. My good friend Nile McCoy, who we fondly called Bowling Ball Head, was with me in the barracks. Nile's name for me was Crazy. He and I'd spent eight months in a four man cubical in New River. The most curious thing about Nile was that no one had ever seen his cock. Living as close as we all did, performing all the necessary functions of living, sleeping, relaxing, studying, and daily hygiene, you'd think someone would have caught a glimpse of it. But no one had. We just resigned ourselves to the fact that someone must have had to see it or he wouldn't be in the Marines.

We kidded behind Nile's back that he had a case of the hidden genitalia, but no one brought this up to his face. I'd seen Nile shrink a man in an instant with his bullwhip tongue. He'd start with something like, "Hey MO FO, look at me! There ain't nothing between you and me, but fear and atmosphere..." Then he'd take in a deep breath, "...and there goes the atmosphere. So jump, Mother Fucker! Come on, Bitch! There ain't no stop sign on my chest. Jump!"

We were lying on our bunks in San Diego when Nile began talking. "You see that shit on the tube?"

"What's that?" I asked.

"Shit about the Chicago eight, you know, Bobby Seale and Abbey Hoffman, and those other guys. They were trying to start a riot with the folks that were protesting the war. They were using some Civil Rights act called H. Rap Brown Law to bust 'em."

"No shit. I heard that the Judge Hoffman couldn't even say the guys' names right," I said, opening up my wall locker.

"Listen, man, I've been thinking. This War's not worth losing my ass over." Nile thumbed his nose, something he did almost every time he spoke.

"I know what you mean. When we saw Walter Cronkite a few months ago say he didn't think we could win the War I started to think about what we we're headed into. In boot camp they got me so fired up I was ready to kill anything."

"That's what boot camp's supposed to do. Give you the balls to charge a machinegun nest and take the brains away that would make you ask the question, 'Why?'"

"So, what are you thinking about? I mean where the Hell could we go?" I asked, sitting back on my bunk.

"Let's think this out a little more. Remember the guys coming back from Nam in New River. They were the angriest men I've ever seen. They hated the VC for killing their buddies; they hated the Hippies for spitting on them in the airports; they hated the lifers for thinking of the Corps instead of them. They said that everyone had fucked them. Do you want to be like them when you come home? That is, IF you come home?"

"Not me, man. But I don't want to run for the rest of my life either. I've heard that the military police track down AWOL's."

"Shit, that's what they want you to think. They can't find enough men to send to Nam. You think they're going to waste good men on tracking down the thousands who have left the country?"

"I don't know, man. Maybe we won't be stationed in such a bad place over there? Remember, man, we're not going in as grunts."

Nile looked at the ceiling and thumbed his nose. "I heard we're going to a place called Phu Bai. You know where that is? It's up by the DMZ. The DMZ's hot, man; that's why the Marines are up there. I'll tell ya what my plan is and you tell me if you're interested. I'm gonna rent a bike and ride around and just see what happens. Maybe I'll keep riding, maybe I won't. I'm just going to leave it up to how I feel, and if you come along you can do the same. You interested?"

"Maybe," I said, taking my wallet off the shelf of the wall locker and putting it in my back pocket. "Let's see what the road has to say about it. Where we getting the bikes?"

"There's a bike place just down the street. I scoped it out. Costs 25 bucks a day. Fred Rasuhour said he'd like to come. That OK with you?"

"Yeah. Has he's been thinking about splitting?"

"Yeah. Said he knows a little Spanish. That might come in handy down in Mexico."

"Sounds like you're ready to go."

"Let's not get too serious now, Crazy. Let's go out, have a good time and if it feels right, we'll go with it. Is that cool?"

"Makes no sense to me, but I'm in."

None of us had motorcycle licenses but somehow we ended up leaving the shop with two Yamaha 250's. It felt good rolling around the San Diego streets. I was alone on one bike; Nile and Fred were on the other. I was following Nile when he suddenly made a right hand turn on to a side street and gunned the motor. His front wheel came off the ground, and Fred screamed, "What the fuck are you doing?" Fred's feet were splayed out on either side of he bike. He'd told us that he'd never ridden on a bike before. Houses flashed by as we sped towards a reddening sun. Gradually, the houses thinned into open fields. I signaled to Nile to pull over.

"You know where we are?"

"Yeah, I think I can get us back. What's the matter, you afraid we're lost?"

"We've made so many turns, I'm not sure where the Hell I am."

"We're cool, leave it to me," Nile said, gunning the bike, his rear tire spitting stones against my legs. Fred gripped Nile around the waist as the bike wobbled into a straight line. The throttle felt good in my hand, and I cranked it as far as it would go and flew by Nile and Fred. Nile tried to respond but Fred's extra weight wouldn't let him catch up. Most of the roads we'd been on were flat, but now they started to rise and dip. I saw a sign that said something about the Baja Desert being 50 miles ahead. I slowed and Nile and Fred came up along side. I looked at Nile; he looked back and tilted his head sideways. I knew exactly what he meant. Do we go or not? I closed my eyes for a second, then shook my head once up and down.

The freedom of the speed and the silent decision not to go back to the ship was exhilarating. I refused to let any fear enter my mind. The white lines on the road flashed past like words on a page; I read them: "You are free! Feel it! Free! Feel it, and nothing else".

There was no plan, almost no money, no water. And we raced towards the desert. The insanity of what we were doing made it all the more intense. The sun was low in the sky, and the bike odometer told me we were well over a hundred miles from where we started. There was already no way to get back before evening muster. We were going to be reported AWOL. This idea made us go even faster. I was in the lead starting up a small hill when the road curved towards the right. Just as I came through the curve a car veered in front of me from a side road. It was about to hit me when I swerved into soft gravel at the side of the road and spun out, falling off the bike while it cart wheeled to a stop in the dirt. I looked up in time to see Nile and Fred run head on into the side of a barn. The car never stopped.

I hobbled over to Nile and Fred who lay crumpled on top of the bike. Nile was holding his ribs and Fred lay off to the side of the bike with one leg sticking out at an odd angle. I pulled up his pant leg and saw the bone sticking through the skin.

"It's broken. We got to get him to a hospital. How about you? You OK?"

Nile couldn't get his breath, but he shook his head yes. I straightened Fred's crumpled body out and saw he was coming around. "You got a broken leg, man. I'm gonna stop a car to get us some help."

"I can't feel anything," Fred said, in a panicked voice.

"Don't move!" I yelled. "Nile, keep an eye on him. I'll stand by the road; maybe someone will come along." It was ten minutes before a truck with a man and women in it came by. They slowed but wouldn't roll down the window and just kept going. I ran back to Nile and Fred.

"I couldn't get them to stop."

"Jump in front of the car next time; he's not doing very good," Nile said, pointing to Fred whose eyes were rolling back into his head. I gently lifted both his legs onto a backpack and went back out to the road. As I stood there my thinking slowly started to come back into focus. Our plans had just changed 180 degrees: we were going back, no doubt about it. Fred's leg was broken, and Nile and I might be looking at a court martial. If the Executive Officer saw how far we'd gone and what time it was he'd have to be an idiot not to see that we hadn't planned on coming back. I looked at the side of the barn where the bike had hit. There was some kind of tin siding with a good-sized dent in it. The two bikes lay strewn in the dirt, Nile's beyond repair. I heard a car coming and stood in the middle of the road. It was a red Ford with a woman driving. She stopped and rolled up her windows. I pounded on her roof.

"We had an accident. My friends are hurt. Please call an ambulance for us. Please!"

She looked terrified but shook her head yes as she pulled away. It was 45 minutes before anyone else came by. Some guy stopped and when he looked at Fred's leg he groaned, "Compound fracture. You guys need help right away."

A siren finally sounded as the sun's last light streaked red in the sky.

Fred's compound fracture left him in the hospital for several weeks. He wouldn't be going to Vietnam. Nile and I reported to the XO who said he'd deal with us after the ship was underway.

Chapter 22

In Country

The USS New Orleans left San Diego and turned its bow into the chop of the blue Pacific, its destination Hawaii. Somewhere in the middle of the ocean Nile and I were called to the XO's office. He was a tall man with white skin shining through his sixteenth of an inch of hair. Looking at Nile he asked, "What were you gentlemen doing with those motorcycles?"

"Riding, Sir?" Nile said, removing his cover.

"Just riding? I've spoken to the owner of the motorcycle shop. He told me that it cost $575 to repair the bikes. I guess you know he's expecting payment, so I had both of your salaries garnished. Do either one of you have a problem with that?"

"No, Sir," we said in unison.

"Very well then. That was quite a distance out in the desert where you had the accident. You must have lost track of the time. Very well then, I hope you two have learned your lessons. No more motorcycle riding when we get in to port. Is that understood?"

"Yes, Sir. Thank you, Sir."

"Dismissed!"

Marines called the Navy personnel on the USS New Orleans "Squids," and they called us "Jarheads," most of the time in brotherly fun. The cargo we carried was 30 CH-53's. Our destination was the coast of Vietnam. Dave and the other men in the advanced party were already in Vietnam preparing the base for our arrival. Our days on the ship were filled with the job of keeping the choppers from corroding in the salt air: we had to wire brush the cording metal and spray cans and cans of zinc-chromate on all exposed surfaces.

When we pulled into Port of Hawaii for refueling and re-supplying the ship, we were given one day of liberty. The first thing Nile and I did was to find a place to rent motorcycles. Then we set out on the streets of Honolulu with our 250CC Yamaha's. At our speeds, we were able to cover the island in a few hours. Twice the police stopped us. We just laughed at them when they said they'd ticket us if they caught us again. "Who cares? We're headed to Nam."

"Don't kill yourselves before you get there," one of the cops said getting back into his car.

On the thirtieth day after leaving San Diego we floated in calm waters three miles off the coast of Vietnam. From the deck of the aircraft carrier I saw Vietnamese fishing boats bobbing between the mainland and us. To them we must have looked like a steel island and our choppers enormous green insects resting on top of it.

The XO announced over the PA system that our destination was Phu Bai Marine Air Base, 30 miles inland. He said it was just south of the DMZ. We loaded into our aircraft, and then one at a time fired up the engines, taxied to the take off markings and lifted off. I watched the tail ramp of my chopper close shut and saw the pilot's thumbs up through the doorway to the cockpit. The chopper shuddered under my feet. It struggled to get its wheels off the flight deck. Its rotor blades spanked the air. I looked at the cargo area filled with crates and wondered if we'd been too greedy when we loaded. We'd packed in anything that we thought might make Nam easier. There were refrigerators, fans, and record collections in those crates. When orders that we were going to Nam had come the vets told us to crate up everything, so we did. I remember Staff Sergeant Murphy saying, "No one looks in the crates. If it can keep you cool or feed you, take it. You'll be damn happy you did." In San Diego I'd carried Nile's 100-pound record collection a mile across hot tarmac thinking his Motown hits had to be the thing that would keep us cool.

The deep whopping of the rotors changed into a whipping purr and the shudder evened out. Looking through the gunner's door, I saw the bow of the ship slip from beneath us. On deck, Squids leaned over the rails, straining to see land so they could go home and tell their girlfriends they'd been to Nam.

I saw the enormous anchor, hanging like a bell clapper against the ship's side; then the aircraft tilted forward, and I could see the green sea sliding beneath us. It was not only the aircraft that had a hard time leaving the carrier; my mind was holding on to the safety of the ship, too. The pilot jerked back on the stick, and the G's started building in my legs. Leveling out at 2,000 feet with the nose of the chopper tilted forward, we rushed toward land.

Within minutes we'd be In Country. I could see the far off jungle and knew the VC's were there. Our Commanding Officer told us that a great achievement for a VC was to blow a million dollar Marine chopper out of the sky. Why not this one? I'd heard stories that a VC would use anything from a heat-seeking missile to a hand slingshot to knock a chopper down.

Questions whirled in my head as fast as the rotor blades: Would we take fire in Phu Bai's Landing Zone? How would I protect myself when I didn't have a rifle? Then the biggest question: Why was I here? I no longer believed in the Vietnam War. I'd even tried to escape. No answers came. My tongue swelled in my mouth and I felt like throwing up.

Would I be leaving this place with war stories like I'd heard in New River-- stories like the one that Trowler told to the whole barracks in the middle of the night? He'd made a hissing sadistic growl at his bunkmate. "Bowen, get out of that rack right now and stand at attention."

Trowler pulled at Bowen's blanket. Bowen gripped it with both hands. "Gimme a minute. I have to get my clothes on," Bowen said, in a shaky voice.

Trowler kept it up, demanding Bowen get out of his rack and stand at attention. "I want you to honor me, Bowen, for what I have done for your lazy ass. I want you to salute me for the beautiful Vietnamese woman I killed. You know what we did, Bowen? We poked her eyes out with a stick and skull fucked her. You hear me Bowen? We skull fucked her. That's what the War is like, man, and that's just what you're headed into."

Hearing that, Bowen leaped out of his rack and ran into the bathroom, leaving Trowler ranting. Who knows if anything like that happened? What I do know is that no one stopped Trowler from ranting. If I made it back home would that be me?

We were gaining land. I took a loose flak jacket on the bench seat and placed it under me; I'd heard that maneuver could save a man's family jewels. I looked at the two 50-caliber machineguns bolted across the forward entrance doors. A door gunner stood behind each gun, the barrels pointing into the azure sky. Neither one of the gunners had ever shot at an enemy. The brass belts of rounds hung from the guns, looking like metal vines growing out of the ammo boxes.

On the green sea our shadow skimmed the surface like a killer whale following us right onto the land. Large rocks passed below and my stomach tightened. A gigantic olive-drab peace symbol painted on a huge gray rock shot past the door gunner's window. I expected blood on the rocks. Back in the states, peace symbols were everywhere, on the sides of buses, buildings, bumper stickers. Every longhair had one hanging around his or her neck. I fingered mine under my tee shirt.

I expected rounds to start coming up through the floor. A veteran door gunner in New River had told me, "When you're being shot at you can see the tracer rounds; they float up from the treetops like stars returning to the heavens. You don't hear them."

After clearing the coast we turned right and were back over water again. My stomach relaxed as we flew up a wide river delta. Water was safe. After ten minutes over the delta, we turned left over treetops and began our descent. Suddenly we were hovering over a large flat area. No enemy fire, no bombs bursting in air. When we landed, there was no one on the flight line except one Marine with hand wands directing the pilot to taxi to a parking spot. Once the rotors stopped it felt as if we'd landed on a stovetop.

Phu Bai Marine Air Base showed no signs of war. Every building had sand bags stacked around it. A metal grid work was lying on the ground; when I asked what it was I was told it was Marston matting-- sounded like something you'd find on the moon. The heat settled on me like someone had slung a hot blanket over my shoulders. I asked a passing Marine, "How hot is it?"

"Welcome to Hell; it's a cool 126 degrees." He accented the degrees as if he were a radio announcer. Ripples rose off the flight line, making the choppers shimmy. Hoisting my heavy sea bag on my shoulder, I asked where barracks were. "It's called a hootch," said the

Marine on the flight line, pointing to a two-story building with a green sand bag bunker built around it. My uniform was soaked through before I hit the shade of the building. I climbed the stairs to the hootch, found my bunk and stored my gear.

Once I got myself settled I went looking for Dave. He'd been in country 30 days now. I went to the Metal Shop and said hello to Gunny Severens. He told me Dave was on mess-duty.

That afternoon at lunch I found Dave. He was dishing out food in the chow line. I didn't recognize him until I was in front of him with my tray; he was dressed in jungle utilities. "Hey Marine, can I get some of that slop you serving?" He slapped a huge heap of what looked like beans onto my metal tray. "Damn good to see you," he said. The second thing out of his mouth was, "This place sucks. How was the cruise? Hope you enjoyed yourself while I was over here fighting your war."

"Thanks, Rhino. I was enjoying the ship's AC just hours ago." White Rhino was Dave's nickname, which Nile had given him.

"You better move on; the Gunny in the kitchen's a hard ass. Let's get together tonight. I'll bring you up to speed on this place. My hootch is right over there," he said pointing out the window.

"Cool. I got stuff Gunny Severens told me I had to do this afternoon. I'll check you out later."

After I filled out some paperwork for Gunny Severens, he told me I was free for the rest of the afternoon. My hootch looked like a chicken coop. The first floor was surrounded with sand bags to about chest high. Nothing protected the second floor where I lived. I climbed onto the top bunk and lay on my back. I looked at the roof and realized there was nothing between me and a mortar-round except for a half-inch of plywood and a thin piece of tin. I got up and tried to write a letter to my folks letting them know I'd gotten here, but I was so hot my sweat kept soaking the paper.

Strange new sounds surrounded me; the constant drone of chopper blades was familiar, but the slapping of screen doors as men came and left the hootch wasn't. I got back on the bunk and somehow fell asleep. The glowing green dial of my wristwatch said 11:30 when I woke. I realized I'd missed my date with Dave. As I lay there in my wet clothes, the wail of a siren sounded. Seconds later a low whistling came across the sky, then a deafening blast. Then another, and another. I counted five. I couldn't see anything. The barracks was alive with movement. I climbed out of the rack and made my way towards where I thought the door was. A line of men had formed and I grabbed the shirttail of the guy in front of me. Outside on the landing there was a little moonlight and I saw men jumping the 15 feet to the sand below. I saw a clear space and jumped. My heels sunk into the soft sand. Following a shadowy line of men, I entered the bunker. We huddled in the dark. More mortar rounds kept hitting. Someone said, "This is the fifth fucking night the Gooks are hitting us."

The hammering stopped and men's faces began to glow in the light of their cigarette lighters. I sat quiet. I didn't want any of these guys to know I was a "Cherry." If they found out I'd have to listen to a bunch of shit about how hard it had been for them, and how inept I was. I was listening for clues as to what to do next when someone said, "Let's get back to bed."

"Keep your ass still until the siren blows twice," a different voice replied,

After 15 minutes, the siren blew twice. I let everyone go out before me. I had made it to the top of the stairs when a sound like someone had put a finger in their mouth and popped it out the side of their cheek was followed by a flash of light hitting among the hootches. The growling explosion ripped into the sky. Men pushed by me while I looked into the dark, listening to the sound of falling debris hitting the roofs. I jumped again and found my way back into the bunker. The mortar looked like it was in the direction of Dave's hootch. "Christ, if it hit his hootch..." I said, under my breath. I sat in the dank sand wondering if I'd lost my best friend. I wanted to go to see where the mortar hit but I hadn't a clue how to find it in the dark. I'd have to try in the morning.

I spent the night in the bunker with as many rats as men. The siren never blew twice. At first light, I slipped out of the hole and made my way to the mess hall. In back of the building a couple of guys were smoking.

"Either one of you guys seen Lance Corporal Deyo? He works on the chow line?"

One of them said, "You mean the White Rhino?"

"Yeah."

"He's stirring powdered eggs. He came in a little shaken up. One of those mortars blew up a Vietnamese hootch just on the other side of the base fence from his hootch." I took a deep breath and headed to the back door. One guy stuck out his arm. "You'd better go around front. Gunny will have your ass if he sees you in his kitchen."

"Thanks, man."

I walked around to the front entrance and got a cup of coffee. Sitting at a table near the chow line I saw Dave carrying a large aluminum pot. He slammed it on the counter and spit out, "I hate this fucking place!"

I went over to him and put my hand on his shoulder. "You OK, man?

"That mortar was only about 50 feet away. It blew the shit out of an empty hootch just on the other side of the base fence. We stayed in the bunker all night. I hate this fucking place."

"I was worried it hit you. I saw where it landed."

"This is gonna be one long fucking ride, my friend. You want green eggs."

"You do have your return ticket on you, don't ya?" I said.

Dave scowled.

In the first month, we lost one bird and its entire crew. Jesus Esposito was the crew chief. He'd been Dave's bunkmate in New River. No one seemed to know if the chopper got shot down or if there was mechanical failure. Jesus was one of our first casualties.

We weren't in Phu Bai two months when orders came for all squadrons on the base to pull out and move down to Marble Mountain. Our squadron, HMH 361, was to be the last squadron to leave. It was hard to believe we were abandoning the air base. No one had an explanation as to why.

Staff Sergeant Severens, the NCO in charge of our Metal Shop, was a large man with a potbelly that bowed out over his brass belt buckle. Tice, one of the guys in the Metal Shop joked, "His face caught fire and someone put it out with an ice pick." He must have had terrible acne as a teenager.

Severens called a meeting and told us that one of us had to stay behind. Pointing his finger at me he said, "Winters, you're the one. You'll report to the captain of the guard tomorrow morning."

"Shit." I slumped and walked out of the shop. Dave followed, "It's only two days."

"I want out of this fucking cesspool. I'm gonna have to stay in a bunker for two days. The fucking rats have taken the place over. Have you seen those bunkers on the perimeter? They're filled with fucking rats. I saw one the size of small dog."

"Two days and you'll be at Marble where there's hot food."

Dave stuck out his hand. We shook like the Black brothers did, with our thumbs hooked and fingers encircled.

Chapter 23

China Beach

When I stepped off the chopper at Marble Mountain, fine grains of beach sand kicked up by the rotor wash ticked at my skin. I had not slept for 48 hours. The two days guarding the perimeter at Phu Bai was over. Tet 1969 was nothing like the previous Tet of 1968 when over 6,000 civilians and 216 Americans had been killed. Headquarters had told us for the past two day to expect a repeat performance. Hue was two miles away from Phu Bai Airbase. The fireworks celebration the Vietnamese set off each of those two nights never gave the hair on the back of my neck time to flatten.

Flying into Marble Mountain Airbase I was relieved to see the base was much larger than Phu Bai. The South China Sea bordered one side of the rectangular base. Hundreds of helicopters were lined up on either side of a mile-long runway: 53's, 46's, Huey's, Cobra gun-ships, every kind of chopper the Marine Corps owned. All had US MARINES painted on their sides. I started to feel safe again.

The routine at Marble Mountain wasn't much different than Phu Bai, including mortar rounds at night. The difference was that when we'd get hit, strike forces were called in from nearby Freedom Hill Air Base. If observers got a mortar location they'd send out Puff the Magic Dragon, a C-47, that would rain lead like a thunderstorm over where they thought the VC were.

The mess hall at Marble sometimes served hot food. We had bread and, if you overlooked the flour worms, you could get it down. We washed gray meat down with a liquid called bug juice, a sugary Kool Aid mixed to disguise the heavy chlorinated taste. This chow was gourmet compared to Phu Bai's.

At Marble the number of missions our squadron was flying dramatically increased. HMH 361 went from the periphery of the War to the center of it. There was more work for us in the Metal Shop. We added a night crew to keep up, and I was put on it. We patched bullet holes and punctures from tree stumps and rocks made when choppers landed in mountain top LZ's. I was sick of filing the ragged edges of holes to make them smooth so they wouldn't stress crack. We'd recently gotten a chopper in that had landed on a landmine. It had hundreds of holes in its belly. Night after night I lay on my back on a roller filing holes and riveting aluminum patches over them. Reaching my arms up over my head for hours at a time made me wish I were doing something more important than getting a chopper back into the war.

I was lucky to get into the same hootch as Dave. There were about ten men to a hootch, but if you were on the night crew you might have most of the hootch to yourself during the day. Dave and I were both on night crew--a good job mostly because you didn't have to deal with the intense heat. Even better was that there weren't many officers or high-ranking enlisted men around at night so the military bullshit slacked off and we could focus on getting work done. We ended up doing most of the work anyway because our birds were flying missions in the day.

Nights would get a little wild sometimes if we didn't have much work. During these slow times we had to do something to help us stay awake, so we might go out and sit on top of the bunker to watch Puff the Magic Dragon work the surrounding jungles. Every fifth round was a tracer round which would stream down from the big plane in luminous ropes providing us with a deadly light show.

Vietnam swung from all-out terrifying excitement to unrelenting boredom. It was on one of those mind-numbing nights that I got my full nickname. Nile had been calling me "Crazy" for some time already, but early one morning it got expanded. We were waiting for our birds to come home from a night mission. We didn't have much information about the operation, but one of the crew chiefs had accidentally overheard his pilot and copilot talking about Cambodian navigational charts, so this meant they'd probably be late, and we had nothing to do until they returned.

Cambodia was supposed to be a big secret. No one was to write home that we were flying there regularly. The bomb squad had just dug up an unexploded mortar round and found Russian writing on it. We were supplying our troops who were trying to stop the Russian supplies from getting to the VC.

There were four of us in the shop: Tice, Plemons, Dave and me. We'd gotten our work done by midnight and were sitting around. Tice had a roll of masking tape and was taping one of his fingers to another. He kept doing this until he had his whole hand taped. He went strutting around the shop poking his taped hand in our faces while making muted sounds as if he were suffocating. I thought he'd gone out of the shop when he sprang out from behind a wall locker and dangled his taped hand in my face. He shook with spasmodic guffawing and dodged my open hand slap.

"Tice, get your ass back here!" I yelled. He sauntered back, careful to keep the workbenches between us. His protruding front teeth along with a tuft of reddish hair on top of an otherwise shaved head made him look like a cartoon character.

"How much tape we got in the shop?" I asked as I lunged at him over the bench.

Reeling back, he said, "I don't know, maybe five, six rolls."

"Go get all the tape you can find, any size; it doesn't matter."

"What for? I got shit to do, man."

"Get it, and I'll tell you."

The inside of our shop was strewn with pieces of helicopters in different stages of repair. A wheel fairing on one bench had the rivets snapped from its hinges. A section of the rotor head had been sprayed with red penetrating die and was waiting to be inspected for stress cracks. Two bare 100-watt bulbs hung from the ceiling. Tice started going around the shop opening drawers and searching shelves for masking tape. He avoided Plemons, who was asleep under one of the workbenches. Plemons was a large man with dark cropped hair on a small, almost perfectly round head. His black eyes seemed to have no pupils. Plem liked people thinking he was a little whacked. I reached down and shook his shoulder gently.

"Plem, wake up."

"What the fuck you want? I'm sleeping."

"I don't think you'll want to miss this. I'm going to find Dave, and I'll be back to tell you what's going on."

Dave was outside the hanger. He was standing with his hands on his hips, looking at the sky. He turned when he heard me.

"See that moon? Make a great picture if I had some night film. Check out how that tail rotor divides the moon into sections?"

"Yeah, that's cool. Come on in; I want your help with something."

He followed me back to the shop. Dave weighed about 130 pounds and stood five feet, ten inches when he signed up. After the first 13 weeks of boot camp, he weighed 190 pounds and was well over six feet tall. I was still struggling with accepting my pimple-faced friend as a large powerful man.

I told Dave we were looking for as much masking tape as possible, and he went down to the tool room to ask Corporal Handy for some. He came back and tossed a new roll in the pile on the bench. Tice rolled another roll of tape at the pile.

"That's got to be enough. What the Hell you gonna do with all of it?"

I pulled a metal chair out of the corner, sat down and said, "I want you guys to start at my feet and tape my entire body from head to toe." Tice glared at me as if I'd said, "Take a helicopter out beyond the flight line, pour gas on it and watch it burn."

Without hesitation, Plem said, "Stick out your feet; we'll start with them."

The room filled with the sound of tape being peeled off the roll. Around and around went the masking tape, up my calves onto my thighs, waist, and chest. I asked for my arms and legs to be done individually, so I could move. When they finished I put my hat on and said, "Now tape my head and face, but leave my eyes and mouth uncovered."

A kind of gut laughter I hadn't heard in months spilled out. Plem's barrel chest made his hanging-out shirttail shake. "Damn, Crazy, you look like you stepped out of a crypt."

Dave showed up in front of me with a can of black spray paint. He danced around me, detailing the strategic areas of my groin, buttocks, and breast. When they finished I strutted around the shop and they laughed.

I walked out of the Metal Shop, down to the tool room. Stepping up to the Dutch door, I spoke to Corporal Handy's back. "Handy, you got a few rolls of masking tape?"

Without turning, he grabbed a roll of tape off a shelf and twisted to give it to me. His eyes bugged and he said in a soft voice, "You're going to get your ass handed to you if someone sees you."

"No one's gonna see me, Handy. Let's not talk about such things. Wouldn't you like to dance?" I gestured with my arm for him to come out and dance with me. "When was the last time you danced with a Mummy like me? Was it back home with what's her name? Come on Handy, you're so handsome… and so shy. You're the head of the tool room. You must have a fine tool yourself. Come on Handy, dance with me!"

Handy turned his back and muttered, "Asshole."

The guys from the shop had snuck up to see what Handy would do, and they giggled when he called me an asshole. I headed back to the shop. As soon as I stepped through the door, Plem took me in his massive arms and we waltzed around while Tice and Dave hummed the Marine Corps Hymn. We were rounding one of the benches, full of ourselves, when a voice bounced off the walls and ceiling.

"What the Hell are you two assholes doing? We're fighting a Goddamn war, not running a fucking circus. Who the Hell is that, Plemons?" Severens stood in the doorway, hands on his hips.

Plemons looked down and mumbled, "Winters."

"Get your fucking ass over here, Winters!" Shaking his finger at me, he continued, "You're a Crazy Fuck. You're going to pay. I got the cure for you. I need a man for guard duty and you just signed yourself up. Corporal Hardman over there at the guard shack told me he's looking for man just like you. You can waltz right up to him and tell him what a Crazy Fuck you are! He likes Crazy Fucks like you."

The next day it started to sink in that I'd be leaving my friends and going on guard duty. I asked Severens how long I'd be going for.

"How much did you fuck up?" was his only reply.

Later he announced in front of the day and night crews that he considered me a dangerous Crazy Fuck. He went on to say that I had wasted government money and that my behavior demonstrated that I thought the war effort was just another place to play grab ass.

I slammed the door of the hootch and flopped on my rack. Nile was stretched out on his rack, a book propped over his head, Aretha Franklin purring a soulful rendition of Never Let Me Go in the background. He didn't look up, so I lay there thinking about how we'd lugged the box of albums from the States. Now when the generators were on it was common to have 15 soul brothers hanging around our hootch listening and dancing to tunes by Booker T and the MGs, Soulful Strut, Friends of Distinction and The Temptations.

Our hootch was also a place like-minded anti-war Marines gathered. Sometimes we'd talk about the War and what the protestors in the States were saying. There was no visible way for us to protest without paying an unbearable price. Dave came up with a name for the group; he called us the Wild Kingdom, named after the Marlin Perkins TV show. He even made a psychedelic peace sign with Wild Kingdom written diagonally across it. I felt sad lying there thinking that I wouldn't be making any of those gatherings anymore. I'd be moving to the guard hootch where I'd get the chance to be a real Marine with gun.

Nile turned from his book and said, "What's the matter? Dave told me Severens called you a Crazy Fuck. It kinda fits."

"You mean the way Bowling Ball Head fits you?"

"Enough of that shit. Tell me what happened."

"I finally got to his fat ass. Seeing me wrapped head to toe with Marine Corps masking tape pushed him over his patriotic edge."

117

"Damn straight! Plem said he couldn't believe the face the son of bitch made when he saw you. Plem told me he said, 'If I catch any of the rest of you assholes pulling shit like that, you'll join him.'"

"So, I'm the example to keep the rest of you fucks in line."

"Shit, man, you'd better wake up. That masking tape could cost you your ass. The VC's been pushing the ARVN's perimeter every night. The ARVN are the only guys between Marble Mountain and us. We all know what ARVN do when they take fire. They run. You'll probably see them running past your guard tower."

"What the fuck am I supposed to do about that?"

"Chill out, man. I'm on your side. Try to hear what I'm telling you."

"Sorry, I'm just so fucking wrapped up with this shit."

"Remember, Severens is a gung ho lifer; his concern is his own ass. He was afraid the officer of the day would see you wrapped in tape, and that would have made it his ass that was on the line."

"The officer of the day did see me. He just turned his head and walked out of the hanger. At least he had a half a brain and knew we needed to blow off some steam. Listen man, I don't want to talk about this shit anymore. Could you give me a hand? I have to move my gear to the guard hootch by this afternoon."

"No sweat, Crazy; I'm off all afternoon. I'm taking your place on night crew."

Nile reached for his boots under his rack. "You know what I heard about guard duty? Grunts run it. They bring in the guys who've been out in the bush for nine months killing Gooks. They want to give them a break before they send them back home."

Chapter 24

The Two Step Snake

It took us two trips across base to get all my gear settled in the guard hootch. To top things off, I pulled duty the first night. The post commander told me my position was Tower 37, located midway down the Marble Mountain beach front, about 200 yards from the ARVN.

The guard tower was made of rusting steel and stood 25 feet above the sand. At the top was a roofed platform measuring six feet by six. There I was supposed to spend hours watching specks floating on the surf, trying to discern if they were Viet Cong suicide squads trying to come up the beach or men fishing.

The tower stood 100 yards from the edge of the surf. I climbed the steel rungs which led to a trap door in the floor. The sound of the surf soon became a deadly lullaby trying to steal my wakefulness. Winds carried sea smells at night and jungle smells in the day. From the tower I saw three rows of intertwined barbed wire and razor wire lying in coils, strung between towers that were spaced at 300-yard intervals. Each tower was occupied at night by a fire team of three men. The towers were abandoned during the day. In broad daylight it would have been almost impossible for Viet Cong to attack from the beach; a steady stream of aircraft crews taking off and landing on the airstrip kept their eyes on the beachfront.

Sandbag bunkers sat at the foot of each guard tower and provided a place to sleep. Two men slept in the bunker while the third stood a two-hour watch in the tower. Claymores were set up at the base of each tower in case of an onslaught. A Claymore land mine is made with plastic explosive impregnated with marble size steel balls. When triggered by a trip wire or a remote pushbutton, it has a killing range that spreads out like a giant shotgun blast. Claymores were positioned in a fan pattern at the base of the tower covering the entire beach in front of us.

We were told that the Viet Cong knew one dead helicopter equaled US troops not being re-supplied and ammo not being delivered-

-that they had halted the War for a valuable moment. Blowing up a million-dollar helicopter was a great deed for a few men dressed in black silk pajamas. So we used high-tech Claymore mines and Starlight scopes that could see at night to keep our birds safe.

Inside the bunker were two cots. Rats and mice hid in the thousands of crevasses between the sand bags. That first night when I pulled the poncho liner up over me and closed my eyes, it took no time before the bunker was alive with mice and rats crawling onto my cot. They were fearless, swarming under my poncho, crawling towards the warmth of my armpits and crotch. I had to wiggle every few seconds to keep them off. I lay awake until my next tour in the tower, my body convulsing at one-minute intervals.

As I waited, I recalled when I was a boy going with my father down to the town dump to shoot rats. Dad taped a flashlight to his rifle, and we'd stand quietly, listening for garbage moving. Suddenly, he'd switch the light on and BAM! Dad's 22 almost never missed. Then we would walk through the garbage and find the rat kicking and squealing. I wished he were there in the bunker with me that night to kill some of the fucking rats.

I must have fallen asleep because when I woke I found my fingertips sore. Mice had nibbled away my calluses. I couldn't wait to get in the tower. I didn't know what was worse- being eaten alive by rats or having my throat cut in the tower by a suicide squad.

The only interruption in the guard duty routine came during rocket and mortar attacks. We'd stay in the towers as observers to report with our radios where we were being hit and from what direction mortars came in. The pandemonium of a rocket attack was designed to make us most vulnerable to VC squads coming up the beach.

In my fourth week of guard duty, I was setting up the Claymores one night for the first watch. Kyle and Bates, the other two Marines on my fire team, had gone into the bunker to sleep. The perimeter guard was mostly made up of grunts. The Air Wingers on guard duty were bad boys like me; Air Wingers were trained to work on helicopters and to put them on guard duty was a waste of their knowledge. Kyle and Bates were both grunts brought in from the bush for their last month in Nam.

120

My watch was from 8 to 10 o'clock. I stood looking at waves gently rolling onto the beach, then fading. The setting could have been a beach resort in some Polynesian island, except for the barbwire. The first hour I enjoyed the sun setting over the sea. When darkness fell I picked up my rifle and looked through the starlight scope. The starlight allowed me to see the body heat of anyone 100 yards away. My eye stayed glued to this device.

Around 9 o'clock the waves' trance was broken by a popping sound. I scanned the beach: nothing. Ten seconds passed: another pop. This time the sky over the sea in front of me lit up. An illumination flare floated beneath its parachute. The night turned back into day. I could see everything on the beach. Leaning back against the steel rail, I relaxed, being able to see again. Then as suddenly as the light had come, darkness returned, and fear crawled back up my spine.

At 10 o'clock I climbed down the ladder to wake Kyle for his watch. I turned my flashlight on his face. His mouth was open and spittle was pooled on his poncho liner. I shook his shoulder; he didn't respond. I pushed harder. Nothing. I put my mouth next to his ear and said, "Wake up!" in as loud a voice as I dared, not wanting to wake Bates. If I couldn't wake Kyle, I'd have to wake Bates, and I was sure I'd get into it with him about it not being his turn, so I kept trying to wake Kyle.

"Wake up, man."

Nothing. No movement. I could see he was breathing. I'd gotten up at 5 a.m. and worked all day filling sand bags, and now this son of a bitch lay sleeping on my time. I gathered up the front of Kyle's utilities and pulled his head up and slapped his face. It was like smacking a dead fish. I slapped harder and harder.

"What the Hell are you doing?" Bates yelled, grabbing my arm.

"This son of a bitch is out cold. It's his turn in the tower."

"Shit, don't you know about Kyle? He hardly ever goes in the tower. He's so fucking stoned every night no one can get him to stand watch."

"Why the fuck hasn't someone turned him in?"

"Cause he killed 30 Gooks in the bush."

I never woke him, and I couldn't get Bates to take my watch, so I climbed back up into the tower, seething. Why was I paying for their bullshit? I didn't give a fuck how many Gooks he'd killed… or maybe I did…

I never felt rested as the hot summer winds blew away the placid days of spring. These winds were the first signs of the monsoon season that we were told would last several months. I watched the sea heave itself at the beach while cumulous clouds piled high. The hulking shoulders of these clouds hid the moon longer and longer each night. Sometimes the wind made the barbwire on the beach coil and spring like a huge Slinky. In my steel roost, I began to feel the building of vengeance.

One night the tower rattled and moaned as the wind whipped at the steel. A figure was coming up the beach; I assumed it was the officer of the guard. He stopped and put his hand up to his mouth, but the wind swept his words away before they reached me. "Halt! Who Goes There?" I yelled. He shook his head and moved on. Then I felt a vibration in my legs, a hammering on the steel of the tower. Looking over the edge, I saw the officer of the day slamming the tower leg with a stick. He screamed up at me, "Why didn't you respond?" I screamed down at him, "I did, but the wind's making too much noise to hear." He shook his head again and moved toward the next tower.

The next night the sky cleared but the wind still blew. A new guy, Mike, replaced Kyle, who'd been relieved from duty and sent to sickbay. Finally, I got some sleep. In the morning I woke up with the light. I unlaced my boots and walked from the bunker out to the seaside by the wire. Looking up, I saw the two men in my fire team leaving the other towers to go to breakfast. Instead of breakfast, I decided to walk. The beach was littered with stuff.

The monsoon winds had died down considerably, but were still tearing the heads off the largest waves. It looked to me as if the guts of the ocean lay on the sand. The legs of a large sea turtle lying on its back moved imperceptibly. Soon the sun would bake the life out of it. Seaweed was strewn far up the beach. Fish of various sizes and colors lay dying by the thousands.

My eyes searched over jellyfish, driftwood, glass fishing-net balls, hypodermic needles and plastic blood bags that had been dumped by the hospital ship floating just off the coast--sea chaff vomited up from the ocean floor. I picked up two of the unbroken glass fishing-net balls--one the color of brown beer bottles, the other light green--and dropped them into a plastic bag I'd found. I'd been swimming in this ocean for three months and had no idea what was in the water.

Most mornings the sea held Vietnamese fishermen floating in woven reed sampans—little floating baskets. Today the sea was too wild for fishing. I found a stick and picked my way up the shore. Flipping over pile of seaweed, I lurched backward as if someone had punched me in the chest. A gray forearm and hand lay glistening in the sand. I prodded it to see if it was attached to anything. I rolled it and saw the hand had two fingers torn off. Near where the elbow should be was a neat cut. I imagined the surgeon's saw out there on the hospital ship hacking the arm off.

As if part of me stepped out of my body to watch, I grabbed the arm from the sand and ran toward the surf. The arm felt like a piece of firewood, the cold flesh triggering me to fling it with all my strength. It splashed in the green surf, disappearing between folds of white foam.

"There, part of you is a little bit closer home," I said to myself.

I started flipping seaweed again. My head was still spinning with pictures of a man stateside hugging his girlfriend with one arm. Looking at my own hand and arm holding the stick I noticed the hair on my knuckles, the shape of my fingernails, and the dexterity of my fingers.

Suddenly something entered my vision making me jump sideways. My eyes froze on a gray and white snake lying flaccid in the sand. The inch thick snake looked dead. I poked it with my stick. Quickly, it raised its head. I stepped back. This must be one of those sea snakes Corporal Hardman talked about. "The venom is so powerful that if it bites you, you're dead before you take two steps," he'd said. Then, pointing at the Vietnamese fishermen floating in their basket-boats, he continued, "The Slopes collect those fucking snakes in their fishing nets and then dump them where our Marines swim during the day."

Some of the snake's tail was in the sand, and I dug it out with the end of my stick. I slapped the its head with the stick, taunting it to strike. It wobbled, moving towards the stick reflexively. The toes of my bare feet dug into the sand. I felt danger and power. Taking the stick in both hands, I wielded it like a batter. When I swung, it was as if I were aiming at the head of Vietnam. The stick moved in an arc from my shoulder and slammed the snake. It's backbone snapped, and it flew for several yards, then lay motionless. I felt a rush of triumph. Something deadly was dead because of me.

Chapter 25

You've Got Two Steps

It was mandatory that we put in four hours on a work detail every day; idle time was dangerous to a Marine. I came in off the beach to get ready for my work detail, opened the door to the plywood hootch, stashed my beach loot of glass net balls and seashells in my footlocker, and headed to the command headquarters hootch. There, I milled around with other Marines waiting for their work detail. Corporal Hardman stepped out of the command hootch and spit in the sand. "Attention," he yelled. I hadn't heard anyone call "Attention," let alone yell it, in months. We were in a war zone, not a training camp. Hardman's utility uniform looked pressed. His cover was starched; his brass was shined; his jungle boots looked like they needed a little polish, but he'd have passed almost any inspection stateside.

"Today we're gonna tear down a sandbag bunker at the base of Guard Tower 24," Hardman said, looking over us.

"Aye, Aye Sir," One of the men at attention said in a sarcastic voice.

Hardman wrinkled his eyebrows and said, "At ease." Then he squatted to pet a blond dog at his side.

At Tower 24 we hoisted rotting sandbags off the bunker and split them open with bayonets. As we disassembled, the bunker mice began running out onto the open beach. Whoever was closest would follow the mouse or rat and crush it with the heel of a boot or smash it with a piece of lumber. We lined them up according to size, like one of those photos you took when you went fishing with your uncle. When we finished tearing down the bunker we had 233 mice and rats lying in a line. A Marine named Blake pointed his bayonet at the line.

"That's the price you pay for fucking with my head night after night," he said.

Endless days and nights passed on guard duty, seeming to loose all natural rhythm. Nights of standing in a steel box waiting to kill or be killed gave rise to unanswerable questions: Why was I here? Did I not believe in this war? Was I a Crazy Fuck like Severens said? What was happening at home?

It was a rule that all Marines had to go to the rifle range every six months. You'd think they'd suspend such a rule during war, but no. The day had come and we were told we'd be marching to the beach to fire weapons with Corporal Hardman. Like I said earlier Hardman was a grunt. An Air Winger like me envied grunts like Hardman. They fought the War in the jungle. We never told grunts that we thought they were hot shit, but we did. Grunts told us that Air Wingers were just spectators watching the War from above, like fans at a football game. What grunts seemed to forget is that Air Wingers were the guys that sat behind machineguns in the open doors of slow moving helicopters. Nothing like hanging suspended in midair, a target the size of a trailer-truck. Grunts preferred to act like the War was theirs, and most of us just kept quiet.

Hardman called us into formation and marched us to the beach. He called cadence as if we were in boot camp. Down the sandy roads of Marble Mountain I scuffed my feet in protest to Hardman's "hup, two, three, four." Then he bellowed, "Stop scuffing your feet, Crazy Fuck."

"Asshole," I muttered.

Hardman screamed, "Platoon, halt!"

Sauntering over to me, he said, "Severens told me you were a Crazy Fuck. Be careful you don't become a Dead Fuck." Struggling not to flinch, I turned my eyes away from his steely gaze.

Hardman halted us the next time facing the ocean. "Line up in two rows and stand at ease."

Fishing boats bobbed in the sea in front of us. Hardman reached into his pack, pulled out a napkin and spread it out. He put bread on it and watched the dog gulp it. He stroked the dog behind the ears and spoke to it in a low voice.

Turning towards us he barked, "Attention! I want the front row to lock and load your weapons and aim at those boats fishing too close

126

to shore. When I give the order Fire, I want every clip unloaded. Then you step back and let the second row follow. Am I understood?"

No one responded. I stared at the ten or so Vietnamese sampans floating just beyond the surf. They'd seen us and were raising their sails, but they stood limp. Makeshift oars popped out over the side of each basket boat, but they moved slowly.

"We can't fire; they're fishing right in front of us," I said, lowering my weapon at the surf.

"Hold that weapon at the ready, asshole. They know the rules. They've been told a thousand times not to be any closer to the shore than 500 yards. You're going to teach those Slope bastards a lesson." Without any hesitation he barked, "Prepare to fire your weapons."

There was the sound of steel on steel as the bolts went home. The front row locked and loaded.

"Stop!" I screamed.

"That's your enemy in front of you," Hardman said as he strutted towards me. Putting his face an inch from mine, he yelled, "Obey the fucking order or you'll be facing a court martial. Did you hear me, Crazy Fuck?"

"Yeah that's me, the Crazy Fuck," I said softly.

"I'm going to give the order to fire and if all your rounds aren't spent, your ass is mine."

Hardman was a killer. Kyle told me he'd seen a string of VC ears in his hootch. His eyes felt like they were poking into me. I tried to calm the gut rage boiling in me by biting the inside of my cheek. I could feel the shadow of a court martial fall over me.

"Fire."

The yellowish streaks of tracer rounds blipped the sea around the sampans. My rifle was aimed at the fishermen, but when I pulled the trigger I spent all my rounds in the sand at my feet. Hardman saw what I'd done and turned away. I didn't see anyone in the boats get hit, but I heard screaming.

The evening after we shot at the Vietnamese fishing boats I walked towards the guard tower under a streaked-red sky. It was as if the sun had cut the gathering monsoon clouds and they were bleeding. I'd skipped dinner and got to the tower an hour early. Working through deep sand, I walked out beyond the wire to where I had killed the sea snake. I found it and it stunk. Pulling a paper sack out of my back pocket, I folded it over my hand and picked up the striped snake, unfolding the bag back over the snake. Lifting my utility shirt, I hid the bag under it. The smell of decay came up through the collar.

I still had a half hour before I had to be back at the tower. I walked to Corporal Hardman's hootch. He lived in a compound with other grunts. They'd separated their hootch from the Air Wingers, piling their sandbags twice as high on their bunker.

Standing at a distance from his hootch, I watched to see if there was anyone inside. When I realized no one was, I casually climbed the three wooden stairs and entered. I looked for something to show me know which rack was Hardman's. There were Playboy pinups and all the odds and ends of stuff familiar to Marines. One bunk was more in order than the others: boots were lined up under the rack; the bed was made with hospital corners; and nothing seemed out of place. This had to be Hardman's. Removing his pillow, I tipped the paper bag and the snake slipped out onto his clean sheet. Carefully I coiled the snake so it looked like it would strike. Smoothing the empty paper bag flat, I took a pencil out of my breast pocket and scribbled, "You've got two steps, Hardass. Love, C.F."

Chapter 26

Luck

Severens stretched out my guard duty stint three and a half months before he let me come back to the squadron. He said he wouldn't have taken me back if it weren't for the fact that two men had been transferred to other squadrons. He needed a metal smith and I was the only one he had access to. It was good to be back with the Wild Kingdom. Most of the men in our shop wanted to work days, so it was easy to get back on night crew.

Nile told me that the lifers were tightening up on the "dissident element" because a chopper had recently been sabotaged. Someone had put pliers into the flight controls causing a chopper to crash on the runway. He said the base commander was trying to weed out the "bad seeds". He suggested that we curtail the meetings of the Wild Kingdom for a while until things settled down. "The lifers might get the wrong idea about us," he said. The truth was all we did was talk about how we hated the War.

I was handed a stack of letters and boxes from Sandy when I got back to the squadron. For some reason only a few got to me on guard duty. Sandy wrote almost every day and sent care packages every couple of weeks. Everyone in the hootch waited for me to open a box. She'd baked chocolate chip cookies and bought pepperoni from the local deli to send.

Brushing the sand off my sheets I secured the mosquito netting and opened the first letter. Tonight would be the first uninterrupted sleep I'd had in months. Nile was playing Roberta Flack turned down low. Her sweet voice in my ears and Sandy's sweet words on the page carried me into the darkness of my exhaustion. Before I closed my eyes I prayed the sirens wouldn't go off.

I woke eight hours later to a warm Sunday morning. Humidity was rising off the wet sand. The monsoon season was tapering off, and we were now getting some long awaited sunny days. I left the hootch at noon and found my way to the beach. I stood under a roofed pavilion enjoying the last few hours before going to work on the night crew. Looking down the beach I noticed a small dark cloud hovering over the sand. It was moving towards me ten feet above the sand. I stepped out from under the pavilion for a better look, trying to figure out what it was. Suddenly thousands of dragonflies enveloped me while others landed in a nearby tree.

One was clinging to the brim of my hat. Another crawled up my arm. I stood still, watching, no impulse to shoo them away. One iridescent insect with double wings like an old biplane crawled over a fold in my uniform and bent its tail around in a complete loop, flexing like some kind of insect yogi.

A faint sound of sweeping interrupted my trance. Turning I saw an old Papa-san sweeping with a broom made of dried grass tied around a bamboo stick. The bugs had caught his eye. He saw that I noticed him and his broom started moving again.

"Papa-san, come here."

He came towards me, head bent.

"Papa-san, what do you call dragonflies in Vietnamese?"

His broom moved. "Papa-san, it's OK. I don't want to hassle you." I stuck out my arm showing him the insect. "Papa-san, how do you say dragonfly in Vietnamese?"

As his head tipped up, I looked into his wrinkled face. His brown eyes were unfathomable, his hair short-cropped and white. A yawning scar running from his left ear to his lower cheek gaped at me. The wound was red and angry. I let my imagination run and saw him standing before an enraged GI who slashed him for not responding to an order. I'd recently seen a crew chief returning from a flight mission get so enraged when a Vietnamese man did not respond to him that he struck the man with his fist. Vietnamese were hired by the US government to do the dirty work on the base.

My mind kept spinning as the old man swept. Maybe Papa-san's wound came from shrapnel from Puff the Magic Dragon while he was humping rockets at night for the Viet Cong. It could be that this shy old papa-san worked on base during the day and for the V.C. at night.

"Chuon," Papa-san said softly. "Chuon."

"Say it again, Papa-san."

"Chuon."

"Do you speak English?"

"Yes, I learn it at the Buddhist temple."

"Papa-san, so many dragonflies."

"Every year they come."

"I've never seen anything like this. At home I've seen a few landing on reeds around the fishing pond, but never so many."

"You are very lucky."

"What do you mean lucky? I'm stuck here in Vietnam. I'm not lucky."

He looked shocked and timidly said, "Vietnamese say if dragonfly lands on you, you have been given great luck."

I looked at the flapping winged insects, wondering if there was such a thing as luck in Vietnam. What did this old man know? He was maybe the age of my father. He looked wise, but all old Asian men looked wise. He learned English in a Buddhist temple. Maybe he was a monk.

There was a low humming sound from the insects in the tree beating their wings. I turned to see them taking off. When I looked back the old man had moved far into the corner of the pavilion and was sweeping, his head bowed.

Chapter 27

Buddha Wouldn't Be Smiling

Marble Mountain consisted of five knife shaped hillocks made of marble. It was the namesake of our airbase and sat less than a mile from the runway. One night in the bunker Kyle told me that a Buddhist sanctuary had been carved into the top of the mountain. "There're Gooks up there right now watching us," Kyle said, pointing to the mountain. "I heard there's a huge Buddha face carved in the marble at the top. That's why the VC hides there, because we can't bomb a fucking sacred place. Bullshit, if it were up to me that Buddha wouldn't be smiling."

At the base of Marble Mountain was a military dump. I'd finally been granted a pass to go off base, so I'd gone to a small village near the mountain and was walking back past the dump. MPs were firing their rifles over the heads of hundreds of Vietnamese who were crawling over the rotting garbage, gathering up military gear, blanket liners, rubber tires, and out-dated tins of food. One MP was screaming in Vietnamese over a bullhorn, "The dump is closed."

Vietnamese women and children scrabbled out of the reeking debris. A reluctant woman was trying to extract a blanket liner from under a large metal wall locker. She strained to dislodge it as an MP walked toward her firing his M-16 on automatic right over her head. She dropped the corner of her prize and ran barefoot through the garbage.

When most of the pickers were off the pile the MP's walked around the perimeter pouring cans of gas on the garbage. One of them lit a match and the fire raced around the circumference of the heap. Still, a few brave Vietnamese darted in and out of the flames grasping at things they wanted. Once the fire caught, a great black swirl of stinking smoke rose and drifted across the face of the sacred mountain.

Chapter 28

Pass

The popping of the metal roof expanding under strong sun sounded like someone was outside throwing rocks to wake me. The temperature quickly inspired me to get out of bed. I'd been planning to ask for a pass. I'd been back in the Metal Shop for a few weeks now and had not had any run-ins with Severens. I couldn't bake in this plywood box for another day. If Severens would give me a pass I'd go to the Air Force base at Freedom Hill. May be I could find Dave who'd been transferred to the Marine division over there, violating Claypool's buddy plan. We could sit in the air-conditioned mess and eat hamburgers. The Air Force had better living facilities in Vietnam than the Marines did in the States. On the way home from Freedom Hill I'd stop at the "Steam and Cream" at the China Beach Army base.

My plan was made. Squinting in the brilliant light knifing through the screened window I reached for the edge of the mosquito netting and got out of bed. It had to be in the 90's already. Swinging my legs over the edge of the bunk, my bare feet skidded on the film of sand accumulated on the floor since last night's sweeping. Nile was still sleeping, and he never had any interest in going off base anyway, so I gathered up my shaving gear and headed for the shower hootch.

The sand on the path worked its way between my feet and thongs. At each step my thongs thwacked against the souls of my feet, throwing little flicks of grit against the backs of my calves. I made my way through the line of plywood hootches.

The spring on the shower hootch door scraped out a ragged note, underscored with a reverberating thwack when it slammed shut. No one was in the shower, another advantage of night crew. Tossing my towel on the peg, I treaded in for a cold shower. No matter how hot it was outside, the shower was always cold.

I wet my hair and turned off the shower. Lathering up, I pressed my fingers into my scalp, hoping to get out some of the aircraft grease from under my fingernails. With one arm I groped for the shower handle, twisted the water on and rinsed off. When I opened my eyes, there was a beautiful Vietnamese woman crouched at my feet. Her sable black hair hung on either side of her oval face. She wore white silk pants and a black silk blouse. Squatting as if she were praying she reached into a rattan basket of clothes and wet the garment in the over spray of my shower.

Her eyes were at the exact level of my crotch. I turned away slowly. She must have been waiting for someone to come into the shower so she could wash her clothes. There were base rules about Vietnamese using water. I was both uneasy and turned on by her seeing me naked. I wondered what she was thinking. She was a gorgeous woman. I was just another Marine to navigate so she could make her meager living from cleaning officers' clothes.

With my back to her I performed a couple of strokes to enlarge my shriveled manhood. Twisting the shower faucet full on, I stepped into a blast of cold water, letting it splash over me; then I shut the faucet off. Half way out of the shower room I turned back and opened the faucet to a dribble. She smiled, revealing her black betel-nut teeth.

When I got back to the hootch I stowed my gear and took out the best set of utilities I had. Severens had to sign my pass, so I headed to the hanger to find him. He was behind his metal desk, but his head was resting on his arms.

"Excuse me Sergeant Severens, could I have a word with you?"

"What do you want?" He said, bolting up in his chair.

"Sorry to wake you, sir, but I would like to go see PFC Deyo over at Freedom Hill."

Severens face was wrinkled from sleeping on his arms. At that moment no one else was in the shop. "Pull up a chair. I want to talk to you anyway," he said.

His massive head was almost square, and it looked like it had been stuck onto his neck as an afterthought. The chair feet squealed on the cement floor when I pulled it over to his desk.

"Winters, you're a pain in my ass."

I stiffened. "Is this off the record or are we talking official?"

Looking around, he said, "Off the record."

"Severens, you're a pain in my ass. You fucked me when you sent me to guard duty."

"You needed that in order to grow up. You think the Marines are a joke. When I was your age..."

"Stop," I said, holding up my hand. "I don't want to hear a father lecture. Not even if it means I don't get a pass."

His face reddened. "Alright, we don't like each other. Let's not make it worse. You're still wet behind the ears and your mouth is prone to automatic." His skin was pocked and tinted with the pinkish glow of a budding alcoholic. "Why the Hell does he keep trying to reform me?" I wondered.

"Are you with me, or on some other planet?"

"I'm here," I said, trying to keep from ruining the day I had planned.

"What I say next I don't want repeated. Do you hear me?"

I nodded my head.

"If you think I sent Deyo to Freedom Hill to torment you, you're wrong. I was ordered to send him."

"What are you talking about?" I asked, sitting up in the chair.

"You know that fucking young lieutenant who's been snooping around here? You know the one I mean?"

"Crawford."

"Yeah. He reported to the CO that your little club of longhaired faggots should be split up. The CO called your group "the dissident element.""

I was spinning. I did not expect to hear what he was telling me. Crawford's face came into my mind. He was a baby-faced lieutenant who'd been hanging around our Wild Kingdom discussions. He'd told us his hair had been down to his ass before he joined R.O.T.C. It was easy to see he'd tried to fit in with us. I remember him telling us one night how much he hated dropping napalm on innocent villagers. He said if he weren't over here he'd be out on the streets of Washington protesting.

A loud crash of steel on concrete broke into my thoughts. A man in the hanger yelled commands. Then I heard the familiar clink of steel on steel and knew a toe bar was being disconnected from the forward landing gear of a chopper.

Severens started again. "Crawford's why Deyo's in Freedom Hill, and McCoy and the rest of you are all getting orders to other squadrons."

"Come on, Severens, you're reaching for straws." He wouldn't meet my eyes.

"Pay attention to what I'm saying. I'm not playing grab-ass with you. The CO wants to know if you guys had anything to do with the sabotage on base."

His words hung in the air. I pushed my chair back a few inches.

"What are you talking about?" I said, trying not to look as frightened as I felt.

"Don't play dumb ass with me. Everyone on the base knows what happened last week when the NCO's hootch door was locked from the outside and a CS gas grenade was thrown under it. The NCO's were screaming like Hell and no one came to help. Officers had to come to let them out. Several of those guys were my friends."

"That's not sabotage. That's just a few hard ass NCO's with runny noses. Everyone on base knows why that happened. Those NCO's were the ones stopping men at random to check if their tee shirts were stamped with their names. When you pull that kind of chicken-shit in a war zone you're asking for it. When a man hangs his ass out of a chopper everyday waiting for it to be shot off, he don't give a shit if his skivvies are marked."

Severens bent forward, lowering his voice. The stale smell of beer rolled over his tobacco stained teeth. "We all know how we lost that chopper at the end of the runway three weeks ago. That pair of pliers wedged into the flight controls killed four men."

I squeezed my hands together below the rim of his desk. Panic was climbing in me. Sabotage was treason. I closed my eyes.

"What's the matter?"

"Nothing, it's the stink from the shitters burning."

"Don't play wise ass with me. Staff Sergeant Green is the head of Metal Shop for HMH 161. You know what happened down there, don't you? He lost his best man in the shop two weeks ago. Someone cut the winch cable with a hacksaw about 50 feet down the cable. It had to be someone who knew how to operate the winch. No VC crept into the compound and cranked up a chopper and undid the winch cable so they could cut it."

"Was this the guy who was being lowered down to help a pilot and crew that crashed?"

"Yeah, when the winch reached 50 feet the cable parted."

"I knew him. We were on guard duty together. He left three weeks before me. They kept getting our last names mixed up. His was Withers."

"He fell 75 feet, landing across one of the chopper blades." The whine of a pneumatic drill from the hanger overrode Severens' voice. "You know any thing about this, Winters?"

"I don't know a fucking thing about this. You're yanking my chain. You know Goddamn well I was on guard duty when all that shit happened. I've only been back in the squadron a short time."

Looking at me, he ran his fingers over his iron-gray bristles.

"Is that right? Sorry, I forgot."

"You're fucking with me, aren't you?"

He yanked open the center drawer of his desk, pulled out his faded green hat and stuck it on his head. Bending over as if someone was trying to listen to us, he said, "Where did you want to go on that pass?"

"Freedom Hill."

He handed me the pass. As I was leaving he said, "All that stuff about Crawford's true."

Chapter 29

Steam and Cream

My first stop was the base armory where I checked out an M-16 rifle. The MP at the gate took a cursory look at my pass, and I stepped out on dusty Highway One. I surveyed the collection of dilapidated huts that Marines called Dog Patch. Kids were everywhere as I trudged up the road.

"Hey GI, you want fuck my sister? She beautiful; she give you a good time. Come on GI. She tight; she want you."

While one kid was telling me about his sister, another was trying to cut open my back-pockets with a razor. I slapped him in the head lightly with the butt of my rifle, and yelled, "Di di mau," which I thought meant get out of here in Vietnamese.

I stuck my thumb out and in no time got picked up by an Army guy driving a six-by. He was going to Freedom Hill too, so he took me all the way. I looked around the base for Dave but couldn't find him, so I went to the mess hall and ate two hamburgers and drank two milkshakes. I couldn't get over how relaxed the Air Force guys looked. It was more like being on a college campus than being in Vietnam. I kept thinking how stupid I'd been for joining the Marines and living in mud and sand and eating bread with worms in it.

It was just as easy to get a ride back home as it was getting there. I had the driver stop outside the Army Base about a mile up the road from Marble. The steam and cream was right near the gate. As I headed there I thought to myself, "Thank God this Army operation is nondenominational and they let Marines in."

I stood in line outside the steam and cream with a group of mud-covered grunt Marines that'd had just tromped out of the bush. When it was my turn in front of the little window, I handed the Army Corporal my rifle, paid 20 bucks in MPC and was given a tag with a number on it. I sat one of the plastic molded seats in the poorly lit, crowded waiting room.

A young woman behind the desk motioned to me to show her my number, and when I did, she pointed to the dressing room. There, I took off my clothes, and stepped through a plywood door into a makeshift steam room. After sweating a while with a small group of naked men, I heard a knock. A heavily accented voice floated through the steam. "Number 39."

I read the plastic disk in my sweating hand. It was my number. Sliding off the bench I stepped out of the steam room into a shower. Then a young woman took me by the elbow and escorted me to a small cubical and motioned for me to lie down on the massage table.

The rule was all you could get was a light massage and a hand job, absolutely no sex. This didn't stop every man that ever came into the place from trying his best to seduce these women. The reality for the woman was that if she got caught having sex, she'd lose her job. One of these girls could make more in a week than the average Vietnamese farmer made in a year.

Her silk ao dai rustled when she entered the room. I lay naked, face down on a padded table, my skin damp from the shower. Her hands rested on the soles of my feet for an extraordinarily long time. I wondered what she looked like. I savored the moment, not allowing myself to turn my head to look. The heat of her hands spread into my calves. My fear-tensed muscles released and her hands moved to my heels, resting there, steady, firm, unmoving.

"I didn't come for my feet to be held." This thought flitted through my mind for a mere second, like a bird leaving a branch. The warmth grew up into my buttocks and lower back, and I felt a faint stirring in my chest. I let myself sink into her hands.

The thought came back. "I should roll over and ask her to squirt her hand full of Jergen's Lotion and stroke me until I come. I should wake up and get what I came for." Again, the thought evaporated. The spasm in my chest was heightening. My breathing started a deepening rhythm. I could feel her thumbs making small circles on my heels.

In the next cubical I heard the sucking sound of flesh being pumped faster and faster until the muffled groans of orgasm sank into silence. I lifted my chin from the mat but a gentle voice whispered,

"No." I obeyed. The movement of her hands released a groan that turned into a sob in my chest. I didn't want her to hear it so I held my breath. Her whisper came again, "Breathe." Pushing my face into the table I muffled a high-pitched wail like that of a small, frightened child. My wail built into a deep belly sob that I hoped no one could hear as I mashed my face into the table. The War was crawling out of me, ripping its way up through my chest and out my throat. Faces of dead men I'd MEDEVACed appeared in my head, treetops with tracer rounds flying at me like flaming birds, Napalm barrels floating in slow motion before bursting into liquid fire. I saw Vietnamese children smiling behind barbed wire fences, their middle fingers sticking up at me.

She held tight to my feet.

I felt myself enter the fear of night after night of waiting to be killed, and my shaking became unstoppable. I had no choice but to let it come. I no longer worried about what she or anyone thought. She let go of my feet, and I drew my legs up under me. Then I heard the sound of a chair being pulled along the cement floor. The tablemat sank as she climbed onto the table. She stretched her body out on top of mine. I felt her breasts through silk on my shoulder blades. Her legs and arms spread to match mine. Together we shook under the power of my war sobs. I didn't dare open my eyes for fear she'd leave.

Chapter 30

Pickle It

When I told Nile that I was considering signing up for door gunner he must have thumbed his nose 17 times in a row before he said, "Crazy is the right name. You hate what we are doing to the civilians here. You complain how the government should just leave these simple people to their rice farming, and the next thing I know you're signing up for door gunner." He looked out the hootch door and struck his head with his open hand.

"I got to get away from Severens…" I started but then let it drop. It sounded stupid and I didn't have a good explanation on why I had to do it. Maybe it had something to do with being on guard duty with the grunts. They'd been out there in the bush fighting a war I only imagined. Maybe I should go out and see first hand what the War was about instead of complaining how unjust and unfair it was without ever really being in it.

Our birds were CH-53's, and most of our missions were re-supply and MEDEVACs. Many of the mission statements coming down from headquarters had Operation Georgia Tar written on them. Georgia Tar was about delivering food, water, ammo, and grunt Marines--30 at a time--all over I Corps.

No clouds in the sky, already 85 degrees at 7 in the morning, I picked up my flight gear and walked by the Metal Shop. Sticking my head in I hollered, "Hey Nile, Plem. Have a good evening."

They would be getting off night crew in a few minutes.

"Going out to waste some Gooks?" Plemons asked, holding his hands in front of his chest as if he were shooting a machinegun.

Setting down the two boxes of M-60 machinegun rounds, I said, "Someone's got to protect your ass. Since you haven't got the balls to do it, I guess I'll have to." Plem looked pissed as I left the shop.

On the flight line I found number 43, the bird we were to fly. I threw my gear in the doorway. The M-50 machineguns we'd come into

142

country with had been taken off, and the chopper was fitted with the more versatile M-60's. Wise, the crew chief, must have finished his pre-flight inspection because he was lying on the bench seat with his hand behind his head. I nodded to him when I stepped on board. Dropping the metal ammo boxes next to where the M-60 rested, I sat down.

I was eager to get airborne. Waiting for the pilots to do their pre-flights seemed to drag on, and there was nothing to do but sweat and worry about the mission. Finally came the thumbs up, and we began to taxi to the runway. Lining up north, the bird rolled a few feet and took off. I never understood why we taxied at all, since the chopper could just lift straight up like we did at every LZ.

Reaching 200 feet at the end of the runway, we dipped sideways out over the sea, beginning a large loop that would take us directly over Marble Mountain. A long plume of smoke snaked its way up into the sky. As we passed through it, the smell of burning plastic filled my nose. I glimpsed yellow flames below and thought the dump must have burned all night long.

My right hand held the machinegun handle and was vibrating as if I had St. Vitas' Dance. Everything in a helicopter shook. Through my flight helmet, I could hear the tower speaking to our pilot. They were advising about heavy cloud-cover in the mountain region of Phu Loc and reminded us that once we gained 10,000 feet we'd be on our own. We hit 10,000 and Captain Nevel spoke.

"Gentlemen our mission today starts with landing on Hill Number 119 where we'll drop the supplies we have on board. From there we will be airlifting a bulldozer to hill 127 which is up near Phu Loc, 30 miles north of Hill 119. Are you with me gentlemen?"

"Yes, Sir," we all replied in unison. I was glad to hear the mission didn't sound like any big deal. I could relax knowing that most likely the LZ's we'd be landing in were friendly. We flew over rice paddies, and I practiced sighting the M-60 at a large water buffalo wallowing in the expanse of shallow water. Soon the rice paddies turned into foothills, then into mountains. Each mountain had an LZ on top of it. They all looked the same: a small circle of sandbags around a roughly flat place hacked out of jungle for a chopper to set down. Sometimes there were plywood outhouses sitting off to one side. Within the boundary of the sandbags were makeshift shelters of strung-up tarps, meager attempts at keeping rain off. Always knots of men in camouflage clustered together, looking up at us hoping it was their LZ we'd be landing on.

Captain Nevel came on the air again. "Gentlemen, Hill 119 is right below us. Let's prepare for landing." Next I heard him ask the grunt radioman on the ground if the LZ was hot. The voice replied that they hadn't had contact in three days. We descended onto a 70-foot circle of dirt. "Door gunners, please take the safeties off your weapons," Nevel commanded.

Wise and I sang out a stereo "Yes, Sir."

Wise was the crew chief but also stood in as door gunner opposite me during landings and takeoffs.

The grunts below were holding their helmets and squatting behind bunkers trying to avoid the powerful backwash of our rotors. Kicking off the safety, I sighted the barrel at the undergrowth searching for muzzle flashes. Out of the corner of my eye I saw a man step into the plywood outhouse trying to get away from the powerful wind. Just as our wheels touched down I saw the outhouse blow over and roll some 50 feet down a slope before stopping. The copilot started laughing into the mike, "Now there's a man that's stepped in shit." We all waited to see if the man would come out. When he did he was swearing and giving us the finger.

We unloaded several bags of mail and two pallets of C-Rations. Wise attached a thick nylon strap to a hook in the center floor hatch. Nevel turned up the engine and lifted the chopper. We hovered 30 feet off the ground while a grunt drove the dozer to the center of the LZ. Lift hooks had been welded at four corners of the dozer. A grunt fastened four chains from the hooks to a central ring; then he stood on the hood of the dozer with the ring in one hand while he reached skyward for the massive strap and hook dangling from the chopper. Catching our hook in one hand, he connected it and jumped down, giving us the thumbs up. Wise was on his belly looking through the hatch at the tension in the strap while he gave Nevel instructions on the lift.

The chopper began shuddering and suddenly swung violently left.

"Bring her back down!" Wise screamed. Quickly, we dropped several feet so the tension was off the strap, and we leveled. Looking out the gunner's door, it seemed to me the dozer was too heavy.

While the chopper hovered, the grunt got back on the dozer hood and worked at adjusting the chains. Once the grunt's thumbs were raised, Nevel pulled back on the collective and a tremor went through the chopper. I gripped the machinegun to keep from falling. It was like trying to stand on the pad of a giant vibrating sander. I could hear the conversation between Nevel and Wise growing tense.

"Maybe we shouldn't take the risk," Nevel said in a tight voice.

"A CH-53 should easily handle this load," replied Wise.

In Wise's tone I could hear the insinuation that Nevel didn't know what he was doing. The shivering in my legs put me with Nevel. Wise was a Corporal, Nevel a captain. No question who was boss. Then I saw it: this was the Marine Thing--a standoff about who had the biggest balls. As we gained altitude, it was clear Wise won.

Ascending slowly, I expected the shaking to stop, but it didn't. We entered thick cloud cover, and I couldn't see more than 20 feet. Nevel tilted the chopper forward, trying to gain speed. The radio remained silent. I stared out the door. Then a flash of green poked out through the white clouds. The co-pilot and I screamed at the same time, "Lift up!" Nevel pulled back hard on the collective and the shuddering got worse.

"We're 100 feet from the side of that mountain, and I can't get this fucking thing to fly," Nevel grunted.

"When you pull back on the collective, trim the rear stabilizers," Wise barked. The shudder changed, and we began gaining altitude.

Another break in the clouds and it looked like I could touch the mountain.

"I've had it. Pickle the fucking thing, Wise," Nevel squawked.

"Hang in there, Captain."

I couldn't believe it! We were going to slam into that fucking mountain because Wise wouldn't back down.

Then the co-pilot chimed in, "Wise, pickle the Goddamn thing. Now!"

The clouds opened and I yelled, "The dozer just pulled free of a tree."

We gained altitude immediately, rising up and over the face of the mountain. No one spoke. The shudder had stopped and we were gaining air speed. We flew in silence.

For ten minutes the jet engine roared in our ears. Then Captain Nevel came on.

"Good job, Wise."

"Thank you, Sir."

Chapter 31

I Could Feel the Impact of Bombs on My Face

The black X's on my calendar were the only joy I could find as the days slowly disappeared. Severens had to yell over the heavy riveting in the shop, "Don't take any tools with you. You hear me?" as he handed me transfer papers. I smiled and walked out of the shop. The papers said I was going to squadron HMM 262. Maybe what I'd heard was true... the War was winding down.

I'd read in an L.A. Times someone brought from the states that the US 1st Division had been withdrawn from Vietnam. Six months earlier some other stateside paper said we weren't flying into Cambodia. What I knew was true was that HMH 361 was being sent back to the States. We'd come to Nam with the choppers, but now they were going home before us.

One of the last air missions I flew was with the 361. I'd taken along my camera to get some shots of the war. We'd been airborne for a half hour when a lot of chatter came on the radio. The flight tower was warning us about a massive artillery barrage going on. They said we were headed into it. The pilot gave the tower coordinates for the LZ we were to supply. The tower came back saying they'd check with headquarters. As we waited to hear, I watched a Phantom jet strafing a small village. The jet had made several passes, and I could see people running from their hootches into nearby trees. I shot pictures of the jet dropping its bombs--bright orange flashes followed by thick dark smoke billowing out over the jungle canopy. I could feel the impact of the bombs on my face.

The tower called back to tell us we were OK and could proceed to the LZ. We'd just doglegged towards the LZ when a radiant flash exploded 400 or 500 yards from us in midair.

"What the Hell was that?" the pilot yelled.

"Shit. It looks like anti-aircraft fire," said the co-pilot forgetting to un-trigger his mike.

"Where the Hell are we? We haven't slipped into Cambodia have we?"

"According to the chart we're right on the line."

"Goddamn! There's another one! Let's get the fuck out of here."

The chopper dropped as if the engine had stopped. Hurtling towards the treetops, my stomach crawled into my throat. I could see small objects on the ground: a tiny multi-colored Buddhist shrine on a dirt road, chickens in the back yards of hootches. Then, suddenly I was forced to my knees, the machinegun handles slapping against my chin as I went down. Both pilots pulled back on the collectives at the same time, leveling us out a few hundred feet over the jungle. Trees fanned out from the rotor wash. When stabilized, we dropped even lower. Skidding just over the jungle we gained air speed until we were going flat out.

"Door gunners keep your eyes peeled. We're so low the VC could spit us down."

Back on my feet and holding the gun handles tight, I flipped the safety off. Below, a green blur flew by for 15 minutes. We made radio contact with the Marble Mountain tower; the pilot reported anti-aircraft fire and gave the tower our coordinates.

When we landed at Marble I crawled under the chopper to find a bunch of jagged holes where scrap metal had punctured the skin.

Chapter 32

Flying Tigers

The call sign for HMM 262 was Chatter Box. The symbol was an open- mouthed tiger with rotor blades in the background. The choppers were CH-46's, smaller than the 53's I'd been used to working on. These birds had two large sets of overhead rotors, but no tail rotor. It was no big deal. I was back to working as a metal smith, and I figured bullet holes in aluminum were the same in any aircraft.

I walked past the 46's in the hanger and noticed rows of yellow figures painted on the cowling of each aircraft, each figure with a conical hat. It reminded me of the gunslingers of the West who carved notches in the handles of their six guns for each kill.

Severens was not on my back anymore, but I missed the Wild Kingdom. Only Plemons had been transferred with me to 262. The calendar hanging in the new hootch showed I had 276 days in country, 125 days still to survive.

262's Metal Shop was run by Sgt. Howe, a pimply-faced man with a large curl of hair above his forehead. Many men were short timers. You had to be in country a year to call yourself a short timer. A short timer was entitled to wear a Seagram's #7 blue and yellow-ribbon through the vent holes of his cover.

I went on day crew and the War seemed to slow down. Most of the work we were doing came from a major accident. One of our birds had landed in a poorly cleared LZ, and a tree trunk pushed through the bottom of the chopper. The landing gear was also damaged. We worked on the chopper for the better part of a month.

The next couple of months dragged along, the only excitement being one mortar attack. We didn't lose any men or birds.

Plemons and I had just had our short timer party. We'd gone to the club to drink 3.2% beer. The next morning as I crossed off the 365th day on my calendar, the hair on the back of my neck stood up. With only 15 days to go, I started contemplating extending my tour of duty just to relieve myself from the pain of waiting. After thinking about being in Sandy's arms brought me back to my senses, I dropped all ideas of staying.

Finally my day came to leave. My relationship with God never seemed to follow me to Nam, but that morning I prayed to Him asking Him to bring me home safe. Somehow I was still alive and would be able to walk onto the freedom bird with all my limbs intact. All I had left was one chopper ride from Marble to Freedom Hill. I sat down on the bench seat of the 46, and its rotors began turning. The last thing I heard before the jet engines stole all the sound was, "See ya in the world, man." It was Plemons.

There was a flack jacket lying on a nylon bench seat next to the door gunner; I grabbed it and sat on it. I was taking my last look at Marble Mountain when the pilot stepped out of the cockpit and said something to the gunner. It was First Lieutenant Deranger. He tucked himself back intro his seat and had our wheels off the ground in seconds. He didn't taxi, but lifted straight up, and when 20 feet up, tipped the nose down and dipped towards the ground, using the slow air speed and the rotor back wash to boomerang us skyward like a circus ride with its chains broken free.

Deranger then cranked the 46 for all she was worth. I realized we weren't headed to Freedom Hill when Marble Mountain slipped under us. Deranger dropped the chopper to treetop level and was skirting the low-lying hills, zigzagging through the valleys. I squeezed the aluminum seat bar. Unlike any other pilots I'd ever flown with, Deranger was making a low, fast approach to the LZ in front of us. Swooping in from the side, he held the chopper a few feet off the ground. This place didn't even look like an LZ; it was just a clearing on the side of a mountain. Deranger kept the rotors cranking hard as he put two wheels down. Looking over the door-gunner's shoulder I saw a small group of grunts running out of the jungle. Deranger had lowered the tail ramp, and they scrambled up it while the door gunner laid a fusillade of M-60 rounds at the tree line behind them. Once the last grunt was on board, Deranger slipped sideways off the mountain. Only then did I realize that I'd been biting my tongue.

The grunts were covered in mud. One man with a shaved head and a long red beard snapping in the wind had come in through the gunner's door. Around his neck was a string of ears; some of them looked fresh. His mud streaked hand rested on a sawed-off shotgun lying across his lap. Two bandoleers of shotgun shells crossed diagonally on his chest. His blue eyes shone. There were no insignia anywhere on him or the other men. All of them wore remnants of uniforms mixed in with Vietnamese garb. One wore black silk pajamas under his camouflage jacket. All of them had on rubber sandals.

They tried yelling at each other over the engine noise. Deranger put the chopper into a sharp turn, and we could see the ground out the side window. The G's from the turn plastered us to our seats. Red beard looked scared, his eyes bulging and sweat running down his face. I smiled thinking Deranger was scaring the shit out of these kick-ass killer Marines. I had to admit he was scaring me too. I'd never flown with a maniac like him.

We weren't ten minutes from the LZ when we dropped into a small base at the edge of a rice paddy. The grunts scrambled off the chopper. Several of them gave Deranger the finger as we took off. From the rice paddy we flew directly to Freedom Hill. When I stepped off the chopper I controlled my urge to kiss the ground. Instead, I stood at attention and saluted Deranger. He saw me from the cockpit and saluted back. I hoisted my sea bag and headed to the building marked Embarkation.

To my surprise there was no line. I didn't have to wait. I handed my papers to a Marine sergeant; he handed me an envelope and pointed to the door.

"The flight's leaving in five minutes. You better get a move on."

I ran to the silver TWA jet and dropped my sea bag on the pile. I took the boarding stairs two at a time. Looking down the aisle, I saw no empty seats. I walked slowly up the aisle looking until I remembered I had a seat number. Opening the envelope I saw I was in seat #115, which I'd passed. Turning back, I found seat #115 already had a Marine sitting in it. I pushed my ticket in his face.

"You're in my seat, man."

He looked up in surprise. "Sorry, man, I just wanted to sit with my friend. Would you mind switching seats with me?"

"No fucking way!" I didn't want to mess anything up. "That's my seat and I'm taking it."

The Marine got up and I sat down.

The instant the wheels left the ground, a deafening roar filled the plane: every man let go of his own death-defying sound. Heads crammed into the tiny jet windows trying to get a last look at Vietnam.

Chapter 33

The World

The Wild Kingdom had its last meeting in Okinawa. Dave, Plemons, Nile and Tice were all there. We spent two days quarantined on base before we could leave. We used those days to celebrate our survival.

I received orders to Norfolk Naval Air Station in Virginia. Dave was bound for San Diego Air Station. Nile was off to Cherry Point, North Carolina, and Tice and Plemons were both going to Jacksonville, Florida. These orders effectively killed any future for the Wild Kingdom. We raised beers, slapped shoulders and said our good byes. We celebrated each other for surviving Vietnam and the Marine Corps. For now, that was enough.

The stewardesses on our flight to Los Angeles were round-eyed, American women, something most of us hadn't seen for a year. As I stepped off the plane in L.A., in the distance I saw a small group standing behind a gate, waving. Green sea bags were hoisted onto shoulders, and we moved towards shrieking voices. Girls jumped up and down; moms cried; fathers stood straight. Once through the gates, some Marines were tackled with hugs, rocked, kissed and pulled into shoulders where tears flowed freely. Most of us walked on past.

At the military customs gate the Corporal asked, "You bringing anything back you shouldn't have?"

'No.'

He waved me through without even looking in my sea bag. I stepped through a set of double doors and, for the first time in 13 months, I stood in the civilian world. I made my way to an information counter and asked where I could buy a ticket for New York. I got a flight that left within the hour.

As I walked towards my departure gate, three men with long hair and tie-dyed tee shirts pointed their fingers at me.

"Hey, look, there's one of those baby killers."

They followed me at a safe distance. I could hear them, and after a few minutes I turned and stepped up onto the seats of a bank of chairs. One guy with love beads and a scraggly off-center beard said, "He wants to kill us, so he can notch his M-16."

I swallowed hard, trying not to jump at them. These guys had no idea what I was about. Suddenly I felt someone take hold of my elbow. I turned to see a man in a blue pilot's uniform.

"At ease, Marine." His tanned face was rutted with wrinkles. "Those kids don't have the slightest idea what you've been through. As close as they've gotten to the War is TV. Leave 'em alone, it's not worth it."

"Who are you?"

"Marine Corps. Korea. Chosan Reservoir." A set of gold wings with TWA printed on them was pinned over his left breast pocket. He let go of my arm.

"You're a Vietnam Vet, aren't you?"

"Yeah, what's it to you?"

"I'd like to thank you, for what you've done for me and our country," he said, stepping back and saluting.

"Thanks," I said, returning his salute.

Briskly, he turned on his heel. The three hippies had disappeared.

I arrived at Kennedy Airport six hours later and took a shuttle to Port Authority bus station where I bought a ticket to New Paltz. On the New York State Thruway I looked out the window at the green apple orchards and felt my eyes drawn to tree line. The bus turned off the Thruway and down Main St., New Paltz. The town didn't look like it had changed much. I stepped off the bus at 7 in the morning. A few people stood outside waiting for the bus to Kingston. No one knew I was coming home. I'd kept it vague so I could surprise Sandy. I'd called my folks from California to let them know I was back.

The summer air was full of smells I'd forgotten. The bus driver dropped my sea bag at my feet. I picked it up and headed into the bus station to use the restroom. I sat my sea bag on a bench, went to the counter and ordered an egg cream from the waitress.

"You drink egg creams for breakfast?"

"Yeah, it's a special diet I'm on." The sweet milky liquid of my youth slid into my stomach. The door opened behind me and I turned, squinting at the silhouette of a large man, the morning sun behind him.

"Is that you, Larry?"

"Ray Conklin. How are you doing?"

He slapped me on the back. "You just get home?"

Ray was my Dad's best friend. He and his wife Peggy played pinochle with my folks almost every Friday night. Ray had been in the Army Air Force in WW II.

"I just got off the bus."

"Let me give you a ride home."

"Ray, I'm not going home."

"Oh, I thought that's where you were headed. Where do you want to go? I own the taxi company here and this trip's on me."

"I'm going to my girlfriend's house."

He smiled. "Of course, let's go."

"Thanks, Ray."

It only took five minutes from the bus station to Sandy's house. In that short time Ray asked if I wanted to make a few extra bucks driving taxi. I told him I'd think about it. When I got out of the car Ray said, "Welcome home son. Peg and I are going over to see your folks tonight."

"Ray, I'll have probably seen them by then, but just in case I haven't, please don't tell them you saw me. I want to surprise them."

"No problem."

When I stepped onto Sandy's porch it seemed like I was waking from a 20-year sleep. I watched my knuckles rap the aluminum door.

There were no lights on inside. I guessed everyone was still sleeping. I knocked again. Sandy's mother, Marie, came to the door. She had a housecoat wrapped around her and was squinting to see me.

"What do you want?"

"Marie, it's me. Larry." I took off my hat and watched recognition set in. She undid the lock, opened her arms and took me in. I held onto her for a few moments, then asked, "Is Sandy up?"

"She's still in bed."

"Can I surprise her?"

"No, you can't. Go sit in the kitchen and I'll wake her."

I went to the kitchen and sat looking at the familiar gray Formica table that I'd watched Sandy do her homework at. I heard Sandy's voice and put my hands on my knees to keep them from shaking. When I heard footsteps on the stairs I expected her to come right in, but it was Marie.

"She's getting dressed. You want coffee?"

"No."

"You two have waited 13 months; you can wait another few moments."

"Larry, come upstairs."

Bolting past Marie, I took the stairs three at a time, and at the top I fell into Sandy's arms. We stood a long time squeezing our bodies together, trying to make them touch in every place possible. She wept into my shoulder. Without letting go of her, I walked us backwards into her bedroom and kicked the door shut.

Chapter 34

Made It

"Dad we need to talk."

"You in trouble?"

"No. I thought instead of just going out and doing whatever I want, I should tell you that I want to marry Sandy. We've been going out for over three years, and I'm ready."

He frowned. "Almost all of those years you were in the Marines. And in case you didn't notice, she's Italian."

"What the Hell's that got to do with anything?"

"Come on, son. You ought to know how the Italians can be. You know Danny, the little shit who works with me. He's five feet four and thinks he's a big man. You can watch him walking around with his chest puffed out tellin' people what they should be doing. He never shuts up. I can't trust a guy like that around high voltage. Mistakes get made when a man is running his mouth. He's your typical Wop--nice guy, but be careful. It seems like you've got no idea what you're getting into. Sandy's a nice girl, but you're talking about the rest of your life."

I squinted at him and, pointing my finger at his chest, said, "You're a frigging a bigot. If you ever open your mouth with this kind of shit in front of Sandy, you'll never see me again."

He recoiled as if I'd hit him. Making a fist, he stared at me. I made a fist. He stood. I tensed. Turning his back to me, he walked into the kitchen. Slamming the back door as hard as I could, I got into my car and barreled down the driveway, stones popping under the fenders like gunshots. Maybe the Marines had given me something.

I'd told my Mom a few days before, making her promise not to tell him. She'd smiled, "You just got back from Vietnam; shouldn't you take some time?"

"I want to marry her. She's a big reason why I came back alive. She wrote me four or five times a week, sent cookies, food, and new socks that she bought with her own money. Ma, the woman loves me."

Mom looked at her hands. I could see that I'd hurt her. I didn't get a single care package from her or my Dad the whole time I was in Nam.

Chapter 35

Getting Hitched

The date for our marriage was set for December 19, 1970. Sandy's father owned an Italian restaurant called Spats, his nickname. He and Marie, Sandy's mom, thought we should have a big wedding, so they could invite local business people and customers they knew. When Sandy asked me what kind of a wedding I wanted, I said, "I'd like a small wedding, just a few friends and family somewhere outdoors." Sandy's look at me revealed that she was stuck in the middle. Sandy told me Spats and Marie had well over 200 guests on their list. I shrugged my shoulders. "Let's do what we got to do then."

I was Methodist and Sandy, Catholic. Spats and Marie insisted we get married in the Catholic Church. I said, "I don't care." I'd given up on church when my parents stopped forcing me to go to Sunday school. Vietnam revived my interest in God a little when I was scared I was going to die. But I'd never even caught a glimpse of Jesus' sandals there. What I did get was a full-face view of Americans' inhumanity and hatred toward a culture they didn't want to understand. As a kid, I thought God and the Boy Scouts were related to being an American. Nam shattered that myth for me; now God and America were nothing more than social window dressing. To me, getting married gave Sandy and me permission to live together. The rest of it was like they said in Nam, "It don't mean nothing."

Before the wedding Sandy told me that we were required to go to sessions with the priest. During these sessions Father Hickey kept asking, "Do you intend to bring up your children Catholic?" Each time he asked me, I shook my head no. I didn't like him telling me what to do. There was too much of an echo of the Marines in his voice. It was the only thing I refused to agree to. Sandy got scared that Father Hickey wouldn't marry us. Instead, he simply stopped asking me.

I looked over the gathering that had come for our wedding and tried to pick out the faces of those I knew. There were only a few. The light coming through the stained glass didn't seem real, and the organ music felt like it was being played in a distant church. While I waited for my bride, I thought how I'd prayed and begged God to get me back home for this moment. Here I was, but it felt like I was stuck in a bubble, watching my life but not able to feel it.

Sandy strode up the isle looking beautiful and happy. She tugged at my hand. I tried to move closer, but I couldn't. My spirit had never gotten off the "Freedom Bird" those few months ago in Nam. I was here in body, but a vital part of me never returned. It felt like I had my face pressed against a window watching myself get married.

The reception was held at John Lapani's Villa, one of Spat's restaurateur friends. Everyone left the church and headed to the party. We stayed behind to get our pictures taken.

"How come you didn't wear your dress blues?" asked my father as he fished for his cigarettes in his coat pocket.

"I want the Marines to be a thing of the past," I said, looking over his shoulder at the door of the church, hoping he wouldn't light up inside.

I'd never seen John Lapani's Villa before. Sandy had made all the arrangements for our wedding while I was down in Norfolk on the Marine base. I peered into the big hall clad in dark wood paneling. It looked more like a rod and gun club than a banquet hall. Corners were broken off several of the ceiling tiles. Tables crowded the edge of the dance floor, each one adorned with folded pieces of paper with the names of the guests written in Sandy's neat print. A band played the music my mother had listened to on the radio for most of my childhood. The thin ties, neat suits and graying hair of the band told me that we wouldn't be hearing any of the Motown grooves that I enjoyed.

It took an hour before my face hurt from smiling. I whispered to Sandy, "When do you think we can get out of here?"

Her eyebrows furrowed. "We haven't even cut the cake yet. Hang in there. Have a drink. Go talk to your friends."

"San, I can't take much more of this. I'm gonna flip."

"OK. We have to wait until the cake is cut, and a half hour after that we can go. My parents will die if we leave any earlier. Can you do that for me?"

I nodded my head, got up from the table and looked for Dave. Dave was talking to Bruce DuBois and his wife, also named Sandy. Bruce stuck his hand out. "Congratulations man, you tied the knot."

"Thanks, Bruce. Hey, Sandy, how you doing? What's it like to be married to this guy?"

Sandy leaned over and kissed me. "Congratulations. You and Sandy make a nice couple." Looping her arm around her husband Bruce's, she added, "Being married is great, isn't it Bruce?"

"Yeah," he said, loosening his tie.

"No parents to deal with anymore," Sandy said, as she straightened my bow tie. "How long have you been back from Vietnam?"

"Six months."

"Did you smoke pot over there?" Sandy asked.

"Not much. I wanted to stay alive."

"Oh," said Sandy.

"I got some in my pocket. Are you interested?"

"No," Sandy blushed.

"What's it like over there? I mean I see all this stuff on TV about the jungle. Were you in the jungle?"

"No. I was stationed on an Airbase."

"Did you fly?"

"Yeah, I was a helicopter door gunner."

Bruce pulled on her arm causing her to have to step towards him. "Did you kill anyone?"

Suddenly a glass was in front of my face.

"Hey, Larry. I got this at the bar. Take it."

I took the glass from Dave's hand as he stepped in front of Sandy and raised his glass. In a slightly slurred, loud voice he said, "I want to make a toast here." Putting his arm over my shoulders, he drew me to him and blurted out, "This mother fucker did not die!" Then, gulping back a year's worth of tears, he threw the champagne glass against the tile floor. Quickly turning, he cut a swath to the door bellowing, "It don't mean nothing."

A circle of heads turned to watch him leave.

Chapter 36

Where Is He?

We left after the cake was cut and no one seemed to pay much attention. We'd said goodbye's to both sets of parents and slipped out the side door. The booze had been flowing, and I could see on Spat's face that he felt like he'd been seen as a father who'd given his daughter a nice wedding.

Sandy had made honeymoon plans for us to stay in the Pocono Mountains. When I opened the bathroom door and saw the heart-shaped tub, I couldn't help but remember taking a shower under a spigot in Nam just six months before.

Being locked in our room for days because of cold weather gave us time to talk about what future lay before us. We decided that first I'd go back to Norfolk to finish my enlistment. Later, I'd get an early out from the Marines to attend Ulster County Community College on the GI Bill in September.

For the first few months of married life I spent most weekends driving from Norfolk Naval Air Station to New Paltz to stay with Sandy for 24 hours and then returning. I didn't do this trip alone; every weekend thousands of military men swooped over the Chesapeake Bay Memorial Bridge heading to various northeastern states.

We had no other choice but to stay in Sandy's parents' house. She wasn't happy that we couldn't get our own place yet. She was tired of being the built-in babysitter for her younger brother, Robbie. Both Spats and Marie worked in the restaurant every evening, and Robbie still needed a babysitter.

A month before I was to be discharged, we found a cottage a few miles north of New Paltz on North Ohioville Rd. We plunked our rental deposit down on the gray frame house with asbestos siding. It looked to be originally built as a summer bungalow. We moved in on September 1, a few days after I was discharged. On September 6 I started classes at Ulster County Community College. Sandy had already begun a job in Kingston as an elementary school art teacher. My major was in recreational education, which seemed ridiculous, but it got me out of the Corps.

Sandy and I moved in the few things we owned and set up house. It was fun having a place to ourselves, not having to worry about someone hearing us in our bedroom. Late that September Dave called from California to tell me he was finishing up his enlistment.

"I'm being discharged in early October and got nowhere to live. I was wondering if you and Sandy could put me up for a few days."

Putting my palm over the receiver I called out, "How'd you feel about Dave living with us a few days?"

Sandy had known Dave in high school. We'd even doubled dated with him and his girlfriend, Donna, before we'd gone to Nam.

"Fine with me," she said, with no hesitation.

"You're in, my man. When you coming?"

"In a few days. Can you pick me up at JFK? I'll call you with the flight?"

"No problem."

All Dave talked about on the way home from JFK was motorcycles. He'd saved his blood money from Nam to buy one.

"I'm gonna get on that bike and ride as fast and hard and as long as I can until I get the stink of Nam off me."

Dave moved into one of the two spare bedrooms. I volunteered to take him shopping for the bike. We located a Yamaha dirt bike with a huge one-cylinder engine. He took it for a test ride out behind the shop. When he cranked the hand throttle the rear tire spit out a plume of dirt. Dave pulled in front of me and gunned the engine.

"Damn thing sounds like a chopper cranking up, doesn't it? I want it!"

The three of us settled in. It was Christmas, and Sandy and I had off from school when a call came in from Nile. I hadn't heard from him since I'd gotten out.

"Hey, Crazy. I just finished a three month tour in the brig."

164

"What the Hell are you talking about?"

He explained that he'd gone AWOL when his mom had gotten ill. He'd asked for a discharge so he could go home to help, but they told him he had to finish his tour of duty. He split. His mom passed a month after he'd gotten home. When he came back to the base, they slapped him in the brig.

"Got any room up there in New Paltz?" he asked. I hesitated. It had been working out with Dave, but we did miss our privacy. I looked at Sandy who was sitting on the couch. She looked back and mouthed, "What?"

"Nile wants to know if we have room for him to come and visit."

She tilted her head from side to side. Pointing at me, she whispered, "Do you want him to come?"

I shook my head yes. Nile and I had been close in Nam, and I missed having him to share stories about the war. Dave had been transferred in the middle of the tour in Nam, but Nile and I stayed in Marble Mountain.

Cupping the phone on my shoulder, I whispered back, "His mom died a few months ago, and he's got no where to go."

"Of course, then," Sandy said.

"You sure?"

"As long as it's not for forever."

In February, Dave and I drove our VW bug down to Cherry Point, North Carolina, to pick Nile up. We packed his belongings into the back seat of the car, and he rode his motorcycle all the way back to New Paltz. There was a build up of ice on the roll bars when he pulled into our driveway.

It felt like old times--even better. I had my new wife and my two best Marine buddies living in our house.

Sometime in late March Sandy turned to me in bed. "When we got married I didn't expect to be living with three ex-Marines."

"Neither did I."

I wasn't surprised she said something. The four of us had been together for two months, but she hadn't made a peep. Most evenings Nile, Dave and I would get into long discussions about Nam, telling stories that she had no way to relate to. I turned towards her side of the bed.

"San, I promise it's not gonna last forever."

As I lay there in the silence I began to see how she'd begun to avoid Nile and Dave. She had to feel resentful being the only one in the house working. Every morning she'd get up early and go off to Kingston to teach, leaving Nile hanging out all day reading motorcycle magazines and working on his bike, Dave riding around on his new motorcycle, and of course, me going off to college to take courses in recreational education. The only time we had alone was in bed.

"Listen San, Nile's been talking about going back to Ohio in a few months. Dave, he's like family. I can't really ask him to leave."

"I'm not really telling you I want them to leave. It's just that we don't have any time without one of them being here."

I pulled the covers up under my chin. "San, I know it's not easy for you. But I'm having a hard time too. It helps being able to talk to Dave and Nile. College isn't really working for me. Kids are throwing spitballs when the teacher turns his back. I left that kind of shit back in high school."

"That's because it's only a community college. No one at New Paltz did that."

"I'm four years older than anyone in the classes. I don't feel like I belong there. The only thing I look forward to is coming home. After Nam everything seems boring."

"It'll get better. Maybe you ought to transfer to New Paltz."

"Maybe I ought to drop out of school and get a job. Taking classes in archery and the history of recreation is a complete waste of my time. I'd rather get high than have an adult man talk to me about the first gymnasium."

166

"You guys are smoking a lot of pot."

"So does everyone. It's the only thing that makes me feel good. It gets me out of my head."

She put her hand on mine. "You've been through a war. It's gonna take time."

"San, Nile and Dave are the only guys I can to talk to. They were there. They know what it was like. Clark, my English teacher, was the only professor who even asked me what Nam was like. The kids in school have one track minds: they either want to get high or get laid."

I lay for a long time in the silence thinking. It seemed no matter how deeply we pushed our arms down into the barrel of our high school relationship we kept coming up with only remnants of what we'd once had. Sandy had been working hard to enter my world, but Vietnam had locked the door. She'd been going to college three blocks from her house. I'd been 10,000 miles away, fighting in a country most Americans had never heard of until their boys started coming home dead.

Sandy had told me that the S.D.S. had organized protests against the War at the college and that she'd felt philosophically stuck between supporting me and what S.D.S. was saying. Many of her professors were against the war. Sandy eventually became aware that the Marines she was living with were not so different from the S.D.S. students. Nile, Dave and I had grown to hate the war. Even before arriving in Nam we'd seen that stopping the spread of communism was simply a bogus doctrine to hide America's financial interests; most Vietnamese were poor farmers whose only concern was a good rice crop. Sandy saw that we had, in our own ways, played a small part in slowing the War down. Nile contributed to an underground military paper, pointing out how American military men were treating the Vietnamese working on the base. Dave led the Wild Kingdom in discussions on why we shouldn't be killing women and children with the unused napalm that should have been returned to base. She saw that our eyes had been filled with hard realities in Vietnam, and it took a lot of pot smoke to settle the feelings of shame that mixed uneasily with the strident patriotism instilled in Marine boot camp.

The next day I came into the house through the back door. Nile was sitting at the dining room table eating something out of a can.

"Hey, Man, what's going down?" I asked.

"Nothing."

"How's the project?"

"Almost done. When you get back from class, we'll fire it up."

That evening Nile came out of his bedroom carting a five-gallon water bottle with brass pipes sticking out the top of it. He sat it on the coffee table and stood back. I walked around the table, inspecting his craftsmanship.

"You really learned your shit working on those helicopters, Corporal McCoy."

Nile had transformed the water bottle into his enormous homemade hookah. Three six foot, clear plastic hoses were stuck on the angled brass nipples. Soldered to a brass pipe that rose out of the hole of the bottle was a large brass bowl.

"I picked up some cheap wine on the way home to fill the bottle."

"Be careful when you pull the cork out," Nile laughed.

That evening Nile, as the master of ceremonies, meticulously unfolded a plastic bag neatly stored in his special wooden box. He took out a small black ball and handed it to me.

"Check out this stuff."

Lifting it to my nose, I took in the sweet, keen smell of black hash.

Dave came in from his bedroom, and I handed the marble of hash to him. He rolled it between his thumb and forefinger and said, "Smells like hand packed Afghani." Tossing the hash to Nile he said, "You do the honors."

I liked to watch Nile work. He moved with economy. First he broke off a small chunk from the hash ball. Then, taking a hatpin from his box, he inserted it into the hash. He reached again into his box for

168

wooden matches and lit one using the edge of his thumbnail. Slowly, he rotated the hash above the flame. A thin line of white smoke streamed off. Nile bent over, snorting a nose-full and then letting out a loud "Ahhhh." Carefully, he placed the hash on a black marble tile on the coffee table. From another plastic bag he took out a large pinch of grass and dropped it on the roasting hash. With thumb and forefinger he squeezed the two drugs together, making his mixture. Using an ace of spades playing card, reminding all of us of the card Marines placed on Viet Cong they'd killed, he scooped the concoction up and stuffed it into the brass bowl of the pipe.

"Shooters look down range and fire on your own dog targets."

This was an expression we'd learned at the rifle range that signaled for us to get ready to fire our weapons.

I struck a wooden match on the zipper of my blue jeans and held it above the brass bowl. Each of us took up a plastic hose and sucked. Wine bubbles danced and smoke filled the bottle as we took in the wine-scented drugs.

Nile sat back on the couch and let out a long, gray plume. He draped his hose over the arm of the couch. Taking off the utility hat he'd worn during his entire tour in Nam, he tipped his head back as if speaking to the ceiling.

"I'm going home."

Dave and I looked at him.

"What are you talking about?" I sputtered.

"I got to go home. I got to go back to my people. No one knows where I am."

"Who's back there? Your mom's gone…"

"Friends."

"When you pulling out?" Dave asked, putting the hose back in his mouth.

"I don't know yet. I have to find a place to stay. I'd like to be out of here in a week."

169

"Shit, man, are you sure? It's fine to stay here. I spoke to Sandy, and she said it's really OK."

"Thanks, man, but I got to be rolling out of here. It's been cool hanging, but it's time to move."

I slumped down into the couch, thinking about the long talks we'd had.

Dave, was shutting down, swimming in his own private pool of history. After a while he said, "Nile's not the only one leaving. I want to tell you guys about this woman Debbie I met. She's a waitress at Barnaby's. We've been going out for a couple of months. We're getting a place together."

"You got to be kidding me. You're moving in with a woman? I thought that wasn't ever gonna be part of your game plan."

"It wasn't, but I like her game and I want to play."

"So, both of you Jarheads are pulling out on me."

They looked at each other and shrugged.

Nile said, "There's another war for me to fight; some call it reality."

Chapter 37

Jumping Ship

It took Nile almost two weeks to get himself together to leave. Dave was gone in less than a week. Suddenly Sandy and I were alone in our house. Darkness filled the absence. There was no one to get high with, no one to share war stories. Sandy listened like she always did, but the War kept eating me. Life was supposed to be good. I'd survived war; I had a beautiful wife; I was in school; and we had a nice car and our own home.

Expecting it would work itself out, we established a pattern modeled on our parents lives. I'd come home from school and do chores like paint the living room or take the storms off the house. Sandy would make dinner. We shopped together for food, did the obligatory visit to parents. Still our best communication was in the bedroom.

Ray, my Dad's best friend, asked me if I wanted to drive a cab at night. We could use the extra bucks, so I took the job. I had no skills other than working on helicopters, which I didn't want to do. The pressure to go to school weighed on me, but college had been more of a ticket to get out of the Marines than a career choice. The language I spoke was made up of anti-war slogans, Vietnamese lingo, and military jargon. No one at Ulster Community College spoke like I did. I was so used to living with daily fear of death that when it was taken away, it was as if I'd been pushing desperately on a door with all my might trying to get in and suddenly someone from inside turned the door knob and I fell into a room I no longer recognized.

One day in Clark's English class, a gawky looking kid who hadn't grown into his arms and legs threw a spitball that landed on my desk. I pushed it to the floor with the edge of my book and glared at him. In the hall after class I took hold of the front of his shirt and pulled him towards me.

"What the fuck's wrong with you? I'm paying for this fucking class, you little chicken-shit. If you were in Nam, you'd be dead. Wake the fuck up!"

The shriveled kid backed away from me.

"You're crazy, man. You're really fucking crazy."

When I got home that afternoon I flopped on the couch. The sun streamed in the windows. I reached for the little box of goodies Nile had left. I rolled a joint, lit it and took a deep drag, trying to stop the shaking in my body.

He's just a goofy kid like I was before Nam," I said to myself.

The sunlight drew lines through the haze in the room. I thought of opening a window before Sandy came home, but sat still.

The gray cat, Malkin, came into the room. We'd recently gotten the cat from the SPCA, and Sandy had named her after some Shakespeare character she'd learned about in college. She said it was in the play Macbeth. When the cat mews, the witch calls out, "I come, Grimalkin." Sandy explained that a malkin was a witch or the companion of witches. She'd gotten it right; the cat had a nasty streak.

Malkin came around the corner of the couch, and I caught her by the tail. Digging her front and rear claws into the rug, she lurched to get away. I held on. She suddenly turned, sinking her needle teeth into the flesh between my thumb and forefinger. As if a trigger was pulled inside me, I grabbed her head, tearing her teeth out of my hand. My blood dripped on the carpet. The room collapsed around me. It was as if my arm were someone else's. I watched it cock back and shoot forward, heaving the cat against the wall. Spittle flew from her mouth onto the freshly painted wall. She lay at the baseboard, quivering in a pile on the floor. My head was jerking from side to side as if someone had attached marionette stings. Vermilion waves coursed behind my eyes when I closed them. I had to make myself unclench my jaw. I thought I heard someone wailing deep within a sandbag bunker. Eyes squeezed shut, I saw my own silhouette flailing into a red night sky. A vortex of sorrow spun inside me and I wanted to vomit. I opened my eyes and made a guttural plea.

"Help me. Please, help me".

I could see the cat's back was broken; its hind legs were limp. I jerked off the couch as if the puppeteer had sprung me back into life. In the kitchen I found a shopping bag. With the moaning cat in the bag, I sobbed, "I'm sorry. I didn't mean it. I'm sorry. I'm so sorry."

In the garage I reached for a shovel standing in the corner. The trees in the backyard were jungle canopy. Elephant grass ticked against my pants. I lay the paper bag on the ground. The fraught moaning freed me to bring the shovel over my head. I swung it down hard, smashing the bag again and again. Collapsing to my knees, I looked up when I heard a cough, like someone clearing their throat. There in the gauzy light stood my father. He had on scuffed up, steel toed work boots, green pants, an over-washed green shirt with a pack of Lucky Strikes in the breast pocket. He smiled, nodding his head. I saw approval in his blue eyes. Someone was next to him. Squinting my eyes, I made out Gunny Webb in his Smokey the Bear hat. His cheek bulged with chewing tobacco, his hands on his hips. Slowly he raised his flattened right hand up to the brim of his hat. I shook my head trying to sort out the confusion, and when I opened my eyes there was Corporal Hardass in spit shined boots, a string of dried up VC ears around his neck. He rocked back and forth on his heels. He held his hand out with his thumb raised.

Chapter 38

The Shrink

When I told Sandy the truth about the cat she took me in her arms and admitted for the first time that our life looked out of control. She told me she understood, but I didn't believe her. It was starting to feel like I could do almost anything, blame it on the war, and she'd forgive me. Or maybe my shame prevented me from seeing that she accepted me.

Somehow we pushed past the reality of the cat, and I began working longer hours driving the taxi. I was still going to school full time. One evening when business was slow Ray, the taxi owner, asked me if I had any interest in buying his half of the company. He said he was getting ready to retire and move to Florida. His partner was Parks Glen, the owner of the bus station where the taxi stand was housed. I told Ray I liked the idea and would like to sleep on it. This might be a legitimate way for me to quit college and start contributing to the running of our lives. I couldn't wait to get home to ask Sandy how she felt about it.

Business picked up at 11 p.m. with a fare to Newburgh. It was 1:30 a.m. when I opened the front door of our house.

"Too tired to wait up. Wake me when you come in. Love, Sandy," read the note on the kitchen table.

I crawled under the covers and as soon as my head settled into the pillow I felt a hand on my chest.

"Welcome home."

"You awake enough to talk?"

"What's the matter?"

"Nothing. Ray just asked me if I wanted to buy his half of the taxi business."

"We don't have any money."

"I know, but he's willing to have me pay him over time."

Sandy pulled herself up in bed.

"How can you run a business and go to college?"

"I'll quit college. I don't want to do it anymore. I feel like I'm wasting my time."

"You want to be a taxi driver the rest of your life?"

"No. But I wouldn't mind making more than four dollars an hour. This doesn't have to be the end of the road."

After a long silence, she said in a soft voice, "If that's what you want, we'll make it work. When's Ray need to know?"

"He didn't say. But I'd like to tell him soon."

Something about this conversation felt strange. I wanted to make a major life change, and in just a few moments I had her convinced. I closed my eyes and imagined being the boss of New Paltz Taxi. I'd never been the boss of anything.

In a few weeks I became a college dropout and part owner of the New Paltz Taxi Company. I was happy; my father was happy; and Sandy seemed to be open to making it work. Ray was Dad's best friend. Dad told me he thought I was getting a good deal.

"Parks is a smart man. You pay attention, and you may come out of this with some money in your pocket."

I wasn't sure what Dad meant about Parks. My work week went from 20 hours to 80, and when I reached into my pocket there wasn't that much money. If I worked hard for a few years I could build the company--buy new cars, fix the old ones--and then the cash would start rolling in.

My four drivers were all men my father's age. I felt their resentment on the first day. I was a young whippersnapper telling them what to do. The second week on the job I called Bill, a man about 60, on the radio and asked him to pick up a fare at Morriello's Apple Orchard. Half an hour later a phone call came in complaining that Bill never showed. When I asked him where he was, he said he'd picked up another fare at the Grand Union.

"Bill, why didn't you call it in?"

175

"I forgot."

"Right," I said, knowing that Bill didn't want to pick up Negro migrant workers.

I was at a loss as to how to handle him, so I mentioned it to Parks. He shrugged his shoulders.

"It'll work itself out."

Bill turned out to be nothing compared to Ken, a part-time driver who worked at night. A college student came in complaining to me that Ken had grabbed his leg and asked him if he was interested in a blowjob. I'd gone to high school with Ken's kids. Parks had told me this wasn't the first complaint about him. I felt embarrassed and ashamed for Ken. I called him aside and asked about the incident. He denied anything happened. Then I told him about the other complaints Parks had heard. He started shaking his head violently up and down.

"Fuck you, you Goddamn baby killer!"

My vision narrowed to his neck. Tight lipped, I spit my words.

"Give me the fucking keys and your night's receipts and get your sorry ass out of here."

Ken raised his fist. I stepped towards him. He swiveled and burst out the bus station door. I followed a few feet behind him. He turned his head over his shoulder.

"You lay a fucking hand on me, I'll go to the police."

"Yeah, that's a good idea. Let's go to the police and tell them where you been laying your hands."

Getting into his car he threw the taxi keys on the ground and drove out of the bus station parking lot with the night's receipts.

Dave came in the next night to fill in for Ken. He sometime drove for extra bucks.

"You're looking really stressed man. Ever think of getting any help?"

"Help? What are you talking about?"

176

"I found a veterans rap group down at the VA hospital in Castle Point."

"What do you talk about?"

"The War and how it's affecting our lives now."

"I thought those things were just a bunch of retired lifers telling war stories."

"No lifers in the group. Just guys like you and me who can't figure out what they just been through. There are some guys that tell some pretty terrible stories, and they ain't making them up. You want to go with me?"

"You kidding? Go the VA? I got no interest in anything military; you know that."

"Just thought it might help. You look like your ass is dragging."

"Let me think about it."

"Cool. Let me know; it's on Wednesday nights."

I thought about it but couldn't see myself near any kind of military situation. After speaking to Sandy about what Dave said, she agreed I was having a hard time. She suggested a therapist named Sam Passier in Kingston. Her friend had been seeing him and had reported that he'd been helpful. I made an appointment with Sam. He was a nice guy and I enjoyed talking to him. I thought we would get right into the thick of it and start talking about what happened to me in Nam, but he was more interested in my childhood, particularly my relationship with my father.

Sam kept asking me, "Do you think your Dad had anything to do with you going into the Marines?"

"He was in the Navy during World War II but never went over seas. My Dad never really laid a trip on me about going in the Marines. All his buddies supported the war, but he didn't really talk about it much."

"Think about the question a little more. It takes a certain kind of man to join the Marines, doesn't it?"

"Yeah, a rock head."

Sam was furrowing his brow so I thought I'd better get serious. "What are you getting at, Sam? Do you know something about me that I don't? If that's true, why don't you just tell me what you're thinking?"

"Sometimes these understandings are better if they come from you, but I'll tell you at little bit of what's on my mind. Your Dad was raised in a family where before he was ten he'd watched his father loose his legs, and just a few years after that his mother committed suicide. The world for him must have become a frightening place."

"I never really thought about that," I nodded. "Keep going."

"Perhaps, out of this fear, your Dad decided he needed to protect his son from this frightening world. The only way he knew how to do that was to help to make him a man as soon as possible."

"Maybe, but how can you make a boy a man when he's only 12 years old?"

"You really can't, but at 12 you'd already learned some painful lessons, like when there's not enough you need to kill. That the only way to secure safety in the world is to work really hard. That play is for kids. All of this was unconscious of course, but it all helped to prepare you for what the Marine Corps would finish."

I forced a deep breath. The truth of what Sam just told me was suffocating. I started to understand what I'd done to our cat--something I hadn't told him about yet. I wanted to leave his office but swallowed hard and waited for him to tell me it was over.

"That's enough for today," he said, putting his hand on my shoulder. "It looks like that settled on you hard. Next week we'll talk about your Mom."

"Great, thanks Sam."

Chapter 39

Here I Am

I waited in front of an idling silver Trailways bus; the sun was warm on the back of my neck as I leaned on my taxi. The day was cool; leaves had not fully come out and the last dull grays of winter were fading under the promise of green. A nice day to be driving a taxi. The memory of standing in this very place with Dave five years before took over my thoughts. We'd been waiting for the bus to Albany to go get our Marine physicals. The War was in full swing, and the body counts on TV kept building. Without my naive ability to not look reality in the face, I never would have gone to Nam. I took a deep breath, allowing myself a moment to be grateful for being alive. I'd promised myself in Nam that every time I thought of it I'd acknowledge my gratefulness for not being killed. Back then I was certain I'd never be standing here again.

The Trailways bus came into the parking lot and I waited for my fare; he was the last person off the bus. His brown wingtip dangled below the bus step searching for ground; the top of his dark fedora bobbed through the bus door. Quickly, I packed away my reverie and waved to him.

Mr. Fedora had on a black knee-length coat. He could have been a businessman or a streaker. He came towards me smiling. I smiled back and opened the cab door. I had been routinely transporting Mr. Fedora, and he never once offered his name. He'd always chosen to go one of two places: the seedy Highland Art Cinema to watch skin flicks or the historic Mohonk Mountain House resort. Today it was Mohonk. He carried no luggage.

Mr. Fedora slid onto the worn seat of the 1967 Chevy. I pulled down on the shift lever and headed west on Main St.. Approaching the bridge over the Wallkill River, he spoke.

"Do you know what God's words 'I Am' mean?"

"Excuse me?"

"Do you know the words that come from the Bible, 'I Am'?"

"No idea what you're talking about." I hadn't looked at a Bible since I'd been confirmed in the Methodist Church at 13.

'I Am' is the only true statement that exists. These ancient words are an invitation to know God. If you understand them, you have no need for other learning."

"Really!"

"If you took the entire world's wisdom since the dawn of man and boiled it down to its essence, it would be contained in this simple phrase: 'I Am'."

I was catching on. He just wanted to talk, so he was giving me a line of gibberish. He wasn't the first fare to unload bizarre nonsense on me.

"Tell me more."

"God is saying he exists and that you are one with him; there's no dividing line. God invites you into his being to become one with him."

Then for a long time Mr. Fedora was silent, as if he wanted to give me time to take in this great knowledge. But instead of pondering this wisdom I wondered why, after all the rides I'd given him, he decided to speak now? He didn't bother to work up to these profound thoughts. He just blurted them at me as if we'd been in hours of conversation. In the silence I could feel myself getting pissed. It must be his mentioning God. In my childhood God had been a background guy. I'd been dropped off at Sunday school for years, and, if I could, I'd kick at the dirt in the churchyard until I could skip out without being seen; then, I'd go down to Buddy's' store to buy candy bars with my collection money. This was the God I took to Nam. He must have fallen out of my sea bag on the first day because I kept looking for him without any luck. I looked but saw more important things through the scope on my starlight rifle, things that wanted to kill me.

I suddenly had the impulse to turn and tell Fedora about my God. If I had it might have sounded like, "Hey man, you want to talk God? Where was your boy in the war? I never saw his face; he was AWOL. I looked for him hard where one of our choppers blew up in front of me with my friends on it. Do you think your God heard those men's screams?"

Tight lipped, I let this internal conversation build inside. Five minutes had passed and neither one of us had spoken. The seed he'd planted in my brain wouldn't stop growing. In the silence, my internal dialog started again.

"Hey Fedora! I think your existential bullshit needs some grounding. Where's your head been for the last eight years, stuck in the Bible? Why haven't you looked up at the TV that's been broadcasting carnage? I've looked and have not once seen Jesus or your I Am God on the screen. Was he sleeping when we all watched the little Vietnamese girl running with napalm burning off her skin?"

The tires of the taxi hit a rut and suddenly I realized I'd better get my focus back on the road. We were halfway to Mohonk and neither one of us had said a word yet, so I asked, "Why are you going to Mohonk?"

"To see the Elementals."

"What?"

"The Elementals, I've seen them before at Mohonk."

I thought, "Here we go. He's speaking more twaddle." As a consummate people watcher I knew I had a gold mine in this guy. If he were a bird, he'd be one that birdwatchers would be dieing to get on their life list.

"What the Hell are the Elementals?" Glancing in the rearview mirror I saw that his eyes were closed.

"Elementals are creatures that give charm and beauty to the wilderness. They're the essence of plants. They appear to us as gnomes, elves, little people, and sometimes fairies. Elementals live on the astral plane of the earth's sphere. They are only seen now in remote places."

This guy was obviously whacked out of his gourd. One cab ride he goes to a porno movie and the next to the mountaintop to commune with fairies. I stayed quiet, not wanting to taint this phenomenal source of hogwash. This would be a great story to tell Sandy when I got home.

"I just read a book called The Coming of the Fairies by Arthur Conan Doyle. Do you know who Conan Doyle is?

"No."

"He wrote Sherlock Holmes."

"Really. He believed in fairies?"

"He saw them; even took pictures of them."

"Conan Doyle took pictures of fairies?"

I pulled up to the Mohonk gatehouse and saluted to the gatekeeper who waved us through. On the two-mile driveway, I looked into the trees to see if I could see any of the fairies Mr. Fedora was looking for. The best I could come up with were the cedar gazebos perched like huge wooden birds at the cliff's edge along one side of the road. We rounded the last curve and, on the rise, saw a grand view of Mohonk's massive stone building.

"Here we are."

Looking in the mirror I could see Fedora with a pen and paper. Reaching over the front seat he handed me the fare and a small slip of paper. I took his money and read the slip of paper: *I Am.*

"Thanks, would you like to be picked up later?"

"No."

As he walked away from the cab, I stripped the gears on the crank as I rolled up the window. Pounding on the steering wheel, I screamed, "Mr. Fedora let me tell you what "I am". "I am" a fucking Vietnam vet who could give a shit about your God, or your Elementals. You haven't got a clue what you're talking about. You want to know about God, crawl into a foxhole. And if you've never been in one, keep your fucking mouth shut. And if you ever find yourself in one, try saying over and over again "I Am," and see how that works. Maybe then you'll find out who you really are.

"About Elementals, I've seen them; they were wearing black silk pajamas and slipped through razor wire in the night as quiet as the sea fog. Real Elementals want to kill you. Mr. Fedora. 'I Am' upsetting you? I'm sorry. Let me give you a small piece of paper to comfort you. Did

182

you say you don't know how to pronounce it? Di di mau. What's it mean? It means get the Hell out of here!"

As I drove home, it felt like Fedora had ripped off my mask only to reveal a killer in me. He wasn't trying to; he didn't even know he'd done it. His mention of God penetrated my deepest wound from the war. Suddenly I was looking in the rearview mirror at a Marine I'd thought was gone. He'd crawled back into me on his knees and elbows and was refusing to leave. There he was, the man who'd wanted to kill VC, and worst of all the man who'd killed his own cat. I knew "I Am" was weak medicine for this ailment.

Chapter 40

Snapped Back

At 6 o'clock one morning I was walking across the bus station parking lot. I thumped my closed fist on the hood of one of my cabs. Three out of the six lined up had over 150,000 miles on their speedometers. I'd co-owned New Paltz Taxi for four years. I'd been averaging 80 hours a week and I was exhausted. I'd sunk all my earnings into the business, and my hope of being a wealthy businessman was as faded as the paint on the old cars.

Sandy and I had recently bought a house and were discussing having a child. My work schedule eliminated that possibility, so I asked Parks if he'd buy my half of the company and he agreed. I had no idea what I'd do for a living but knew that if I didn't get out of the taxi business, my marriage, to quote Dave, "was going to fold like a cheap camera."

The building tension between Sandy and me disappeared with the decision to quit. I was spending more time at home and looking around for what to do next. I'd come home early one night and we were watching television when a sudden newscast interrupted Mork and Mindy. The newscaster announced that the North Vietnamese had just taken over Saigon.

"It's over. All that American blood for nothing."

"Thank God. It's been enough," Sandy said, turning up the volume on the TV set.

"It has. But I can't help thinking of the waste. That whole fucking War was a waste--a waste of life, time, and money. Just look at how happy those bastards are sitting on their tanks. Those are the guys I was trying to kill, and they won."

"Nobody won," Sandy whispered.

The images on the TV were hitting my face like arrows. I wanted to kick the TV screen in and at the same time go out in to the street and scream out my relief that it was over. It felt like fabric inside me was being torn. I'd managed, so far, to keep a steady trot going away from those 1969-1970 years and suddenly world events were reeling me back in. I reached for the phone.

"Who you calling?"

"Dave, I got to tell him what's going on."

Chapter 41

The Last Ride

Alex Minewski was a steady taxi customer. He was an art professor at New Paltz College and, in fact, had been one of Sandy's teachers. When he found out I was a vet he began asking for me every time he called for a cab; For the past few years I'd been taking him to his classes at the college, grocery shopping and to art openings.

Alex was over six feet tall with thinning gray hair. His narrow chin hung down, suggesting the handle on a hand-held theater mask. His busy dark eyes measured everything. Years of hard drinking flushed his cheeks, and his mouth held an Emmett Kelly-like pathos.

Alex's limp came from a wound to his right leg while fighting in India during World War II. His wife Natalie told me that, after he was shot, he'd spent two years in and out of various military hospitals. His leg never completely healed. The leg pain became the locus of 20 years of drinking.

Before coming to teach at New Paltz College, Alex worked in New York City as a picture framer. During this time he continued his own painting. He also studied at the Art Students League. In the early 60's he quit drinking cold turkey. Sobriety plunged him deeper into his artwork. He told me he painted with a vengeance, neglecting to sleep many nights—only dozing in the chair of his studio.

Alex had been telling me for years about a remote island off the coast of Maine called Monhegan. He and his family had been going there for years. I mentioned to him that I was selling the Taxi Company at the end of June.

"Why don't you take me and the family to Monhegan, and this could be your swan song to New Paltz Taxi?"

"How far is it? And how much room would you need?"

"It can't be more than 400 miles. If we took that big yellow van we'd have plenty of room."

"That's a damn interesting idea."

"You could bring Sandy and make a vacation out of it. Come out to the island and stay with us for a week."

"I'll get back to you after I talk to Sandy and come up with a price."

Sandy thought it was a great idea. We were both tired, her from teaching the whole year and me from the out-of-control schedule I'd been working at the taxi.

The next time Alex got in the cab I told him, "I'll do it."

"Great. Let me tell you a little bit about the place. It's an artists' colony. Many artists from New York City come there for the summer. It's also a small fishing village; several of the locals fish for lobster during the winter months. You have to take a mail boat out to the island, and cars are not allowed."

"I can do it for $250."

"We're on. Pick us up early next Saturday. Pull up by the back door so we can load."

"This will not only be my last taxi fare, but the largest."

When I pulled into Alex's driveway all the legalities to sell the taxi were in place. If things went right I'd return to signed papers. So what if the wheels fell off my taxi dreams; like they said in the Corps, "It don't mean nothing."

During the first hour of the trip we accomplished introductions. Sandy and Natalie had the common ground of both being art teachers. The conversation flowed naturally as little 9 year-old Andrew, the Minewski's son, crawled into the backseat and fell asleep.

Alex rode shotgun and started telling me about how he'd been one of Merrill's Marauders in Burma. He gesticulated with his hands to make his points. If you'd been looking at us from outside the van you'd think he was telling me about a fistfight he'd had. I'd seen a movie about Merrill's Marauders and knew that only a few men survived. Alex had never spoken to me about the War before, and it felt good to be talking to a soldier. He described Burma's beauty, the colors and the textures of the terrain. This vibrated pictures of Vietnam loose in my mind.

After eight hours of driving, we arrived at Port Clyde, a small town located on the coast of Maine. From there we'd take the mail boat, the Laura B, out to the island. We parked the van on the lawn of a retired fisherman for five bucks a day. Alex told us that trucks were the only vehicles allowed on the island. In the summer they were used to haul guests' luggage to one of the three hotels. In the winter the trucks were used to haul lobster traps to the wharf where the fishermen would unload them onto waiting lobster boats.

The Laura B. pitched as we steamed out beyond the sight of land. Sandy and I held the rail. Alex and Natalie kidded us about not having sea legs. We arrived at the wharf and Carl, an island fisherman, loaded our things into his truck and delivered them to the cottage. I helped Alex unload the truck while Natalie and Sandy went into the house. For the next several days Sandy and I explored the island. Then, Alex asked me to go for a walk with him to Lobster Cove. We sat on rocks and looked out over an expanse of sea.

Alex began telling me stories about the war. His voice rose and pitched with feeling. It was as if he were following a musical score he'd written years ago that he'd never had a chance to play. Now he was dusting off his keyboard and fingering a haunting melody. Alex was only a few years younger than my father and he was interested in what had happened to me. The sea washed against the rocks as we spoke about how wars feed upon human souls.

Alex said his experience in India rattled him so deeply that he shook for the better part of his two years waiting to get out of the hospital. He'd been frightened that he'd never walk again. He explained that he started drinking to keep the tremors out of his limbs so he could draw. I didn't tell Alex I was smoking pot almost everyday to keep my own fears numb. My neck was in constant pain. My shoulders always up around my ears. Not even when I slept did the fear release. A few weeks ago Sandy had leaned over me when I was asleep to kiss me goodbye before she went to work. Feeling something on my face, I sprang up, grabbing her around her neck before I realized who she was.

"Alex, there's something I'd like to ask you. It happened five years ago just after I got out."

Alex looked in my face. "Let me guess. When you came back from Vietnam you thought everyone was looking at you as a killer."

"Not exactly, but close."

"That's what I thought people were thinking about me when I told them I was one of Merrill's Marauders. Then the Goddamn movie came out."

"I killed our cat. I didn't plan to do it; it just happened. It sank its teeth into my hand, and I threw it against the wall. I couldn't stop myself."

"A cat."

"Yeah. It bothers me, sometimes more than the things I did in Nam. There, it was my job. Killing my own pet makes me a real killer."

I lowered my head to break the gaze between us. Alex put his hand on my shoulder and squeezed. Tears ran through my beard onto my jeans. For a long time we rocked with the sea.

"You are a killer because you have taken life. There is no repair, only the grief you must carry. There is no salve for this pain. Your choice is to carry it or drown it in vodka or drugs like I did."

He stood abruptly and walked away. I followed him as he limped along the path.

"Alex, stop!"

When I came upon him, his eyes were full. I put my arm over his shoulder. We walked arm and arm the rest of the way home looking at the ground.

Chapter 42

Another Beginning

After the Monhegan trip I came home and signed the papers, selling my half of New Paltz Taxi. I'd made an arrangement with Alex before leaving Monhegan to rent a station wagon at the end of August to bring him and his family back to New Paltz.

Within a month I found a job. Ted Lasher, the Town of New Paltz Supervisor, was a man I'd known since I was a boy. Ted ran a gun and fishing tackle shop on Jansen Rd. My brothers and I would catch crayfish in small streams and sell them to Ted for a nickel apiece. Then we'd spend all the nickels in Ted's soda machine, walking home with empty pockets.

I was taking Tom Miller's job as water superintendent; he was retiring. The hardest thing about the job was that it was only 40 hours a week, which meant I'd have a lot of free time. Within my first year, Ted lost the election and Bill Yeaple became the new Supervisor. My job description changed under Bill to include running the town landfill and establishing its first recycling center.

The slow pace of the town job allowed me to renovate our house. When we moved in there was no shower, so my first project was to remodel the bathroom. Next was the spare bedroom, which was to be for the child we were planning. Sandy had just received tenure, which meant if she had a baby, her job was guaranteed. We were reading books together on natural childbirth and thinking of maybe having our baby at home.

I had just placed a Pete Seeger album on the stereo. Pete was cranking out Sailing Down My Dirty River when Sandy came in through the front door. Setting down her book bag she reached for the amplifier knob and turned the volume down.

"I want you to check something out. I found a magazine article at school today." she said, taking it out of the book bag and handing it to me.

In large print the title read, How To Increase the Odds of Having the Sex Child You Want. I skimmed as she waited. The author described a method of checking body temperature to determine the ovulation cycle that indicated when to have sex to increase the likelihood of having the gender you wanted for your child. Sandy and I had discussed wanting a boy.

"Looks good. What do you think?"

"I'd like to try it."

Placing my hand on her inner thigh, I asked, "How about right now?"

"Save your energy for later, I'm not sure if I'm at the right temperature."

"I am."

"I'll get dinner started."

A few weeks had passed, and I was pulling up the covers when I glanced at the calendar on her nightstand. The big black X's through the numbers reminded me of the calendar I kept in Nam. I noticed that today's date had a circle around it.

Sandy smiled. "Tonight's the night."

"Tonight's the night," I repeated, twisting off the sidelight and feeling some performance anxiety building.

"Do you think it's going to work?"

Guiding her hand to my penis, I said, "It's always worked before."

"That's not what I mean."

"If it doesn't, we'll have fun trying." I pulled her close, visualizing that somewhere in the tiny cracks between us a son was going to spring to life.

"Remember, it's got to be in as far as you can get it when you come."

"How could I forget? And you remember you're supposed to come so the acidy of your womb is just right for our boy."

"Let's make this a lovely experiment."

"One that might last the rest of our lives," I said, moving my hand from her breast to between her legs.

Chapter 43

We're Pregnant

"I missed my period," Sandy declared.

We stared at each other in disbelief. The first time and we'd scored! Many of our friends had tried to get pregnant and failed. We decided to wait to tell our parents, just to make sure. When she missed it the second month it was time to announce the good news.

We decided to tell my family first. They'd be easier since they never got mixed up in our lives the way Sandy's parents did sometimes.

When we came through the front door of my parents' house, Dad was groggy; we'd awakened him in his recliner. Mom sat in her cushioned rocking chair reading. We said our hellos and I sat on the slate fireplace hearth; Sandy took the wingback chair. I could feel the coolness of the stone seeping through my pants. Dad was looking out the bay window at the birdfeeder. I looked out to see what he was watching, and there was a sudden movement in the feeder. Then I saw a gray squirrel leap onto it and start eating birdseed, his tail twitching.

"The squirrel's winning, huh?"

Dad reached underneath the walnut end table, and an electronic shriek squealed out of the speaker he'd fastened to the bird feeder. The squirrel continued nibbling sunflower seeds, its tail shaped in a question mark."

"He's got yah Dad; I think he's used to it."

Mom put her romance novel down. It had a picture of a buxom woman holding onto the leg of an angry man. Sandy sat across from Dad with her legs crossed and her long black hair draped over one shoulder. A haze of smoke hung in the room. I saw Mom's freshly crushed cigarette in the ashtray on the end table.

Clearing my throat I waited until everyone was looking at me.

"We came to tell you something. We're having a baby."

Mom's face lit up. "Congratulations!"

Dad got out of his recliner and shook my hand. He moved towards Sandy and gave her a half-bent hug with one arm.

We told them the due date was May 3. Then we gathered up to leave.

"Sandy will you be going back to work or staying at home to take care of the baby?" my mother asked, stuffing her hands into her apron.

"We've decided I'm going back. We need the money."

"Who's gonna take care of the baby?"

"Mom, we haven't figured that out," I said. "Give us a chance to have it first, will ya?"

"Maybe we can help you out," Mom said looking at Dad.

He looked out the window at the birdfeeder.

"We haven't gotten that far yet, but thanks for the offer," I said, touching Sandy's elbow, guiding her to the door. Before leaving I looked at Dad.

"You need a louder buzzer."

"I'm working on it. Ray got me this alarm off one of the machines at IBM before he retired. He said it'll blast the ears off that squirrel!"

Back in the car Sandy asked, "How come you rushed us out of there?"

"You can never tell how my old man might act. We were ahead of he game so I thought we should get out when we could."

"What do you think he might have said?"

"Probably nothing, but there's been nothing I've ever done that he's approved of and I can't imagine having a kid opens up a new category. You ought to know by now there are some things my old man and I haven't worked out yet. Remember the car I told you I stole and had to pay for."

"Yeah, the guy's name was Bostrup, wasn't it?"

"Yeah, we never talked about how he handled it with me, not before I went to Nam and not since I'm back. Another thing, he's never even asked me what it was like in Nam, not a Goddamn word. I go a world away, risking my life for the values of him and his buddies, and he acts as if I went off to summer camp. I've seen more life than him and he still looks at me like a kid."

"You got a lot on your mind about him don't you? All I can tell you is that he seemed happy to me when you told them. Do you think we shouldn't consider them taking care of the baby when I go back to work?"

"Let's wait and see how they really are with it before we make a decision. They've had four kids and it seems to me they're ready for retirement, not raising more kids. And to tell you the truth, I can imagine my old man laying some kind of a trip on our kid."

"He might be different with his grandchild. We're going to need someone we can trust. And your mom would do most of the child care."

"What about your folks?"

"They've got a restaurant to run; they've got no time." Sandy looked out the car window.

Chapter 44

Beginning the End

Before I turned from DuBois Rd. on to Jansen, I reached for Sandy's hand. "It went pretty well with my folks. What do you say about going over and telling yours? Let's just get it over with."

"I'm not sure I'm ready. I don't know how they're going to take it."

"What do you mean? It's good news! What can they say?"

"Maybe it's just me, but I've never talked about having a baby with my mother."

"I got to make a turn; do we go or not?"

"We have to do it sometime. They're going to see my belly anyway so let's go."

"Listen, we've been married five years. We both have jobs. We've been going together since high school. I'm 27, you're 25. We're old enough to have a kid. How could they have a problem with that?"

I took her hand as we pulled into their driveway. The headlights lit up the restaurant sign: Spats' Fireside Inn.

Sandy's parents lived behind and above the restaurant. Once a week we'd eat dinner with them and Spats would dominate all opinions and dictate the movement of each family member. He'd orchestrated several disastrous vacations for us. I'd come to understand why Sandy welcomed the distance from him that our marriage offered.

We made our way to the kitchen door and knocked. Sandy's mom, Marie, let us in. She hugged Sandy and made a smacking sound several inches from my cheek.

The dark wood paneling of the living room made the room seem small. The smell of tomato sauce permeated even the living room. The restaurant kitchen was just down the hall. Open or closed, Marie always had something on the stove.

Spats sat in an alcove off the living room working on menus. They were stacked on his desk. Looking up, he nodded a hello to me, and Sandy went to kiss him on the cheek. Marie asked us if we wanted fresh cannoli's. I said yes and she disappeared down the hall.

"Changing the prices or adding new dishes?" I asked, sitting down with my back half facing him.

He put down his pen. "Damn customers are so sloppy. I have no menus left that are presentable."

Spats' salt and pepper hair was perfectly coifed, his black shirt was buttoned at the top and his gray slacks had knife-creases. Marie ironed his underwear. I wondered how sloppy the menus really were.

Marie returned and handed me a plate with two cannolis, then went to sit next to Sandy. Spats watched me eat, so I quickly reached for the napkin Marie had folded on the plate. Sandy and her mother were chatting away. I looked towards Sandy and saw her take a deep breath and reach for her mom's hand.

"Mom, Dad, we've got good news."

Spats looked up. Marie was at the edge of her chair.

"We're going to have a baby."

Marie's breath was audible. Spats pushed the menus to the floor.

"What?" he said.

Sandy's face looked horrified. "I'm pregnant."

Spats began mumbling, and Marie's face froze in a painful smile.

"We just told Larry's parents, and they wished us good luck."

"You're not ready to have a baby," Spats snapped.

"Yes, I am."

"You've got no idea of the dangers involved."

"I've graduated college. I'm a teacher. I want to be a mother. We've been planning this for a long time."

"Stupido! Stupido! Stupido!" he squawked, dropping his head into his hands.

Marie began crying.

"Spats, we've been together eight years, married for five. We're old enough to have a kid," I said, standing up.

"What the Hell do you know? You think because you're running a dump now that qualifies you to know how to run a family?"

"What did you say?"

"You work at the dump. What the Hell do you know about being a father?"

I turned towards him. "Don't ask me what kind of father I'm going to be. What kind of father are you right now? Your daughter announces she's going to have child and you act like an asshole!"

"Shut up!"

"You shut me up, asshole."

"Spats please stop. Let's sit down and discuss this," Marie squeaked.

"There'll be no more discussion," I said through clenched teeth. "I'm going home." I looked at Sandy. "Are you coming with me?"

When I saw Sandy hesitate I barreled down the hallway to the kitchen door. Reaching for the doorknob my hands were shaking so much I couldn't open it. Fidgeting with the lock and growing more and more enraged at not being able to get out, I bellowed, "Let me the fuck out of this house. Now!"

Spats came down the hallway. With his head down he undid the lock. The door sprang open from my pushing, and he flinched. I ran into the dark.

After starting the car I revved the engine, my eyes riveted to the kitchen door hoping for Sandy to come out. She didn't, and the tires threw gravel as I pressed the accelerator to the floor.

It was midnight when the bedroom door opened.

"You awake?" Her head peaked around the door jam.

"How'd you get home?"

"My father drove me."

"So you decided to stay when I asked you to come with me?"

"I didn't know what to do. I was so upset." She was crying.

"I can't believe you stayed there after the shit he gave you. Your father's an asshole."

"Yes, he is. But he's my father."

"He only gives a shit about himself."

"Yes, he does. But he's my father."

"I don't care if he is your father. I'm finished going there."

Chapter 45

My Dad's Second Chance

It was Sandy's eighth month when I made a truce with Spats. There were no apologies; we simply agreed to tolerate each other for the sake of our wives.

Sandy delivered our son Jamie on May 3, 1976, exactly nine months from the day of conception. We'd wanted Jamie's birth to be perfect and hitting the due date made us feel like we were off to a good start.

With accumulated sick time and maternity leave Sandy was able to spend the first six months home with Jamie. None of the people we'd considered to take care of Jamie seemed to be right; I swallowed my pride and asked my mother if she'd do it. She agreed and Sandy went back to teaching.

While Sandy had been home with Jamie, my Dad had heart bypass surgery and was forced to retire from Central Hudson. To my surprise Dad and Jamie really hit it off. By the time Jamie had turned two, they were riding around together on Dad's riding lawnmower. Dad had fastened a car seat to the hood of the tractor and would strap Jamie into to it.

I, myself, was struggling to connect with my son. Somehow I could never even calm Jamie down. For the first few years Sandy could pick him up and plug him in to her breast and he'd settle right down. I'd pick him up, rock him, shake him, rub his back and he'd just go on wailing.

Now, there was my father giving him what I couldn't. It made me feel crazy. I think his open-heart surgery actually opened his heart. His fear of dying opened his eyes. When I dropped Jamie off at Dad's house in the morning, he'd run into his grandfather's arms.

Chapter 46

Bad Man

It was clear that taking care of a rambunctious two-year-old was more than my Mom and Dad could handle.

Sandy's best friend, Cindy's, son Jack was a year older than Jamie and was going to daycare with a woman named Margaret in neighboring Gardiner. Margaret was a soft-spoken woman with sadness in her dark eyes. Her three kids were in high school. Her husband had left her for another woman. Daycare was how she was making ends meet. When we went to visit Margaret, toys were scattered around a large backyard; it looked like a playground for kindergarten kids. There were three kids there when we visited, and they were having a good time going up and down a silver slide that dropped into a sandbox. After our talk with Margaret, as we were leaving, Jack wrapped his arms around Margaret's leg. She rubbed his blond head lovingly.

When Sandy and I got back into the car we looked at each other, and I said, "Margaret's the woman to take care of our Jamie."

Sandy nodded.

In September Sandy went back to teaching. That same month we sold our small house in the village and bought a larger one five miles away on Forest Glen Rd. in Gardiner. The new house had two rentable apartments and six acres of land. The apartments would help defray the cost of the mortgage and gave us a large back yard. Jamie was old enough that he wanted to be outside, so I started taking him with me when I worked on the yard.

The house was only ten feet from the road. The road dead-ended at the Wallkill River, but enough traffic passed that I decided to build a fence in the front, both to block the road from view and to keep Jamie safe.

I was working on the fence one afternoon, cutting rough slab wood on a table saw. Jamie was playing in the back yard. Every couple of minutes I'd come out with a new piece of fence to nail up and check on Jamie. He was at the edge of the lawn trying to pick up a rock, but couldn't find a handhold. I went back to finish nailing up the slab. Then I heard Jamie's earsplitting yell. "Daddy, Daddy."

I ran into the back yard. Jamie's face was contorted in a scream. As I ran towards him I kept trying to figure out what was the matter. I didn't see blood. He was jumping up and down, crazily slapping his hands against his pants. When I reached him I lifted him into my arms and felt a sharp sting on my forearm. I instantly knew what was happening. I shifted him to my other arm and looked down to see a yellow jacket drive its stinger into me for the second time. Jamie had stepped into an angry nest of bees, and they'd swarmed up his pant leg. He writhed in my arms.

The bees were diving at us, so I ran across the lawn undoing the suspender straps of his overalls and pulling them off. I slapped at his bare legs to kill the stinging bees. A swarm followed, plunging at our heads. Bees were stinging our faces. I took the stairs two at a time, pushed through the door and stepped into the kitchen. Sandy had heard the commotion, and I saw the fear on her face.

"He's been stung."

Welts were coming up on his legs and face. He franticly wiggled and screamed until he was out of breath. It took an hour to calm him down. A call to the doctor kept us vigilant for a bee sting reaction. None came.

The next day while I was feeding Jamie breakfast, Sandy leaned over to kiss him and asked, "What did that bad man do to you yesterday?"

I flinched at her words. Was she joking or was I a bad man because I wasn't watching Jamie the way I should have been? I turned away; I didn't want her to see she'd hurt me. I'd always feared I'd end up being like my father. Sandy was a teacher. She knew about kids; she taught them all day. I was an ex-Marine, a "Bad Man."

Jamie seemed to be having some difficulty at daycare. He came home cranky and upset. I asked Sandy if she knew anything about what was going on. She said Margaret mentioned that Jack sometimes got angry and Jamie got some of it.

"She says that's normal for boys, that her boys get into fights on the playground all the time."

"Don't you think you should talk to Cindy?"

"I will, but you know Jack's dad is pretty tough on him sometimes. He uses words like stupid and idiot when he talks about him."

"He calls a three-year-old stupid? What's the matter with him?"

"He's angry. Maybe it's that hunting accident where he blew part of his foot off."

"The hitting has got to stop."

"Boys will be boys. Anyway, I don't think we'd ever find someone as good as Margaret."

Chapter 47

Backing Out Before It Got Started

Sandy and I had read about giving birth: <u>Birth Without Violence</u> by Frederick Le Boyer. We'd wanted to bring Jamie into the world gently, starting with a warm water bath. We didn't want drops of silver nitrate put in his eyes. We didn't want him to suffer the pain of circumcision. We wanted him to come into life like a feather floating on a soft summer breeze. I still carried sore memories from my own childhood and wanted to make sure I did not repeat what had happened to me.

The only Le Boyer wish we got was that he wasn't circumcised. The county health commissioner would not allow such a bizarre, New Age request as not putting silver nitrate in a child's eyes in one of his hospitals. I was used to complying in the Marine Corps, so we bowed to authority once again. I gritted my teeth, but not even Sandy knew how I really felt.

Jamie was a colicky baby, crying and kicking in his new bed long into the night. I tried to help by getting up and rubbing his back, but it never seemed to work. After a few minutes, Sandy would come into the room in her housecoat offer him her breast, and then tell me to go back to bed.

For a while she expressed milk, which I tried to feed him from a bottle, but he knew the difference and turned his head away, so I stopped trying. As he grew older and started to crawl, he and I would sit on the couch where I read to him. These times were good, but I couldn't sit still long without feeling a restless urge to get to fixing the house or work on one of my many projects. I needed to be always doing something. Sandy made more money than I did. I couldn't get used to that, so I worked on the house, did side jobs after work, and cut cords of firewood for our wood stove. I was doing what I thought a husband and father was supposed to.

Sometimes before I fell asleep at night I could feel the connection with my son fraying. Sandy just had to plug him in to her breast and they'd set in a reverie while I fidgeted in my chair trying to think of the next chore to be done.

One day shortly after Sandy had gone back to teaching she asked me if I'd pick Jamie up at the sitter because she had to attend an important meeting after school. I said sure. She told me exactly what to feed him when I got him home.

That evening when I picked Jamie up we had a nice car ride home. I carried him into the house. When he didn't see his mom, he squirmed in my arms and started howling. I rocked him but that didn't work, so I got his baby food from the fridge. I sat him in his highchair, spooning applesauce up to his open mouth. He spit it out and continued to blubber. I lifted him from the highchair and sat him in his windup swing, cranking it up. This was always a surefire way to calm him. He paused while his little lungs filled. Then so did the house--with his wailing.

The room seemed to shrink. I felt helpless to help him. "Stop it," I yelled and then bolted out the back door leaving him in the swing. I ran into the garage and pounded my fists on the workbench.

When I came back into the house his crying had softened to a whimper, but when he saw me the screams started again. "Ma Ma," he hollered between sobs. I picked him up and ran out the front door to the car. I belted him into his car seat and took off, explaining to him that we were going to look for Mommy. As I circled around New Paltz, he gradually stopped crying. Every 15 minutes I passed by our house on Grove St., looking for Sandy's car in the driveway.

When I finally saw her car there, I pulled in behind it. She was at the door, looking scared.

"What happened?" she said, her forehead wrinkling.

"I can't do this again. The only way I could get him to stop crying was to ride around looking for you."

"I'm sorry; I had to go the meeting. He looks upset."

She took Jamie out of my arms.

"Did the Bad Man upset you, sweetheart?"

205

By the time Jamie turned three, I had surrendered most of my responsibility for raising him to Sandy. Her confidence in taking care of him gave me permission to step back. Whenever I got angry around Jamie, I felt the stored up rage from my childhood and the War trying to push its way out. I didn't want to dump this on my kid. I felt shame when I handed my crying son to his mother; I'd seen other fathers comfort their kids and knew I should be able to.

To everyone watching us--our parents and friends--we looked like a perfect couple: we had a beautiful tow-headed three year old, owned our own home and were both working good jobs. What they didn't see was the churning inside me. My anger was coming from so many different places that to contain it was becoming impossible. I was angry at my father and how he raised me. I was pissed off at those in power who had sent me to into a senseless war, risking my life and bending my spirit. I was enraged at myself for being unable to father my own son. I'd be provoked by something as simple as Sandy coming home late from work. I wanted to yell, and some times I did, like one of my DI's in boot camp. Usually, I choked it down, causing it to build up inside. My therapist told me I had a deep sadness under my rage, but I couldn't reach it.

I didn't plan to have an affair with my good friend Bob's girlfriend. At a party at our house everyone went out to get food and left Judy and me behind. I'd been drinking heavily and found myself lying naked with Judy on our living room floor. This sexual connection with Judy set into motion the disintegration of both my marriage and a good friendship with Bob. I had no explanation to offer either Sandy or Bob.

My betrayal tore open the door for me to leave Sandy. I believed that if I didn't get away from my son I would become another Winters father to him. So when I told Sandy I was leaving, I had this strange feeling I was protecting my son--from me.

The rush of being with Judy--a forbidden woman--took over my life. Being with her was all I allowed myself to think of. Our relationship furthered my isolation from everyone.

Jamie grew older, and I left Judy for what turned out to be a series of new relationships, always convincing myself that sex was love. In each one I looked for a person who might help me make a family so I could bring the son I so dearly missed back into my life. Every time I'd leave the arms of a lover I'd be forced to look at myself and quickly realize I didn't like me.

In time I began to see that I was the angry man standing outside the circle of my family and friends. What I brought into every relationship was the Vietnam frequency of bedlam, chaos, and long work hours. Pandemonium came with the morning coffee. After years of failed relationships and a profound loneliness for my son, I recognized that if I didn't figure out how to un-make the Marine I'd become, I would loose it all.

Chapter 48

A Good Man

Jamie was about six. He was sitting in my Datsun pickup truck with his baseball cap pulled down over his eyes. I'd just picked him up from his mother's house, and we were going to spend our every-other-weekend together. He'd just started telling me about a man his mother had started dating.

"Bob's his name; he's from New Hampshire."

"How come you haven't told me about him before?"

Jamie looked down at his hands.

"Do you like him?"

"Yeah, he took us out hiking in the mountains. He carried me on his shoulder, just like you do."

I looked out the side window so Jamie couldn't see my face. I knew I had no right feeling hurt. This news of Sandy's boyfriend seemed to have activated a landmine in me. Within a month of finding out she had a new man, I'd bolted from New Paltz. I was imploding, and I didn't want Jamie or anyone else to see it.

I decided to move to Monhegan Island to get away from Sandy and her Good Man. On the island I'd be starting another career—the third since I'd gotten back from Nam. The year before, I'd quit my job as New Paltz Water Superintendent and gone into carpentry. Now I worked alone as a carpenter, carrying my own financial weight for the first time since I got out of the Marines.

Before I left for Maine I signed our divorce papers. As I prepared for the escape, I was fully aware that I was abandoning Sandy and Jamie again. What I could not sort out was why I had such feelings of rejection. While married, I never was sure if I was living in Sandy's dream or my own. For ten years we'd coasted on the strength of our childhood romance. Sandy's letters during the War were such powerful reminders to me of her love. Perhaps I married her out of a sense of duty. Our marriage had been a healing place for me in the beginning. Sandy had made a safe nest for me, even letting my friends move into it. Her kindness and taking care of everything confused me, and I wasn't sure what my responsibility as a father and husband were.

Chapter 49

Throw Me the Anchor

Before I left New Paltz, Jamie had been coming to me every other weekend. I felt obligated to have something interesting for him to do. If we weren't going somewhere or doing some activity he'd pout around the apartment. It always took several hours of fussing and complaining for him to adjust to the transition from Sandy's house to mine, which I translated into him not wanting to see me. He didn't like the kind of food I cooked. He often refused to eat anything but peanut butter and jelly. He seemed reluctant to tell me he didn't want to come. He already understood it would hurt me, so he complained instead.

Both my parents liked Sandy. She continued to take Jamie to see them. Sandy's keeping in contact with my folks was good for Jamie, but it all reinforced my image as the "Bad Man." I knew they were unhappy about the affair I'd been having and the subsequent divorce, but we never talked about it. Now, 400 miles away on Monhegan Island I hoped I'd be insulated from all of them.

After a few months of working as a carpenter on Monhegan, I secured a job with Sherman Stanley, the most prolific of the six lobstermen on the island. As a supplement to the $50-a-day he was paying me, he provided a small cottage for me to live in. The island rumor was that Sherm was not an easy person to work for. He pulled well over 600 traps and expected his man to work from 5 a.m. to 5 p.m. I figured that I'd worked for Don Winters and for the USMC; what could this guy do that I hadn't already seen?

January 1, 1982, was the opening day of the 6-month lobster season on Monhegan. This was the only place in the US that had a lobster season; everywhere else you could fish them anytime. All night long a loose piece of roof flashing had been slapping back and forth in a gale wind. I peeked at the alarm clock; its red numbers punched 1:17 into my dilated pupils. Sherm's last statement to me was, "See ya at 5 on the beach." But I was sure he wouldn't go out in winds like these.

Yesterday, Lexi, one of the youngest fishermen, said, "If it's too rough we ought to agree to put off trap day until it's calmer." Of the six fishermen in the fish house three nodded their head, but Sherm and his son, Shermy, had kept still. Pulling the covers up over my shoulders I vowed that I'd get out on the roof on my first day off and fix that flashing.

The alarm made its 4:30 belch and I rolled out of bed. I felt for the steep ladder stairs and climbed down from the loft into the one-room kitchen/living room. Lighting the oil lamp, I dipped a pitcher into the five-gallon bucket and filled the coffee pot. As I waited for the water to heat I thought to myself that I'd never worked on a boat. I wasn't afraid of the work but I wondered if could I handle the seasickness. Being a stern man on a fishing boat couldn't be any harder than picking truckloads of rocks all day, but could I pick lobster traps with my stomach in my mouth?

I grabbed a carton of milk out of the gas refrigerator, sniffed it and poured it over a bowl of Life cereal. I could make coffee, reach the refrigerator, do the dishes and eat--all within two steps. I'd fitted the cottage out like a ship—everything within hand's reach. Sitting at the table, I opened the refrigerator, pulled out some bread, baloney and mustard and made myself lunch while spooning in cereal. I didn't realize I had to bring lunch until Sherm mentioned it to me the night before on the radio. I thought we'd come in for lunch.

The red light of the CB flashed, then squawked, "You up, Larry?"

Clearing my throat, I picked up the mike. "Right here, Sherm. We going out in this wind?"

"It's the finest kind of day. See you on the beach in a few minutes. Over and out."

"I'll be there. Over and out."

There were no phones on the Island; everyone from lobstermen to housewives communicated by CB radio. I spooned and envisioned what I was supposed to wear. A week earlier Sherm had given me a list of gear I needed.

"Hoffman's in Camden is a good place to buy Helly Hansen Oilskins," he said. I had only 200 bucks to my name, but I spent over a $100 on the yellow oilskins and knee-high black boots two sizes too large so they could accommodate heavy wool socks and down booties. I splurged for a ten dollar Sou' Easter hat, which made me look like a real Maine lobsterman.

I was pulling my second boot on when the CB rattled again. "Hey, Shermy. You there?"

"Right here, Lexi."

"The weather radio says there's an eight-foot sea running. I can see a strong Sou' East wind blowing right into the harbor. I'm going to give it a few hours to see if it dies down."

"Me too. Call me in an hour," Shermy replied.

My cottage was at the edge of a meadow. Friends affectionately called it "the Ghetto on the Meadow." It was tucked into the side of a hill 400 yards from the sea. On a clear day I could see the winter-gray ocean through the evergreens. I stepped onto the trail cut into the side of the hill and made my way to town. I put my lunch, a change of socks and two pairs of extra gloves in the five-gallon wallboard compound bucket I used to haul water from the town well. When I reached town, which was essentially the one store on the island, it was only another hundred yards to Sherm's fish house that sat right on the beach.

A light dusting of snow crunched under my feet. I'd use the bucket to bring water home when we came in tonight; that would save me a trip. The wind cut into my face. Reaching my fingers between the rubber collar of the oilskin jacket and my bare neck, I dug down in search of the wool jacket collar and pulled it up.

I stepped around the fish house. The sea in the dim morning light had white fog rising from it; its rhythmic pounding grew louder as I moved toward the door. Reaching up in an automatic gesture to stroke my beard, the rubber glove froze onto the hairs of my face.

Light spilled out of a crack in the fish house door. I trudged up the three steps, feeling exhausted from the friction of the oilskin's rubbing. The fish house was lit by an old oil lamp sputtering in the corner. Sherm stood with a pitchfork raised above a wooden barrel; with feet set, he drove the fork down into the fish inside.

"Morning," I said, looking around for a place to put my bucket.

"Morning. Get yourself one of them forks in the corner. We got to fill five of these short wooden tubs with herring."

I drove the pitchfork down into the barrel of fish, the tines spearing their soft bodies. Scales and blood splattered onto my new oilskins. I could taste the salt on my lips that flew up from the brine in the barrel.

"Grab the rope handle."

I took hold of my end of the full tub with both hands and following Sherm's lead, sidestepped awkwardly down the beach to the edge of the surf.

"Now we've got to go get the punt."

I didn't know what a punt was. I followed him, hoping I'd figure it out. Next to the fish house lay a small wooden dinghy. I grabbed its rail and we carried it down to the tubs.

The morning light was just beginning to eat at the shadows; white waves were cresting onto the beach. Sherm's boat, the *Phalarope*, tugged at its mooring in the harbor.

I looked at the ten-foot punt and then at the five, 40-pound tubs of bait fish and my five gallon bucket and wondered how it would all fit in. Then I glanced at the breakers on the beach and thought to myself, there's no way.

Sherm nodded at the tubs of fish. Lifting one of the tubs I sat it on the floor in the center of the punt. Sherm jumped into the boat yanked it to the side and barked, "Hand me that one." I gritted my teeth and thrust it at him. He grabbed it, swinging it like it was an empty laundry basket. I handed him the fifth tub waiting to see where he'd place it. There were two on the floor of the stern, one in the middle, one on the back seat and he placed the fifth on the front seat. Where the Hell are we were going to sit, I thought.

Without saying anything Sherm grabbed one side of the punt and began to drag it into the surf. The bow of the punt pivoted, hitting me in the back of the knees. Regaining my balance I took hold of my side and together we strained to drag the punt into the surf. Sherm motioned with his hand to stop when the bow was afloat.

I watched him as he stood poised, both hands on the gunnels, knees bent, looking out into the dim light in the harbor. I didn't know what I was doing so I took his pose and waited for him to make a move. I felt the punt shift and saw Sherm lunge his weight forward. I did the same. The bow of the punt entered the trough of a four-foot cresting wave. I felt the numbing edge of cold water that had climbed above my knees and down into my boots. Sherm was in the punt grimacing, "Get in Goddamn it before we capsize." I gripped the side of the punt with one hand, a tub of fish with the other and muscled myself aboard. Sherm sat on top of the tub of fish in the center, manning the oars. I seated myself on the tub of fish on the stern seat. The slimy fish moved under my butt. I reached into the air for something to grab but was sitting too high to reach the gunnels. The punt pitched and Sherm pulled on the oars. I looked into writhing sea and felt it would be only a matter of moments and I'd be trying to swim the 50 feet back to shore.

Sherm's face wrinkled, his blue eyes glinting in concentration. The punt pulled forward with the power in Sherm's arms. The heavily laden boat plowed towards the Phalarope and I tottered on the tub of fish like frightened child.

Once beyond the breaking surf we entered a rolling sea. Sherm plied the oars and we rocked our way slowly forward. I looked out beyond the protected harbor at waves that reminded me of the monsoon in Nam.

The creak of the oars in the locks, the wash of sea on the beach allowed me to drift away for a moment. I couldn't do anything until we reached the Phalarope anyway. I thought of Alex who'd introduced me to Sherm. It was as much his romantic notion of working with Sherm as it was mine. The sea bobbed us and I wondered if I'd ever make a decision that wasn't impulsive or guided by what someone else thought I should do.

"Wake up, get hold of that Goddamn rail or we're going to pound the shit out of the boat."

I took hold of the Phalarope's wire rail with my rubber-gloved hand. It immediately slid off; ice was covering the wire. Sherm reached into his bucket and handed me a hammer.

"Crack the ice off so you can get a hold."

The entire boat was coated with two inches of ice. After cracking the ice so I could get out of the punt, Sherm handed me the tubs of fish. "Take your hammer and start cracking off all the ice you can reach. I've seen a lobster boat sink right here in the harbor just from the weight of ice. Water vapor condenses on the cold surface of the boat; it can build two inches in 24 hours."

Out on the bow I started sliding back and forth, "You slide off the boat, you'll go right on down with all that clothing you got on; that water's thirty-three degrees. Chip the ice on the wire rails first so you got something to hold on to."

"Christ." I muttered under my breath. On the wharf 300 yards away were 200 wire lobster traps we'd stacked there yesterday. Not one other boat was out.

With the ice knocked off the rails and deck the Phalarope sat higher in the water. Sherm motored to the wharf and I jumped off and tied us up. I then started handing the traps to Sherm who stacked them in the stern of the boat. I counted them out loud Sherm said that we'd be able to take 60 in one load. When we reached 40 Sherm had to stand on the edges of the lower traps to be able to stack the remaining traps. I hopped into the boat and tossed a rope over the pile to secure it. Sherm hit the throttle and we headed out of the harbor with the stacked traps towering several feet above the cabin.

The Phalarope nosed past the lea of Manana, the small island protecting Monhegan's harbor, a raw blast of wind caught the boat and I could feel the shudder in my legs. I began right there to understand what the fishermen meant when they said, "We entered the teeth of the gale." In the wave troughs we could not see land. I pressed my knees hard against the gunnels to keep my balance like Sherm had showed me. We fought the wind for 15 minutes before Sherm turned the wheel, bringing the stern into the wind.

"Bring me that set of traps." Sherm pointed to the top of the stack. I stumbled across the lurching deck covered with piles of warp. Warp is the rope tied to the lobster buoy and the trap; it could range between 25 fathoms to 75 fathoms in length depending on the depth of the water it was to be set in. The coiled warp was stacked four feet high on the deck. There was nowhere to stand but on top of it. Because of the boat pitching and the ice that had formed on the tie down rope it took several minutes to get it untied. In the end I had to take off my rubber gloves to get the knot out. Pulling the two traps free, I lugged one in each hand back to Sherm, who motioned for me to sit them on the gunnels. Stepping back I got my foot tangled in the warp and fell on my back on the pile of rope. Reaching a hand to me Sherm said, "You'd better get your sea legs fast or its going to be a long day."

"Right," I said, trying to decide who I hated more, Sherm or the ocean; it felt like they were both thumping the shit out me.

"Watch your feet in the warp," he said, pointing to what looked like thousands of loops. If you get your foot caught in one of them, the weight of the sinking double traps and the power of the boat motoring away will pull you in."

Looking down at the warp he was standing on I asked, "What should I do if you get pulled in?"

Sherm looked squarely at me. "Throw me the anchor."

"What do you mean, throw you the anchor?"

"Yeah, that's just what I said, throw me the anchor. It'll only take a few seconds to get hypothermia and I might as well get it over quickly." Laughing he turned his back.

I looked all day for another boat, but no one was on the sea but us. As the sun started sinking we set the last of the 200 traps. As we tied off to the mooring my stomach felt like it had migrated up into my chest. I'm not sure why I didn't puke but I didn't. Maybe it was because I couldn't handle the shame it would bring from Sherm, or maybe it was that I'd burned every ounce of energy in my body and the effort would have killed me. While hauling the punt up the beach Sherm asked, "You want to come up to the fish house for a drink?" I nodded yes and followed him up the fish house stairs.

A warm blast of air hit me like a pillow hammer. I grunted hello to the six men gathered around the workbench. Each man was holding a give-away glass from McDonalds: Porky Pig, Roadrunner, Bugs Bunny. Shermy, popped a Coke and, together with Bacardi 151, poured a Yosemite Sam's glass full and handed it to his dad. Looking at me he asked, "Want one?"

"Sure," I said, moving a coil of rope off a stool so I could sit. My head was already floating above my neck like a balloon on a string. Warmth reeling off the woodstove; I lifted my feet off the floor to the rungs of the stool and realized this was the first time I'd sat down all day.

One at a time the fishermen asked Sherm questions about our day. No one commented on the fact that we'd been the only ones to set traps. Lexi asked, "How many did you get out?"

""We got a few out."

I knew that the man who sets his traps first got the choice fishing; the rule was that you did not crowd another fishermen's fishing grounds. The few traps Sherm was talking about were set in the choicest sites. Why else risk your life, I thought to myself.

I saw hairy knuckles wrapped around a full Daffy Duck glass in front of me. "Thanks," I said taking the glass and bringing it to my lips. I swallowed a long deep draft. The bitter rum and the sweet coke cut the mucous in my throat. I felt the cold glass stealing the heat from my hand and I sat it on the bench.

I wondered if being Sherm's stern man had anything to do with the sideways glances I was getting. Were they wondering about my lack of brains in choosing to work for him? Lexi's girlfriend told me in years past that Sherm had eaten stern men at a rate of one a month. Today I knew why.

After finishing my drink I grabbed my lunch bucket and said good night. Stepping back out in the cold I made my way to the town well. I had to drop the heavy steel bucket three times to break the ice. Taking hold of the rope I groaned, "Another damn rope." My bucket full I lumbered up the narrow path, faint moonlight reflecting off the snow. The weight of the water bucket pulled me off balance and it was hard to walk. I decided tomorrow I'd take two buckets, filling each one only half full. The pain in my arm made me wonder if I could make a yoke that would go over my shoulders like the ones I'd seen the Vietnamese carry water with.

When I got in the house it took a long time to find the energy to get out of my clothes. Down to my long johns I reached into the refrigerator and took some ham out of a cellophane wrapper and shoved it in my mouth. That was dinner.

Two weeks passed and we'd been out everyday except Sunday. I bathed in the hot water I'd poured into my lunch bucket. There were purple bruises above my kneecaps, from pounding against the gunnels. My forearms and wrists ached from grabbing and pulling rope. The muscles of my hands ached from squeezing the handles of the pliers used to open the heavy yellow rubber bands used to band the lobster claws.

Monday morning came quickly. It had been good to have a day that I was not pitching and pounding on the sea. I'd been able to write a letter to Jamie and to my folks. Just a few minutes of sitting still brought up the feelings of distance that I had created. The routine of getting up early and making my way to the fish house was more manageable now than at first.

The sun came up as we pulled out of the harbor. We started pulling traps just on the backside of Manana. Sherm hooked the lobster buoy with a gaff, grabbed the warp in his hand, placed it into a hydraulic winch and pulled the trap out of the deep to the side of the boat. While doing this he maneuvered the boat so the bow would break into the oncoming sea. I was at the table working with the crabs and lobsters we'd just emptied from the last two traps. I was sorting lobsters by measuring them with a brass tool that I'd hook over their shells. The small ones I'd throw back, the keepers I'd band to keep them from chomping me, or more importantly each other. The crabs I'd break the claws off and then spear onto the bait line. A few days ago I'd been pinched because there were so many lobsters on the collection table I couldn't get them all banded before Sherm had another trap to empty. Sherm saw me break the claw off the lobster that had hold of my thumb, "A one-claw lobster's worth half the price."

I thought to myself, "What the fuck's he worried about? He's selling lobster for five dollars a pound and last week we pulled in over two tons in one day."

I was pulling the bags of rotten bait off the bait line and threading a new bait bag on with the hook as I watched flocks of seagulls descending to the gunnels to gulp the festering filth. It was as if they'd found a fine delicacy; they couldn't get enough of the rotten fish covered with sea lice.

Looking over the side of the boat I watched for the rising traps, the green warp spinning off the hydraulic winch into a pile at Sherm's feet; the double traps becoming more and more visible until they'd break the surface of the olive sea. Sherm hoisted them onto the side of the boat; I undid the door and reached into the withering life inside. The trap was filled with the greens and blacks of lobster, the multi oranges of rock crab and the shiny brown of small cod flapping around. I pulled the crabs out first. Most of the time there were more crabs then lobsters in a trap, sometimes as many as 20 of them. I'd grab both crab claws in my rubber gloved hand, twist them off and toss them into the five-gallon bucket at my feet. It was one o'clock and the bucket was three-quarters full.

Sherm positioned the boat to set the next pair of traps. I was banding and saw him out the corner of my eye when he pushed the traps overboard.

"Larry!"

I turned to see Sherm loose his grip on the wheel. There was a wrap of rope around his ankle and he was being pulled towards the stern of the boat. I grabbed the warp and with all my strength I pulled back. With a moment of slack I made two quick turns around the stern bit. Bolting to the wheel I pulled back the throttle. Sherm bent over and released the loop from his ankle.

"Thanks," he muttered as he walked by me to the wheel.

As we carried the punt to the fish house Sherm asked, "You think you'd like to come up to the house for a drink."

"Yeah, that would be nice."

Barbara brought out crackers and cheese, and Sherm made the rum and Cokes. I had two drinks before I stood up to leave. Barbara was working in the kitchen and I thought for a moment they'd invite me to eat. I stuck my head into the kitchen, thanked Barbara for the crackers and headed toward the door.

Sherm followed me outside. When I reached the end of the shoveled path he said, "Thanks for today."

I raised my arm over my head and kept walking.

Chapter 50

Change in the Compass Setting

My days were so full of hard physical work that nights in the cabin existed only for eating and sleeping. I'd listen to a few minutes of public radio and fall asleep. One evening I got a call on the CB from the postmaster telling me I had mail at the post office and should come pick it up. It was a card from Jamie; I recognized Sandy's handwriting in the address before I opened it. Jamie had drawn a house with three stick figure people. The two large stick figures were holding hands. The third figure stood a short distance away. A black crayon curl of smoke was coming out of the chimney. The drawing jolted me back into my former life. There was something about that curl of smoke that hurt. I remembered the cords of wood I'd cut and split to keep us warm. Cutting wood, remodeling the house—that was what I'd thought a father was supposed to do. The card was signed in his wobbly handwriting: I love you Daddy. Below, Sandy had written: I'll be seven in a month.

It was April and I could almost see the end of my commitment to Sherm, which was June 1. Jamie's letter made me realize I needed him back in my life. I wrote Sandy to see how she'd feel about him coming up to stay with me at the end of June when she finished school.

In a few weeks I got her reply, and to my surprise she agreed. She'd written that he asked every day where I was. She even offered to drive him up to Port Clyde. All I had to do was come over on the ferry and pick him up. She said she'd come get him at the end of the two weeks. She and new husband Bob were planning a vacation in Canada and had it all worked out.

Jamie's coming gave me something to look forward to. Day after day Sherm and I worked, sometimes in gray storms, others in brilliant sunlight. The routine had grown so rote that weeks passed with no words of substance spoken. Ever since I saved him from being pulled out of the boat, I knew he respected me. Shoulder to shoulder, 12 hours a day, we became a fishing machine.

Spring was lengthening the days, so Sherm squeezed me for the extra hour. My sea legs had long ago come, but my stomach had never migrated completely back to where it belonged. I'd become so sensitive to breaking off the crab legs that the cracking began to feel like it was happening in my own chest. Sometimes when Sherm wasn't looking I'd toss a crab back into the sea.

I marked days off my calendar like I did in Nam. It was a visual way to see that I was getting closer to seeing Jamie. On June 1, Sherm and I pulled in the last load of traps. We piled them on the wharf, then hauled them up to stack in the side-yard of his house. Lifting the last trap off his truck, I stacked it then stuck out my hand.

"Never had to throw you the anchor, Captain."

Sherm smirked and reached into his pocket. He pulled out a wrapped wad of bills. Peeling off a $50, he handed it to me.

"That's your bonus. You did a good job. At first I didn't think you'd make it."

I took the bill and shook his hand again. "Thanks!"

Neither one of us mentioned next season. For now, I'd already lined up a carpentry job that I planned to finish before Jamie came.

Standing out on the bow of the Laura B., I scanned the waiting crowd at the Port Clyde wharf. I spotted Sandy first, with her long black hair shining in the bright sun. Jamie was holding her hand, and even at a distance I could see he'd grown. I leaped off the boat before the gangplank was tied off and pushed my way through the crowd. When he saw me he yelled, "Daddy." I picked him up in my arms and drew his head into my neck. It felt like years since I'd seen him. I turned my back to Sandy because I could not stop my tears.

The boat was only going to stay at the wharf for 15 minutes so we were forced to quickly settle our plans for picking up Jamie. Sandy handed me a bag and said, "His medicines are in there: asthma medicine, baby aspirin."

"Anything else I need to know?"

"He likes to be read to before you put him to sleep."

222

"I remember. How you been?" I asked.

"Good. Bob and I had a nice wedding. We're going to visit his folks in New Hampshire. Then we're going up to Nova Scotia, and we'll stop on the way back to get Jamie. How are you?"

"I'm a little tired; been working hard all winter. Where's Bob?"

"He's up by the car. He thought it would be better for me to do this alone." She paused, then continued, "Your folks have been calling. They're wondering if I'd heard anything from you. I take Jamie over there almost every week so they can see him."

"Thanks. I only wrote them once since I've been up here." I lowered Jamie back to the wharf. "You ready sailor? Were going out on that big boat."

"I want Mommy to go to."

Sandy reached down and lifted him.

"I told you in the car that Mommy will be back in a little while to take you home. Daddy misses you and he wants to spend time with you. Be a big boy and go with Daddy."

She shifted him off her hip and handed him to me. I took him in my left arm, and bending towards Sandy, I pulled her to me with my right arm. The three of us hugged for a long moment.

"Thanks, San," I whispered.

Jamie and I hiked the island, taking different paths everyday. Sometimes we went to the cliffs on the seaward side of the island where we watched gannets dive into the ocean for fish; other days we walked through Cathedral Forest looking for fairy houses that tourists made from bits of bark and moss. I'd made plans for us to go fishing on Sherm's boat. He took tourists for $25 each. We caught mackerel and some cod that were over half Jamie's size. Sherm was nice enough to only charge me half price.

Jamie and I were becoming recognized as father and son on the island. We gathered hellos from many locals as I walked to the general store with him perched on my shoulders. At night I read to him from one of the books Sandy had packed.

The two weeks were passing quickly. I was starting to daydream about Jamie growing up with me on Monhegan. The bond I'd broken by leaving him was mending. Sandy wrote me from someplace in Nova Scotia, saying she and Bob were going to take the ferry out to Monhegan so I didn't have to take Jamie into Port Clyde.

When the day for Jamie to leave had come, I waited until the last minute before going to the wharf. As Jamie reached the top of the hill, the Laura B. was already nosing into the harbor. Hoisting him on my shoulders, I stood far back in the crowd so that Sandy and Bob would have to work their way to us.

Bob stuck out his hand. "Hey, Larry. I'm Bob."

"Hello, Bob. Nice to meet you," I said, lifting Jamie off my shoulders so he could hug his Mom. Bob had a beard like mine, except it was red. With a frog in my throat I asked if they'd give me a few minutes alone with Jamie. Bob tousled Jamie's hair before they moved off to the other side of the crowd.

"Jamie, I'm gonna come home and see you soon."

"When, Daddy?"

"I think I'm going to move back home."

"You gonna live with me and Mommy and Bob?"

"No, son; I'm going to live with Grandma and Grandpa until I get my own place. You can come and see me there."

"Why don't you come now?"

"I can't; I have things I have to do here." I squeezed him tightly, then pushed through the waiting crowd toward Sandy and Bob. Handing him into Sandy's waiting arms, I took his face in both hands and kissed him, then stepped back quickly.

"Goodbye."

Turning and waving, I headed up the steep hill away from the wharf. When I reached the top, the Laura B. was un-mooring. She cut her usual circle in the harbor and headed out past Manana.

Three weeks later the undercarriage of my Datson pickup scraped the dirt when I pulled out of the old fisherman's lawn parking lot at Port Clyde. It had taken me two trips on the Laura B. to get all my things back to the mainland. As I headed out of Port Clyde I thought of the last turn I'd be making on the eight-hour drive before me; it would be onto DuBois Rd. to the house I'd grown up in.

I'd been out of Mom and Dad's house for more than ten years. When I pulled up the driveway I looked over at the leaning barn, remembering how Pete and I had hidden there waiting for Dad to come home. After getting settled in I asked Dad if I could build an addition to the barn both to hold it up as well as to put all my tools in. He agreed, so while I was looking for carpentry work in town, I built a shed style addition on the barn after straightening it up.

I regularly saw Jamie, bringing him to my parents on weekends. They loved having him in their house again. I soon found work doing small jobs. Life in New Paltz had started again.

Part II

Chapter 1

The Unmaking

A March rain dripped down the bay window of my parents' house. I sat in my father's chair looking out at the birdfeeder; the gray squirrel sat with empty paws. I hadn't put birdseed in the feeder since they'd left for Florida two months before. The phone rang; it was my best friend, Peter.

"Hey, Man, what's up?"

"What are you doing?"

"I'm looking out the window. But sitting in my own shit would be more truthful."

"Have you been working?"

"Yeah, I got a few small jobs lined up. I'm doing alright."

"What's bothering you? Lack of female companionship?"

"No. Well, maybe; it's a drag being alone. I can't wait to see Jamie on the weekend. He's the only one I'm hanging out with."

"My Dad needs some work done on the porch at the Moreno Institute. Lots of people walking around down here. You think you might be interested? "

"What's the Moreno Institute?"

"It's where I've been training to be a psycho-dramatist. My old man lives here with Zerka. She's the queen of psychodrama. You remember what I told you? Psychodrama's group psychotherapy where people act out their problems. Anyway, my Dad runs the business for Zerka. You interested? It might be a few weeks worth of work and you could check out what I'm doing in the theater."

"You acting?"

"Not really. If you come down and look at the job I'll explain it to you."

Yeah. Where's the Institute?"

"Beacon. I'll give you directions."

Peter and I had been friends for several years. We'd met when I owned the taxi company. I was standing in the bus station speaking to a friend about a book I'd read by A. S. Neill about the Summerhill School. We had been talking about 15 minutes when I was interrupted by a young-looking man with white hair.

"Hello, my name's Peter. I couldn't help but overhear what you were talking about. Are you a teacher?" He held out his hand.

"No, I own the taxi company," I said, shaking his hand.

"I've been listening to you, and I want you to teach at the new school I'm opening."

"I don't have a degree."

"That doesn't matter. I'm a professor at Brooklyn College. I'm on my way to the City on that bus that just pulled in. Can I give you my number, and can we speak?"

"Call me, my wife's a teacher." I handed him a card off the taxi counter.

I never did teach at Peter's Unison Learning Center, but I did help him navigate some of the local contractors and politicians while he was building his school.

A few years later, around the same time, both Peter and I divorced our wives. Divorce was painful for both of us, and the pain became part of how we bonded. I stayed in touch with him through phone calls and letters, and once I was back from Monhegan, we spoke often.

I pulled into a driveway almost hidden accept for a small sign that read Moreno Institute in faded black letters. The drive was lined with huge beech trees; their wrinkled bark reminded me of elephant skin. A large white clapboard mansion sat atop a gentle hill. When I got out of my truck, I caught a glimpse of the Hudson River below. I climbed the front stairs to a wraparound porch. I decided to look around a little before I knocked; maybe I could figure what Peter's dad wanted me to do. The porch needed a paint job, and some of the balusters were broken, but otherwise it was in good shape.

Merlyn, Peter's dad, was a wiry white-haired man with thick, black-framed glasses that magnified his sad eyes. He introduced himself and explained that he wanted a bench built. After getting the details I gave him a price. I started working at the Moreno Institute the following Monday. While sawing and assembling the porch bench, I noticed men and women coming and going from an entrance in the basement. They'd go past me early in the morning, come out for lunch and go back in the afternoon.

"What's going on in the basement?" I asked Peter while he helped me carry lumber from my truck.

"That's the theater. You want to see it?"

"I got to finish what I'm doing. I'm running a little behind. Merlyn's asked twice when it's going to be done. Is he always so uptight?"

"Don't worry about him. He's nervous about a large group of students coming next week; he wants the place to look good for them. Listen, if you won't come down now, how about this evening? There's going to be something they call an open session. It costs five bucks to get in, but since you're working here you can come free. It starts at 7. Meet me here at 6:30. What do you think?"

"I don't have to do anything, do I? I've been hearing some strange sounds coming out of that place."

"You don't have to do anything but watch."

"Cool. I'll meet you right here."

The theater was a long narrow room with a round stage at the end. There were only a few windows high up on the walls. Lighting strips with red, blue and green bulbs were in lines on the ceiling. Peter and I sat in metal chairs near the middle. At 7 o'clock there were about 25 people. A one-armed woman came out from behind a curtain and sat on a stool in the center of the round stage. Her empty sleeve was pinned neatly. Her small features looked both old and young. Her thin lips bowed into a smile.

"Good evening. I'm glad you all attended tonight's open session. My name is Zerka Moreno, and I will be the director for this evening. I want to start with what I call a warm-up. The way this works is that I want you to pair up with someone you don't know. After you introduce yourselves I want you to find out each other's ages. The oldest one of you will ask the question, 'Why are you here tonight?' Then you are to listen to the answer without asking any more questions. I will tell you when to stop, and then we will reverse the question."

I found out my partner's name was Tom, and he was 60.

"Why are you here tonight, Larry?"

I started with how I was working on the building because my friend Peter had asked me to come and work for his dad. By the time five minutes was up I'd told Tom I was divorced and a Vietnam vet. I had no idea how it all got opened up.

When it was Tom's turn, he told me that he was a professor at a nearby university and that he'd protested the War. He went on to say that he had doubts in himself that he didn't often share, such as how he felt for not standing up and fighting for his country. He went on to tell me he'd also been divorced for a few years and was afraid of heading into his old age alone. His children had distanced themselves from him since the divorce, and he was here tonight to be with people who might understand. He said he'd been coming once a month for the past few years.

I was blown away at how much we'd gotten to know each other in ten minutes by only asking one question. The voice volume in the room increased dramatically as people got comfortable. Zerka asked for silence, but it was obvious people did not want to stop. Two hours later the psychodrama ended, and Peter and I took a walk.

"What did you think?" Peter asked, pulling his wool watch cap down over his ears.

"I've never seen anything like it. That gal that was the protagonist, what a story! I was crying when I heard her speak about how she had to give the baby up for adoption. I was afraid she was going to call on me to play a role; she was looking right at me. I would have flipped. Do you know Tom, the guy I was talking to in the beginning?"

"Yeah. Nice guy. He comes every month."

"I'm gonna have lunch with him. We really hit it off. I can't get over how much we shared with each other in ten minutes."

"Powerful stuff, isn't it? What do you say you sit in on some of the sessions I lead?"

"You lead? You mean you do what Zerka was doing?"

"Yeah. That's why I'm here. I'm training to be able to make a living at doing what she does. I'm almost a director, just a few more months."

"I got to finish the porch; maybe when I'm done I'll come down."

Chapter 2

A New Story

I'd been hooked by Psychodrama. Now I was lugging in the last of the four hand-hewn beams that I'd saved from a renovation. I was using them to make a loft bed in the tiny bedroom I was given at the Moreno Institute. I'd moved out of my parents' house before they'd gotten home from Florida, to start my Psychodrama training. It felt good to be with people again. I was living with Peter, and eight psychodrama students who were also in training.

Peter seldom mentioned his degrees from Harvard and Oxford. His focus was on becoming a trained psychodramatist. This was a step into his father's world, at the same time freeing himself from his father's support.

After the experience of the open session Peter talked me into using my VA education benefits to start training at the Institute. I worked out an arrangement with Merlyn and within the month moved my things from my parents' house into the Institute to begin attending training sessions. It was in one of these sessions that I got a full dose of what this new form of psychotherapy was all about.

Our group was training for a two week period. By the end of the first week the group was growing tight because of all the psychological pain from the many psychodramas we had done. Every session I'd seen had been gut-wrenching in some way. Each psychodrama was directed by either Peter or Christina, a woman from Finland also training to be a director.

In Friday's 3 o'clock session I was chosen to be the protagonist. Somehow I'd avoided being chosen until then. Peter was the director and asked the group to do a warm-up before we got into my material.

"I want each of you to pair up. Sit on the floor facing each other with your knees touching. I'm going to say words or short phrases out loud. All I want you to do is keep eye-to-eye contact with your partner. I will tell you when to switch partners. Have you got it?"

The group responded with a collective murmur.

I was paired up with a beautiful woman named Maria, from Brazil. Her dark hair hung down covering her breasts. Her eyes were almost black. I played the role of her father who leered at her when she was a teenager. I felt such shame in playing that role, but I was assured by Maria and Christina, the director, that she chose me because she felt she could trust me. I was sure she'd seen the killer in me and wrote off what Christina had said.

I was spinning into Maria's eyes when Peter shouted, "Sky!" It echoed in the theater. A few moments passed and I heard "Earth!" then "Fire!" I felt like I knew the theme Peter was following, and it was easy to keep my eyes locked with Maria's. "Free love," said Peter his tempo picking up. "Jungle, snakes, longhairs, clamors, old man politicians, napalm, no bras, Gooks, Fire power, Body bags, pot-smoke."

Peter was in full swing and firing words out in a stream of unpredictability. Maria saw me flinch. I could feel my body heat rising. Maria offered me a tissue and smiled. The theater was growing smaller. Peter's warm-up was working. Maria reached for my hand as Peter yelled, "Find your next partner!"

I did the exercises with Jim, Sharon and Helen before we finished. The 60's and 70's were a whirlpool of feelings spinning inside me, and at its center was a dark vortex of shame I called Nam. What I'd packed away in my psychic attic was about to be brought down.

"Larry, come up to the stage."

I worked my way through the others who were sitting on the floor. I came to the round stage and sat at the first step of the three steps. Peter sat next to me and put his arm over my shoulders.

"I could see that you were being stimulated by the warm-up."

I nodded.

"I want you to close your eyes and let your mind be free to wander to a time and place that you are ready to bring to this stage today."

I closed my eyes and the swirl of loose memories spun faster and faster around the inside of my skull until a vision of the South China Sea came clear. The waves washed on the sand and out beyond the surf, sampans bobbed on the sea. The picture behind my eyes grew more vivid and Peter's arm tightened around me as I pulled back from the memory. Then Hardman sauntered before me, the brim of his Marine Corps cover shading his blue eyes.

"Have you got something for us?" Peter asked, lifting his arm from me.

"NO!" I said, louder than I intended.

"Good. Lets go with it."

I wondered if Peter had heard me. It was as if he could see inside my head.

"You don't have to tell us the story. Just give us one of the elements of the scene you see."

I took a deep breath. "I'm standing at the edge of the sea."

"Let yourself feel the sea breeze and the sand under your feet. When you're ready, let us know if we can enter this scene with you."

"I don't know. It scares the Hell out of me."

Peter looked away.

"I'm so ashamed of what I did."

"That's why we're here, Larry. Shame is what solidifies our souls, not allowing them to engage in the free flow of life. There is not one of us here today that doesn't carry a load of shame. I know you know this, especially after watching all the psychodramas of this past week."

"Yeah, but none of them had to do with killing."

I had my eyes closed and it seemed like the movement in the room stopped. Peter shifted his body; I felt his torso and thigh touch mine. He whispered, "We can do this, brother. I'm here with you."

I opened my eyes and looked at the group at my feet. Every eye was holding me; a few heads were moving up and down.

"Do it, man," said Jim, a therapist from Arizona.

"All right. Let's get to it," I said, standing up and pacing the first level of the stage, with Peter walking on the lower second level right next to me. As we walked Peter asked questions.

"What year is it?'

"April 1970."

"Where?"

"Nam."

"What happened?"

"I let people be killed."

"You want to tell us the story?"

"No."

"Will you do it anyway?"

Wringing my hands, I nodded.

"Well, come up to the center of the stage and sit on the stool with your back to us, and tell us the story. If you want, you can keep your eyes closed."

I closed my eyes and allowed the images to come.

"There was a regulation that the Marines fire their weapons periodically. I'd been placed on guard detail because I acted out by having my friend wrap me from head to toe in masking tape. My sergeant caught me, and I became the volunteer for guard duty. Corporal Hardman was squad leader of the guard detail. He marched a small band of us down to the beach to fire our weapons. Hardman was a grunt, brought in from the bush before he went home. Man, he was a sick dude who had a string of VC ears hanging in his hootch. He personified what the Corps wanted all of us to be--gung-ho idiots that would charge machineguns never asking questions because it was your job"

"Slow down," Peter said, taking hold of my arm again. "Let's get what happened on the table first. Give us the rest of the story line."

"He marched us to the beach. Out in front of us was a small fleet of sampans fishing. He told us they were breaking the 200 yard rule and that when he gave the word we were going to fire on them."

"I thought you said you were going to the beach to fire your weapons because it was part of the regulations," Peter said.

"I did. Hardman just decided that this was a great way to teach the fishermen that they shouldn't come so close. At night the VC sometimes came ashore with satchel charges to blow up our aircraft. That's why there was a 200 yard rule. But it was broad daylight and no one could ever make it up the beach without hundreds of Marines and flying aircraft seeing them."

"OK, so what happened next?" Peter stepped back.

"We lined up and loaded our weapons. Hardman told us to fire when he gave the word. I was a Lance Corporal, so Hardman outranked me. Before he was able to say Fire, I yelled Stop!

"Every man in the line looked at me. Hardman's face lost all expression. I swallowed hard and told him that there was no reason to fire on the innocent people and that we could simply wait for them to move out of range. They'd seen us and were plying sails and oars to get away as fast as they could.

Hardman said, 'I don't give a shit what you think. If you don't fire that weapon and keep your mouth shut, you're busted.'

Hardman screamed, 'Marines, come to the ready, aim, fire!'

I aimed my weapon at the sand and discharged all my rounds at my feet. Many of the others fired at the sampans. Tracer rounds were landing around the sampans."

I lowered my head.

"How do you feel now that you've told that story?"

I could hear Peter moving behind me on the stage.

"I should have stopped the bastard, but I was afraid for myself. Peter, I feel so ashamed. I knew better. I didn't want to be there. I hated the war. It made me into a bastard like Hardman. I don't think I want to do any more of this."

I felt his hand on my back.

"Open your eyes and raise your head."

I opened my eyes and before me sat the group, many with tears on their cheeks.

"How'd you guys end up in front of me?"

"Look at the support in their faces, Larry. Can I take a moment to tell you what I heard in your story?"

I turned around.

"Today you are a man of 30. When the story with Hardman happened you were a boy of 20, a boy who had never been out of his small town. You went from the Boy Scouts into the Marines with almost no time in-between. What you're doing right now is judging yourself from the moral position of a grown man. Today you're a grown man who knows so much more than the boy who went to Nam."

"Yeah, but anyone alive knows it's not right to kill innocent people."

"True, but the level of fear and confusion from the War was your only reality. Your values were untested until then and you did the best you could. If you could have the opportunity to face Hardman today is there anything you'd like to say to him."

"I'd like to tear his fucking head off!" I bellowed.

"Would you choose someone from the group to role-play Corporal Hardman?"

I looked over the three men in the group. "Jim?"

"Love to."

"Jim." Peter rubbed his chin with his forefinger and thumb. "I want you to stand off to the side of the stage. Larry, take these gloves. The rest of you go to the closet and bring out the pile of metal chair bottoms and put them at the foot of the stage."

After Jim had taken his position and the chairs were stacked in front of the stage, Peter said, "OK, Larry. I want you to role reverse with Jim who is now Hardman."

239

Peter then put up his hand. "Stop just a minute. I want to explain what I am doing. The reason we role reverse Larry into the role of Hardman is to inform Jim how to play the role with authenticity. So Larry, now I'm going to speak to you as if you are Hardman, and I want you to answer me as if you're him. Can you do that?"

"Yeah," I said, moving to change places with Jim.

"Hardman, I hear you had that group of Marines shoot innocent people fishing in the surf. Is that right?"

"Fuck, yes. They didn't belong there and you can be damn sure the ones we didn't hit will never come that close again."

"You got any feelings about killing those people?"

"That's my job. That's what the Marines trained me to do and I did a fucking good job of it."

"This guy, Winters, he thinks you're a murderer."

"He's a fucking pussy, a longhair in disguise. We'd a lost the fucking War the first day if all Marines were like him."

"Hardman, I think Winters has got something to say to you."

"Fuck him" said Jim.

"Role reverse," Peter yelled, causing the group to look in his direction. "Larry, put the gloves on and pick up one of those chair bottoms. Each time you tell Hardman the truth you can heave the chair bottom as hard as you want against the carpet hanging behind the stage!" He glanced at me, "You with me?"

"Yeah," I said, putting the gloves on and looking at Jim. Peter was whispering in his ear.

"What's the matter, Winters? You feeling sorry for yourself? They were fucking Gooks!" Jim screamed at me.

I almost dropped the chair bottom.

"What are you doing standing there? You a fuckin' pussy, Winters? You afraid to throw the fuckin' chair, just like you were afraid to shoot the fuckin' Gooks?" Jim screamed, his face red. Peter urged him on.

A click, like the safety coming off an M-16, tripped inside me. My vision narrowed. I gritted my teeth and stared at Jim, who stared back at me with his Hardman eyes.

"YOU FUCKING ASSHOLE. I SHOULD HAVE TURNED MY RIFLE ON YOU. YOU'RE THE PUSSY! YOU SAW THE KIDS ON THOSE FUCKING SAMPANS. IT TAKES REAL BALLS TO KILL KIDS."

Jim stepped back, and I heaved the chair bottom with all my strength, smashing it against the carpet.

This went on for 15 minutes, chairs bouncing on top of each other. The group watched, the women huddling together and the men raising their voices each time a chair hit. My energy ebbed and I felt the exhaustion in my limbs. When I'd thrown every last chair bottom, my legs buckled. I lay on the floor allowing the weeping to come. My body heaved; snot dripped into my beard. It was much more then Hardman; it was my childhood, boot camp, and Nam terror all spinning crazily inside me. It was breaking the well-erected barricades of my embarrassment, shattering through the many walls of guilt, stomping my fortified inhibitions and making me stand naked in the truth.

My free fall into myself stopped when I felt hands laid on me. Someone took my head in his lap; a hand rested on my heart. Slowly the tremor settled.

"When you're ready, open your eyes."

The group surrounded me. Peter was holding my head, stroking my hair. Someone handed me a tissue.

"My friends, you have just witnessed the beginning of the un-making of a Marine."

Jim had hold of my foot. We locked eyes.

"Ya know, Hardman was just a boy too," he said.

Chapter 3

"It Don't Mean Nothing"

Dave called. "Can you meet me at P&G's in an hour?"

P&G's was been the local watering hole Dave and I had been meeting in for years.

"I'm there," I said.

I pushed open the bar's heavy oak door, and a cloud of smoke crested out over my head. A thumping downbeat vibrated the grimy window glass that framed Main St., New Paltz, in hundreds of 6 by 10 inch rectangles. Standing on my tiptoes I looked over the heads of the packed crowd. My eyes were drawn to massive shoulders draped in the familiar olive drab. I pushed, squeezed and excused my way through sweating bodies.

It had been months since Dave and I'd spent any time together. When we were younger it had been great sport to come to P&G's for a Friday afternoon happy hour. As high school seniors we were just old enough to drink and plenty old enough to ogle the abundant college girls. As I yelled to Dave over the music it felt like we were trying to recapture a lost ritual of our youth.

Dave told me about the Vietnam Veterans' ticker tape parade he'd been to with the Vet group he belonged to. It was held down in New York City.

Cupping his hands he yelled into my ear, "We lost the dragon fight, brother."

I shook my head. "Yeah, and the parade's ten years too late."

It was too loud to talk, so we drank in silence with 70's music filling the empty spaces in our thoughts.

P&G's was like a reservoir collecting the river of college students flowing down Plattekill Ave. from campus. I drank my Margarita and Dave downed his Scotch. As we downed our third round, a deep bass cadence from the band The Police began pounding our eardrums. Dave nodded at the dance floor and we entered the crowd of dancing bodies. A couple of girls were standing together so we muscled our way toward them. Dave and I are both pretty good-sized men, so when we started bumping and grinding, the crowd made room. With the booze warm in our blood we strutted our old-man asses into a room full of kids whose parents knew a lot more about Vietnam than they did. We stomped out our own homecoming parade, marching to hard pounding rock and roll. The NYC parade was no more than an act of contrition for a bunch of battle weary old men. We danced because we made it back alive. We danced before a country that begrudgingly tipped its hat many years too late.

At midnight we headed out toward DuBois Rd. where my folks used to live. I pulled off the road near my old house. I yanked too hard on the truck's emergency brake and a metal-to-metal squawk sent a warning into the woods.

"Let's go up behind the house," I said, opening the truck door.

Drunkenly we navigated our way, arms outstretched, catching tree limbs so they wouldn't slap our faces. Dim shadows and the crackling of the dried leaves stirred up some of the old hyper-vigilance from Nam. How many times had Dave and I stood wide-eyed, waiting, gripping our rifles and imagining what was out there? We found a couple of large trees and sat down. The damp of the earth seeped up through the seat of my pants.

Dave started.

"Remember when I got transferred from Marble Mountain to Freedom Hill?"

"Yeah, that's when I got transferred to 262 with the 46's."

"Something happened there that I never told you."

"You mean when you got drunk and started giving Gunny a lot of shit?"

"No. It's when the hootch next to mine took incoming."

"No shit. Why didn't you tell me?"

"I guess because it rocked the shit outta me. It was about 11:30 at night. I'd just gotten back to the hootch from drinking at the club. I'd been asleep a half hour. It felt like something exploded inside my dreams. When I woke up I had sand in my eyes and mouth. My ears were ringing. Another blast came and I realized the VC was dropping mortars. I kept running my hands over my body feeling for blood. Faintly, I heard screaming. I reached for my flashlight under my pillow but was afraid to turn it on, so I felt my way out the door of the hootch. I climbed over things that weren't there when I came in. The screams kept me moving. I looked for the silhouette of the hootch next to us. It wasn't there. A jagged angle of what looked like roof tin glinted in the moonlight."

"You must have been shitting bricks."

"Cement blocks. I crawled through the rubble towards the moaning. It was so fucking hard to see anything. I took a chance and put my hand over the flashlight, letting only a little light come through the cracks in my fingers. I knew the light could be a target for some fucking sniper to zap me."

I shifted a little, reaching for some dry leaves to put under my butt. I wanted to ask questions, but he was on a roll. I saw Dave's silhouette; he was rocking.

"Keep going."

"I shined the thin light beam and saw a leg sticking out from under a pile of stuff. I turned off the flashlight and started pulling stuff off the guy. He moaned and I told him he'd be OK."

"Was anyone else around?"

"Not yet. The fucking warning sirens were going, too late as always. They made it impossible to hear anything. I got the debris off the guy and was holding his head in my lap. The sirens finally stopped and a voice shouted, 'Anyone in there?'

'Over here, a guy's been hit,' I called.

'How bad?'

A light shined on us. I told him to turn the light off.

'The perimeter's covered. We've got to be able to see what's going on,' he said. 'Relax, Marine, I'm the lieutenant of the guard.'

When he shone his flashlight I couldn't believe what I saw. The hootch took a direct hit. The lieutenant radioed for the base ambulance. I'm telling you man, I've never been so scared. It turned out two Marines in that hootch got killed. The mortar vaporized them."

Dave rocked on the balls of his feet. I heard the tree branches brush against each other in a gust of wind.

"I got the Cross of Gallantry. Sometimes, I think that was the only worthwhile thing I did there."

I could tell he was weeping by the long the spaces between his words. I inched closer and placed my hand on his knee. He rocked forward into my arms and we held each other. My tears came when his chest heaved against mine.

We sat that way for a long time, tired from the Too Late Parade.

Chapter 4

The End of Another Beginning

My training at the Moreno Institute lasted almost a year until the Veterans Administration investigated and found the education I was receiving was not something they wanted to pay for. I left with a large bill to pay back to the VA.

I found an apartment in New Paltz with a room for Jamie and returned to working as a carpenter. An architect friend, Chuck Silver, suggested that I meet a carpenter named Dan Guenther.

"Both you guys do good work, and I've got a big job coming up with no one lined up to bid on it. If you like each other, maybe you can team up," Chuck said, jotting down Dan's phone number and handing it to me.

I liked Dan immediately. He stood six-foot-six, with shoulders slightly hunched as if he'd been ducking doorways all his life. He told me he was an engineer by schooling. We decided to give Chuck's job a try and together worked up a bid. We got the contract, and it took six months to finish Mary and Melba's house in Stone Ridge. This was the first of many homes we built together.

A few years later, I was perched on top of a 24-foot ladder. A single bead of sweat dropped from the tip of my nose and I watched it hit the plywood floor below. The August sun beat on us as we fastened roof rafters to a ridge board. Dan thrust the beveled end of the 2-by-12 up to me on the ladder where I caught it with my free hand. The 80-pound plank stopped at the end of Dan's extended reach, and if I didn't catch it at that very moment, it would fall. The split-second timing we'd worked out felt good. These choreographed moves were the result of working together for two years.

"Here she comes," Dan yelled.

"Got it," I said, grabbing the rafter. Lining it up with the pencil marks, I quickly shot several nails into it with the nail gun.

As I waited for Dan to heave me the next rafter, I took surveyed the view. I looked down at the ball field behind the middle school, at the roofs of other houses on the street. Raising my eyes to the Shawangunk Ridge, I saw the Mohonk Mountain fire tower. I breathed the air in deeply, taking in where I lived. Then I noticed a white Ford station wagon turning at the beginning of Joalyn Rd. It looked like my Dad's new car. It wasn't unusual for my parents to stop by the job site to see how we were progressing. After Dad's medical retirement, he and Mom had put Dan and me on their weekly sightseeing tour.

"Hey Dan, I think my folks are coming. Let's get this next one up before they get here so we don't have to stop."

At the last pneumatic pound and hiss of my nail gun, I heard the car door slam.

"Larry, come down here! Something's happened to your father!"

I heard the panic in her voice. As I climbed down the ladder, the pressure in my temples started to build. I didn't run to the car; I needed time to sort out what to ask her. Had he had another heart attack?

After just a minute with my Mom, I took off my nail belt and yelled, "Dan, I got to go to the hospital. It's not good."

"Go ahead. Don't worry about this. I'll take care of it. I'll give you a call tonight. Call if you need anything."

It was 11 o'clock when I entered the hospital. It had to be more than 35 years since I was in this hospital as a six-year-old kid. The tile corridors started kicking up old memories: The children's ward where a nurse with cold hands undressed me while my father talked to a man with a large mustache and white coat.

"Is this going to hurt him?" Dad asked.

"Mr. Winters, it's a simple hernia operation."

An iodine odor stung my nostrils as I walked into the elevator, shaking loose another set of memories: Ten years ago at the same hospital I'd been sitting in the waiting room waiting for Dad to come out of surgery. They were doing bypass surgery on his heart. When he woke up from the operation he'd changed. I wasn't sure what it was. His eyes didn't pierce me. His face was soft, and tired. He looked scared.

The fear and sadness of these memories was weighed on me. I knew what lay before me was more serious than in the past. The doctor had told us he had lung cancer and was not expected to live six months. I came into room 426, and Dad looked like a child curled up in bed. It was as if an invisible sheet had been lifted over his face. I held onto the doctor's words, hoping I'd be able to make peace with him in six months.

I'd never had an honest talk with my father. I knew I should try and make that happen before I lost the chance. Sam, my therapist, had told me I had legitimate anger towards him and should get it off my chest. He reminded me that I'd been beaten as a child. And there were the puppies, of course. Sam said anger was in the way of my longing for his love.

I'd been coming to the hospital every day for a week and had not been able to do much more than report the everyday occurrences. He was sleeping when I entered the room. He looked tired; the pale skin of his neck was bunched. His once-powerful arms lay on top of the sheet like decaying fish. There was a faint smell of urine and I noticed the catheter bag was dripping onto the floor. I looked at my arms, moved my fingers, and watched the muscles swell.

I left him sleeping and wandered the corridors looking into doorways. An old woman was trying to get herself out of bed; her nightgown was high on her thighs, leaving her silver pubic hair exposed. I turned my head away hoping she'd notice. In the waiting room the blaring TV did its numbing job.

I stared blankly into a magazine, trying to pump myself up to speak with him. I stood up and sat back down deciding to give myself a half hour. I wondered how I could still be afraid of him. He was a frail, dying old man. But he's my old man. Maybe it was all those years of being poked by those sharp blue eyes of his, or being kicked around the living room with his steel-toed work boots.

I passed a nurse as I entered his room; she had changed his catheter bag. "Hey, Dad, how you doing?"

"Tired."

"You want anything?"

"Yeah, this pad's all wrinkled. Can you straighten it out?"

The nurse came back in, and we rolled him onto his side and straightened out the foam pad and sheet, then rolled him back and repeated the procedure for his other side.

Pulling a chair next to his bed, I bit my lip.

"Dad, I want to talk."

"Go ahead. Talk."

"I mean I want to talk about us, about how it was growing up."

"That was a long time ago."

I had planned to spend the whole day with him. Mom had spent the last three days with him, coming early in the morning and leaving at eight. I told her I'd take a day off work and spend it with him so she could rest.

"There's something I wanted to talk to you about," Dad said, pulling the pillow down behind his head so he could sit more straight.

"OK, you go first. I'll tell you what's on my mind later."

"I want you to take care of your mother's affairs. She's not going to know what to do with the money when I am gone. She'll need your help. I want your mother to get married again if she wants. But I don't want some guy taking all her money. I want you to make sure of that."

"OK, I'll take care of it."

I was touched that he would give his blessing for Mom to remarry. That short conversation drained him. His eyelids started to shut. I held his wrist while he slept. An hour passed before the nurse's aid came with lunch.

"Would you mind feeding him?"

"Sure, I'd be happy to," I said looking at the food on the steel tray. "I'm gonna let him sleep. I'll feed him when he wakes."

As I sat there holding his wrist, I could feel the lines of the room softening. Never in my life could I remember touching my father for so long. Tears dripped down my cheeks.

When he woke, I asked if he wanted to eat. He nodded yes. I placed the bib around his neck. After 15 minutes of picking up tiny forkfuls of applesauce, turkey with gravy and mashed potatoes, I stopped. Most of his meal was still on the tray, and the other part of it was on his bib. A stroke had taken the muscle control from the right side of his face.

"Could you take me to the bathroom?"

"Yeah. What do I need to do?"

"You have to help me lift my legs over the edge of the bed. Then disconnect the catheter tube."

He could hardly stand so I lifted him by the armpits and steadied him as we made it to the bathroom. I pulled the IV rack with my foot, trying not to pull out the tubing from his arm. Once he was on the toilet, there was no way to close the bathroom door; I couldn't get all the contraptions inside. He was in plain view of two other patients in his room. I turned my back to him to give him some privacy.

"I can't wipe myself."

"Do you want me to do it?"

"Please."

A flood of feelings came upon me. My father was asking me to wipe him. The only ass I'd ever wiped other than my own was Jamie's. I pulled a handful of toilet paper from the roll. Working my way through the tangle of tubes, I pulled his nightgown to the side and reached in to wipe him. His large balls hung in tired skin. I realized that hanging flap of skin was where I'd come from. I would never be any closer to my beginnings than now.

I helped him back into bed, and by the angle of the afternoon sun coming in the window, realized it was time. In a few hours one of my brothers or my sister would be coming to visit.

250

"Dad, I want to talk about what it was like growing up around you. It's time to let you know the truth. Will you listen?"

He turned his head. "I can listen."

"You spanked, beat and kicked me so many times that I'm still afraid of you. You worked me like I was a hired man but I was just a boy. I picked up so many fucking rocks and shoveled so much dirt, by the time I got to high school I was ready to retire."

I forced myself to look into his face. Tears were in his eyes. Part of me enjoyed this; part of me was ashamed that I was taking advantage of him. His tears settled into the creases of his face, catching the fluorescent light. He raised his hand weakly.

"Slow down son. I can't keep up."

Sitting back in my chair, I felt a warm flush in my body; my limbs were vibrating. Together we sat silent for a half hour. Then he spoke.

"You think you had it bad. Let me tell you about my father. When I was 14 I had to carry him on my back out to the wood lot …"

I listened to him for the few minutes until he fell asleep. Pulling my chair to the bed I took his hand. A peace settled between us. As he slept, I talked as if he were awake and listening.

"Dad, you never asked me about Vietnam when I came back. It hurt. I didn't know what to do. I came back broken. I wanted you to tell me how to put myself back together."

I went on for a long time until there was nothing left to say. The warm sun slanted lower through the window. I watched it slowly move over the sheets until it shone on our hands. I didn't want to move. This was the first time in my life that I didn't need anything from him. He woke and we talked about the fishing trips we both had loved, of times in the woods where he'd taken me hunting and showed me how to respect a gun. I retold the story of how he'd grabbed the doctor who roughly pulled the fishing hooks out of my brother Pete's fingers. In the quiet we made some peace.

"Dad, I love you."

Through tears he choked, "I hated that you joined the Marines. You never even asked me. I prayed you'd come home. I know I didn't know how to be your father, but I've always loved you."

Suddenly he shifted and started talking about his mother.

"The day before my mother died I brushed her hair. I loved the feel and smell of her hair. She wore it like a robe around her. I would brush it a hundred strokes."

It felt like we'd been opening the leather skin of a hardball for hours. We were slowly unraveling the tightly wrapped yarn and now had found its soft rubber center.

Mom, Peter, John, Sharon, and I were all there when Dad passed. Pete read the Twenty-third Psalm as we stood around his bed. It was not easy for our family, having never developed the language of feelings. Awkward hugs, private tears, the handing of tissue boxes, and longing looks were about all we could do.

There lay the man who'd shaped me.

I wanted to run away to my new girlfriend, Helise.

Chapter 5

Flashes of Light

My father's death went quickly. I stepped into his role and took care of Mom. We sold the house on DuBois Rd. that we all had grown up in. Mom and Dad had lived there 40 years. One day I drove down the road and passed the old homestead. I couldn't help but think about the old forts and tree houses we'd built in the woods. I mused that the people who bought the old house would never know about the hard work that had gone into the place. They wouldn't know that the 300-foot driveway was three feet thick, made with hand lifted stones. Or that their septic system was dug by hand—by me. Did they know that the acre of lawn once was a vegetable garden that had every rock picked out of it? There'd be no way for them to know about the amount of sweat and broken fingernails that went into the place.

Jamie was 16 and my role as his father was shadowy. My patience grew short and my jaw tightened like my father's. I noticed he'd cringe like I used to. He still came to me every other weekend. By the time Sundays rolled around and we'd figured out how to be with each other, I'd have to bring him back to Sandy's.

I'd been building houses with Dan for several years and was now in my late thirties. My knees and elbows ached from long days putting on roof shingles. One of the houses Dan and I renovated got featured in the New York Times Sunday edition. The article made me feel like I'd reached something as a carpenter. It also helped me to start thinking about moving on.

That's when I got another call from Peter. He was working as a Psychodrama therapist at a psychiatric hospital called Four Winds.

"If you go back and finish college, I can get you an internship working here. You can finish your psychodrama training at Four Winds with me," he said.

Peter's words and my aching body fired up my imagination. I soon spoke to Dan about changing our work schedule. I suggested we compress our workweek into four ten-hour days. I explained that I'd use my day off to return to college. Dan liked the idea. By the beginning of the New Year I'd started at Empire State College where most of the required work could be done outside the classroom. This commitment to college allowed me to take the internship at Four Winds. On Fridays, I car-pooled to the hospital with Peter.

Around this time I attended a mask-making workshop and met a dark-haired beauty named Helise. We'd paired up to help each other make our masks. She lay on her back on the floor while I placed wet plaster strips on her smooth face. Her almond brown eyes peeked at me through the wet plaster of the mask. By the time the workshop ended, Helise told me she'd been divorced for over a year. We exchanged numbers and within the week had made arrangements to go on our first date.

We went out for a year before we began staying overnight at each other's homes. Both of us were cautious after the pain incurred by our previous relationships. We moved slowly. I, being more impulsive, was ready sooner than Helise, but her steady, careful approach held more wisdom.

I was finishing my internship at Four Winds when we finally decided to move in with each other. Helise owned her home so we decided I'd give up my apartment. Four Winds asked if I wanted to work there full time. I wanted the job but still owned the business with Dan. I asked Dan if he was OK with me selling my part of the business to Sally, a woman who'd worked for us for many years. Dan agreed Sally would make a good partner, and two months later I sold the business to her.

A few months later I needed to build a shelf in Helise's house. I went to the basement to cut a piece of lumber and found I didn't own a circular saw. Things were changing; never before in my adult life had I not owned a circular saw.

When I started full time at Four Winds it was the first time in my life that I felt like I was doing what I was meant to. The challenge of learning to become a group therapist excited me. My own years of personal therapy turned out to be my best training. I liked dealing with people who death had visited; it was familiar.

Attempted suicide was almost a requirement for a patient to get into the hospital. My job as group therapist most often entailed working with patients that wanted to take their own lives. I had a very short time to understand why and to create an intervention that helped them to want to live. I loved the work.

Four Winds was a battlefield for depression. I was a soldier on that battlefield.

Chapter 6

Finally Back

Helise and I had been living together for seven years when we decided to get married. Life had been good. I was working at Four Winds Hospital and had settled into the long commute. I listened to books on tape, which allowed me to enjoy many books I'd never had time to read. Helise helped me through the death of my Dad, and we had built a good foundation of caring.

We set the date for August 20, 1994. Elizabeth, Helise's daughter was 20 and had just graduated from college. Jamie had turned 16 in May, had just gotten his driver's license and was itching for a car.

We had a large potluck wedding in Peter and his wife Susan's backyard. Peter was my best man. It was a sweltering afternoon as many friends and relatives gathered. Jamie and Liz stood at our sides under the chuppah held by my sister Sharon, my brothers, John and Pete, and Helise's brother Barry. Steve, a Rabbi friend, performed our ceremony.

Dark sweat blotches on my purple silk shirt grew larger as I danced wildly with Helise to the Klezmer band. My Methodist family stood watching like farmers lined up against the barn wall, as our friends and Helise's Jewish family did the Hora. Helise's mom, Shirley, looked at the potluck table and wondered what her family could eat. Unbeknown to Helise, Shirley had come with her trunk full of kosher food: whitefish, whole smoked salmon, bagels and kasha. A knot of folks from Brooklyn sat around that table for hours while the rest of the guests circled, wondering what they were eating.

Late that night, on our way home after cleaning up, Helise and I held hands in the car as we drove home.

"Finally," I breathed. We'd navigated lumps in Helise's breast, my Dad's death, and our children in all manner of tantrums. We'd stayed together through these life storms, making us strong for what ever lay before us.

Helise squeezed my hand.

"Finally what?"

"This is the first time since 1970, when I left Vietnam, that it feels like I'm really back from Nam."

Chapter 7

The Good Father

A warm breeze blew my tie over my shoulder as I walked across the Four Winds campus headed for the administration building. It was one of those summer days that draw buds out. I let my hand skim across the tips of the yews that bordered the sidewalk. Plucking a red berry, I crushed it between my fingers and brought it up to my nose for a sniff of that sharp clean spike of evergreen. I pushed open the front door and walked into the mailroom. Thumbing through my mail I noticed a letter that had been opened. Scrawled diagonally across its corner was Check this out! Peter. I took the letter out of the envelope and read the first page:

People to People is sponsoring a trip to Vietnam for U.S. Specialists in Post-Traumatic Stress Disorder and Creative Arts Therapies.

I stuffed the rest of my mail back into my box and put the Vietnam letter in the inside breast pocket of my jacket.

At lunch I remembered the letter and pulled it out. It said a psychologist named David Read Johnson was taking health care professionals to Vietnam to study the effects of Post-Traumatic Stress in the Vietnamese culture. I read on to find out that 30 people were going and the cost was $4,000 per person. Instantly, I knew I had to go. I had no idea who David Read Johnson was or how I'd get the 4,000, but I was going.

Without thinking about it, I left lunch and went straight to Sam Klagsbrun's office. Sam, the owner of the hospital, was the man who'd hired me. I knocked on his door.

Sam had once told me the story of his family fleeing Belgium when he was a boy. They walked across Europe to escape the Holocaust. They eventually came to the United States where Sam went into training to be a rabbi. He did not finish, but instead went to Yale to become a psychiatrist.

"Come in," he called.

I stepped into his office.

"Sit down." Sam gestured to a chair across from him.

"Sam, this is hard for me. I know the hospital has come on hard times. I know that no one's been sent to training for a long time. But I have an opportunity that I have to make happen."

Sam shifted in his chair and pushed his glasses up on his nose.

"What's on your mind?"

"I want to go back to Vietnam. The trip costs $4,000, and I was wondering if Four Winds could help me?"

"What do you mean? Are you a Vietnam Vet?"

"I never told you about Nam. I didn't think war and healing work mixed. I spent four years in the Marines and 13 months in Vietnam."

He let out a laugh. "You mean to say I hired an ex-Marine to work with my patients? Not only a Marine, but a Vietnam Vet? I must have been out of my mind!"

I fidgeted in my chair and looked down at the envelope I was crumpling in my hand. I thought to myself, "I jumped too quickly. I should have asked Peter how to approach Sam before barging into his office."

I ran my finger between my neck and collar. I looked around his office at the paintings of naval ships. Two old high-mast ships were firing cannons at each other in a pitching sea. A World War II battleship cut through the crest of a wave. There was a three-mast ship sailing in midair above the ancient city of Atlantis. The ship's clock on his desk rang every half hour.

"Sam, were you in the Navy?"

He smiled faintly. "I was a psychiatrist in the Navy. I worked mostly with a disorder called battle fatigue; today it's called Post Traumatic Stress Disorder."

"That's what this group of doctors and therapists are going to Vietnam to study. They want to see if the Vietnamese people suffer from PTSD."

I went on to explain that People to People was a quasi-governmental travel agency set up by Eisenhower. Their mission was to match up professionals from the United States with corresponding professionals in other countries.

"On this trip they plan on having Vietnamese doctors and therapists at treatment facilities and hospitals meet with doctors and therapists from the US."

Sam leaned back in his leather chair, placed his wingtips on the edge of the coffee table and looked at me with a serious expression.

"How do you feel about going back?"

"It scares the Hell out of me, Sam. I haven't had a good night's sleep since I'm home."

The phone rang and Sam got up to answer it. I wondered what he was thinking. I watched him write something down. He said good-bye to the person on the phone and came back to his chair. Before he sat he handed me the piece of paper. It had the figure $2,000 written on it.

"The hospital can't afford it right now, so I'll give you $2,000 out of my personal account. Will that be enough for you to make it happen?"

"Yes, but I can't take it!"

"Larry, if I didn't think you were doing an excellent job here I'd never offer it. Please take it and let's not talk about money anymore."

I felt like Sam had just hugged the breath out of me.

"I don't know how to thank you," I stammered.

"Tell me the story when you come back."

I shook his hand. I wanted to put my arms around him, but was too afraid I'd fall apart.

Chapter 8

You'll Be Sorting That One Out the Rest of Your Life

A few weeks later I kicked at pebbles in the Four Winds parking lot while waiting for Peter to pick me up to carpool home. I couldn't predict where the stones were going to land although I was trying to aim them. I had the same feeling about Sam's gift. It felt it absolutely the right thing to do but it had also unleashed a bulldozer inside me. The big steel blade was moving through a cemetery, exhuming old memories. Now that I'd gotten what I'd asked for, was I going to be able to handle it? Two weeks before I'd seen the movie Platoon and still hadn't been able to calm down. The only thing getting clear was that I needed help sorting it out.

Peter's car pulled up in front of me and before I got in I kicked the last of the stones I'd lined up with the toe of my shoe. It flew up, hitting the fender of Peter's car.

"Hey! What the Hell are you doing?" Peter squinted at me as I got into the seat.

"Sorry, I wasn't paying attention."

"Did you check out that Dan Jones flyer I gave you this morning?" he asked as I fastened my seatbelt.

"I took a look at it. Could be a nice trip. When are you going?"

"What do you think about both of us going? Take a little break from Four Winds and do some men's work with Dan Jones?"

"You know this guy Dan Jones?"

"He was the therapist of John Lee, the guy who wrote The Flying Boy. I've done some training with John. He loves Dan."

"Yeah, I remember you telling me about him," I said as he pulled out to pass a trailer truck. "I think it will help me sort out why I'm going back to Nam."

My mind drifted back to when I'd told Helise I wanted to go back. She'd brought her hand to her face.

"Do you have to?"

"Yes, I have something to finish."

"What?"

"I don't know. But I know I have to go. I think I left something there. Maybe I'm going back to validate that part of my life. I really can't put words to it."

She shook her head. "If you've got to go, go. I'll be frightened, but I'll handle it. Vietnam is something I won't ever understand."

"I don't either; that's why I'm going," I said, swallowing a lump of fear.

Peter's voice brought me back.

"You'll be sorting that one out for the rest of your life."

"Let's go!"

Chapter 9

Welcome Home

The month passed with most of my anxiety about going to Nam absorbed by the intense work at the hospital.

Peter and I flew to Santa Fe and were driving a rented car into the foothills of Rose Mountain, the site of the Dan Jones workshop. I pushed down on the accelerator as we climbed the steep blacktop. After ten miles the road narrowed and turned into gravel.

"I'm not sure why I decided to come out here," I said. "I hope we're not going to have to hug trees and read crystals."

Peter tilted his seat back.

"Dan's supposed to be a good therapist, isn't he?" I asked.

"According to John Lee."

"We'll find out when we get there."

The horse and cattle farms were thinning out and the landscape changed to ponderosa pine and shrub oak. Our car's wheels filled potholes as the road abruptly turned into a one-lane dirt path. A sharp scraping came from the bottom of the car as I tried straddling a rock.

"There's a house." Peter pointed at a distant tin roof. We bumped our way towards it.

"Looks like an old hunting cabin," I said, rolling down the window.

Its slabwood siding was sun-bleached and elk antlers were nailed randomly all over it. I pulled into a driveway of fist size stones where several cars were parked. A knot of men looked up as we thudded to a stop. We got out into the gritty cloud of dust we'd just stirred up, and a balding man with a wide smile and a tee shirt that read Dow Jones came at me with his hand out.

"Howdy. I'm Dan Jones. Welcome! Believe it or not we're only at the base of Rose Mountain." He pointed to a rugged trail behind two dented pick-up trucks. "We've got another five miles to go. Why don't you guys put your gear in one of those trucks?"

Before we took off, Dan had all of us stand together in a circle and introduce ourselves. Hank was by far the oldest man in the group; he had a head of white hair and a Texas drawl. The tallest man in the group was Brent who couldn't look into my eyes. Brent stood next to Mike, a powerfully built man whose sleeveless tee shirt showed his biceps. Jake's guitar was at his feet and his hair was in a ponytail. Pete wore a cowboy hat with a sweat stain; he spoke so softly I couldn't make out what he said. There were several other men. When the circle broke up Peter and I tossed our gear in the back of one of the trucks.

The driver came over. "Name's, Andy. You're gonna get to see a truck rock climb."

We crawled up the stony flank of Rose Mountain as I gripped the side of the truck bed with both hands to keep from being rattled loose, my ears popping every few hundred yards. Dan told us the camp was over 6,000 feet and warned us of altitude sickness.

It was almost dark when Andy stopped the truck near a cluster of sheds.

"We're here, gentlemen," he said, pointing to a small A-frame building. "Peter and Larry, that's your sleeping quarters. It's small, but there's a nice loft. Just throw your sleeping bags on the mattress and you'll be set."

After stowing our gear, we stepped out into the thin evening air. Sheds were scattered among the trees on the hillside, some for housing the men, others for storage. It could have been a lumber camp in the 1920's.

We trudged up the hill to the mess hall. When we got there men were sitting around picnic tables eating and talking. The sun lit the uppermost branches of the soaring firs. The bass melody of male voices was comforting. Several men spoke with a Texas twang. Dan was from Austin and he'd brought along some of the men he worked with.

After a dinner of spoon bread, salad and sautéed tofu, we were told to meet in the main lodge for a briefing on the week's events. It was almost dark. We were surrounded by silhouettes of the massive pines, their branches feathering into the star-speckled sky. The stillness of the mountain made me whisper as I asked Peter, "What do you think, brother?"

"Place is high and wild. I think we're going to have a good time here."

I opened the door of the main lodge and a yellow light spilled onto the stone steps. Oil lamps were bolted to the wall. Below the lamp brackets were directions on how to use them. Another note read, Take off your shoes.

In the large room men in socks stood before a bank of windows, looking out at the black shoulders of the mountain. The white pine board floor had a large Persian rug with meditation pillows strewn like mushrooms in a semi-circle on it. A fire crackled in the fieldstone fireplace. On the mantle was a gourd that rattled when I turned it over. Another rattle was made from a turtle with its neck and head stretched over a stick for a handle.

Several drums were piled in a corner of the room. Peter took a large, skin-covered drum. Placing it between his legs, he began with a simple rhythm. Other men picked up drums and joined him and within minutes all of us were pounding. Our sound moved slowly from a desperate rattle to a cacophony to an indomitable cadence. A loud yelp silenced the drumming. Everyone snapped their heads around to see Dan Jones sitting before us, with arms raised. Looking around he welcomed each one of us with his eyes and a nod.

"Gentlemen, make yourselves comfortable, sit or lay any way you like. I'm going to tell you about our plans for the week. I want every one of you to keep in mind that we can change this agenda at anytime and as often as you want."

"Rose Mountain is a sacred place. Cougar and black bear roam around out there." He pointed at the bank of windows. "Those trees have never been cut. In this purity we will do our work. Each man brings his trouble and pain, as well as his joy and love. Together this week we will use bodywork, the Native American vision quest, and the sweat lodge as healing tools. When we come to the end of the week a

265

community of men will have formed around the simple act of telling the truth. Your willingness to tell your truth will bring the sacred to this gathering."

Sitting cross-legged, Dan allowed a long pause. "I will meet all of you in the morning in this room. Sleep well."

The next morning Dan made some introductory remarks and asked who was willing to break the ice and work.

A tall man with long, gray-streaked brown hair and snaps on his shirt raised his hand.

"What's your name?"

"Chris," said the man, rocking and shoving his hands under his butt.

"Chris, what did you bring here today that we can help you with?"

"My brother died last year of an overdose, and I haven't been able to feel anything."

By the time we ended, Dan was able to help Chris begin to forgive himself for not being able to help his brother.

By the third day I'd witnessed men working on issues as varied as divorce, child abuse, sexual abuse, abandonment, and bigotry towards gays. No one had mentioned Vietnam.

Back in the A-frame after dinner, I was taking off my shoes when Peter asked, "Why you holding back?"

I flopped on the bed. "What do you mean? I haven't seen you rushing out there."

"I'm thinking of going tomorrow."

"I'm not there yet. Not a man in the bunch even remembers Vietnam."

"Bullshit! That guy Brent, you heard him at dinner tell us he was in the Air Force. He's a colonel. He's your age; he had to be in the war."

"Maybe. I keep thinking most of the guys here were protesting the War."

"Do what you want. I'll back off. If anyone knows how hard this topic is for you, I do. Just take care of yourself."

The next morning Peter told Dan of a recurring dream he'd had since childhood. Peter's work with Dan went on for almost and hour, and by the end of the session Peter lay in Dan's arms sobbing. When Peter's chest stopped heaving, he re-entered the men's circle with snot dripping from his nose. Handing him a tissue I stood and hugged him.

"Good work, brother."

Dan sat crossed legged with the empty pillow in front of him. His eyes were closed, and he breathed deep relaxed breaths. Without thinking I stood and walked toward the pillow. I sat, copying Dan's body position. I closed my eyes and in a few minutes I felt Dan's hands touching the backs of mine. I looked into his face. He acknowledged me with a slight bow of his head. He squeezed my hands gently and asked, "Shall we start?"

"I guess so."

"What'd you bring?"

"Fear."

"Where does the fear live in your body?"

"My belly," I blurted out. "It's like someone's squeezing my guts."

"Use your imagination and become that fear. Feel how it shrivels and trembles. Reach into it and give it a voice, Larry."

I closed my eyes and tried to feel it, but I couldn't. I opened my eyes and saw that Dan was stretching his head and neck towards me for my answer. Lifting his eyebrows, he urged a reply. I shook my head.

"Dan, the best I can come up with is 'Don't go!'"

I imagined Dan was wondering, "What the Hell's 'Don't go' got to do with fear?"

Dan stood and motioned me to stand facing him. "Choose someone to be your fear," he said in a sharp voice that I hadn't heard before.

I recoiled a little and pointed at the older man, Hank. His belly hung over his belt and his graying goatee contrasted with a reddish completion.

"Could you do it?"

He acknowledged my finger with a nod. When he stood, popping sounds came from his knees.

"Jesus Christ, Dan," he grumbled. "Why don't you have some chairs for old men like me? It sounds like artillery going off every time I stand up."

"I wish you'd said something earlier, Hank. I'll make sure there's a chair here for you next session."

Hank moved his chin up and down. "Don't worry about it; I was just kidding."

"Hank, stand behind Larry and put your hands on his shoulders."

I felt the weight of Hank's warm hands and let my shoulders drop.

"See if you can find that fear again and repeat those words loudly."

"You mean 'Don't go?'" I yelled, tensing my jaw.

Dan raised his arms and squeezed the air with his hands, a hand-signal to Hank, whose fingertips sunk into my shoulder muscles.

"Say it again!" Dan barked.

"Don't go!"

"Louder!"

"DON'T GO!"

Hank's fingers dug deeper. I flinched when he hit my collarbone, but his fingers kept probing deeper.

"Hank, please repeat 'Don't Go!'" Dan said.

Hank boomed right into my ear, "Don't Go!"

"Louder, Hank."

I'd had enough. I wasn't going to put up with this shit anymore and tried to jerk away from Hank. That's when Dan brought his face up into mine.

"Who put that fear in you, boy?"

"The Marine Corps," I shot back, eye to eye.

"The Marine Corps, huh? Who told you 'Don't Go?' "

"Nobody."

"This was during the Vietnam War?"

"Yeah." My chin jutted at him.

"Your folks wanted you to go?"

"Not really."

Dan rolled up his shirtsleeves. "You're a therapist, aren't you?"

"Yes."

"Well, take that damn therapist hat off and put it on the hook over there."

He reached up to his balding head and removed an invisible hat, tossing it towards the peg.

"Now take yours off."

I took off my imaginary hat and walked over there and hung it up.

"Oh, and by the way, leave it there until you go home."

I felt exposed.

"Hank, please come here," Dan said.

Dan took hold of Hank's elbow and walked to the side of the room. They stood with their heads together, whispering. They walked back and Hank went to put his hands on my shoulders. I flinched and pulled away. He held on to me.

"It's OK, son. I'm not going to hurt you this time."

I let his hands rest on my shoulders. He didn't pry or dig, just squeezed gently and repeated, "I'm not going to hurt you, son."

"If you want, Larry, lean back into Hank. You can trust him, he won't let you fall."

I didn't trust Hank, but I leaned back anyway.

"It's OK, son."

If there's something in there, let it come," Dan whispered softly.

I coughed and a yelp came up into my throat. Hank pulled gently back on my shoulders. I let him pull me into his chest. He whispered, "Don't go, son."

Hank wrapped his arms around my chest, and I let my weight settle into him. I saw Dan motion to a man in the circle to get some pillows. Then he helped Hank to sit down while he held onto me. I felt lost inside myself.

"Open your eyes," Dan said, touching my shoulder.

The men's circle had moved closer. My hands were on top of Hank's hands and Dan placed his hands on top of mine.

"Larry, it's time to tell these men about, 'Don't go!'"

Everyone nodded.

"My folks didn't want me to go to Nam, but they didn't try to stop me. I don't know if it was that I was so Hell bent on going, or they just didn't care. I had to get away from my old man. I just couldn't live around his criticism any more. I signed up with a friend, Dave, and we booked out on the Marine's Buddy Plan. I didn't know what I was doing. I was angry and confused. I'd never let my own boy go to war. They let their boy go off to war without even a squeak."

Dan bent closer. "It sounds like you wanted them to hold on to you. Why?"

"I was scared. I thought I was going to be killed. I was just a stupid kid who didn't know what he was getting into. I needed someone to stop me."

Suddenly a chorus of voices began. "Don't go, son. Don't go. Please, don't go."

I stiffened. Hank's embrace started restricting my breathing. Looking down at the white hair on his ropey forearms, I knew this old man still had some power. I knew I couldn't trust the bastard. I tried to break free while the litany went on. "Don't go, son. Don't go…"

I pushed but Hank's arms tightened. The men's circle had moved away from us. "Don't go, son. Don't go." Each time grew louder. Dan nodded, and three of the largest men and Peter stepped out of the group.

"Larry, imagine Hank's your father and he's not going to let you go," Dan said.

"This is Bullshit!" I spat out. Hank locked his fingers over my breastbone and tightened. "I've had enough of this shit!" I yelled. "I'm tired of playing this fucking game! Let me go!"

The chant picked up. "Don't go. Don't go…"

Buckling forward, I lifted Hank off his knees. I got one of my own knees under me. Hank didn't loosen his grip. A large man moved to Hank's back to support him, which pissed me off.

I struggled to get a full breath, then forced my other knee under me and made a lunge to my feet, carrying Hank with me. His grip released and I took a deep breath. Thinking I'd won the game, having made it to my feet, I relaxed just as Hank snaked his arms back around me.

Peter's voice came from behind. "Get that old bastard off your back. He's just saying 'Don't go.' He really wants you to go! Who's gonna protect his ass if you don't go?"

Hank boomed, "Don't go, son. Stay here with Daddy!"

I doubled my efforts to break free. A few men were spotting us. Hank released my chest and grabbed me by the waist. John, the huge man who had been supporting Hank's back, grabbed me around my chest encompassing my arms. I'd been thinking all along that if I really wanted to I could break free of Hank, but I didn't want to hurt him. With this other guy locked around me, though, I wasn't so sure. "Fuck it," I thought and started bucking. That's when Dan and Peter each grabbed a leg. I bucked some more, the group screaming louder and louder, "Don't go, son!"

I was trying with all my strength to break free. I lifted Peter completely off the ground as he rode my leg like a bronco. This caused them, all of them, to tighten their grips until I gave up and lay limp.

Chest heaving, my wet cheeks pressed to the floor, I could feel them relax. What moments before had felt like a brutal restraint, suddenly felt like an embrace.

Hank whispered, "I really don't want you to go, son, but you're a man now and it's up to you."

Dan had the men release me. I lay alone on the floor, washed-out, flooded with feelings. I wanted to stop crying, but at the same time, felt like I'd spent years of my life waiting to begin.

After a long while Dan asked me why this story had come up.

"I just realized something. It's not about my parents not stopping me from going to Nam. That has some truth in it, but the real truth is I'm planning a trip back to Nam in October."

"Why?"

"I think I left a piece of myself over there and I need it back."

Dan brought his two hands together in front of his face and bowed his head. "I understand." A long silence settled in the room. "I want you to sit still and listen to these men before you. There is no need to reply. This is a time to take what is offered. Are you with me?"

I nodded.

Hank cleared his throat and I turned to face him.

"There's something I have to say to you." He ran his hand through his white hair. "I supported the war. I would have sent my own son. I'm not proud of that now." His voice caught and it took him several moments to gain composure. "If that fucking War was today and you were my son, you'd be going over my dead body. I mean that!"

Hank stood. Desolate sobs erupted from him as he staggered towards me. I stood, and we embraced.

"I had a boy your age. I lost him in an automobile accident when he was 16."

Hank shook in my arms. He grabbed my shoulders and pushed me back. Looking directly into my face, he said, "Welcome home, son."

When Hank sat down, Dan stood.

"I hated the Vietnam War. I protested it in the 60s. I was at the head of the pack, screaming at the politicians. I'm truly sorry for what you lived through but I would do it again in a heartbeat. I got out of the Marines just before the War started. I know what the Marines are like. I respect you." He snapped his right arm up into a salute. "Semper Fi, brother. Welcome home."

Sobs erupted from a man sitting in the back. Dan moved toward him pulling me with him, the group parting for us. He reached out to Brent who sat crab-like with his head buried in his arms. Squatting down, Dan stroked his back until he quieted enough to speak.

"I've avoided you from the first day. When I heard your friend say you were going back to Nam, I stayed away from you. I'm a Colonel in the Air Force. I enlisted in 1969 but didn't go. Worse yet, I didn't want to go and did everything I could to get out of it, including having my father an, Air Force officer, speak to one of his friends who made arrangements to keep me Stateside."

His hands move up to his face. "I'm so ashamed of myself. I should have gone. It was my duty, but I was afraid of being killed."

I reached over to Brent and rested my hand on his bony shoulder.

His friend Mike stood and came up to us. He sat next to Brent and put his arm around his waist.

Looking at me, Mike said, "I admire you for going, for doing what I was taught a man's supposed to do when his country calls. I hid out in college smoking pot."

Looking into this man's face I said, "Let me tell you something, I didn't believe in the War any more than you did. The problem was, after I got there, there was no place to run."

"But you went. The way I was raised that's what a man does. I was a boy hiding in college screwing co-eds, while you were having your ass shot at. Ever since the War ended I've been haunted with the fact that I'm a coward. It's because of men like you that I have freedom. Remember, in the end you went, regardless of how frightened you were. Your going means something."

He reached his free arm towards me, and I grasped his powerful hand.

"Welcome home, man."

Peter stood and draped his arm over my shoulders.

"A man's got to come home before he can leave again," he said. "Welcome home, brother."

Chapter 10

Nam the Second Time

The 6-hour flight from New York to L.A. left me fidgeting in my hotel room. My black, multi-pocketed backpack lay splayed across the bed like a gutted bear. I caught myself fiddling with the contents for maybe the tenth time. I shuffled socks out of one compartment, replacing them with the first aid kit. I re-wrapped the bag of medications and hypodermic needles so they'd take up less space. I was shifting the large sheaf of wooden chopsticks from an inside pocket to where I could get them more easily when their paper sack split, spilling them on the floor in a literal pile of pick-up-sticks.

I took out the Leatherman multi-purpose knife (with pliers and screwdrivers) and fingered its smooth stainless body to calm myself. It felt like I'd been packing the same stuff over and over for two months. My goal was to take everything I needed, at the same time trying to carry the bare minimum. I pulled out my leather bound poetry journal and flipped through the last few poems I'd written. Poems had been my therapy since I'd gotten back from Nam. Almost no one knew I wrote them until Peter encouraged me to do a poetry reading with him the year before. It was about 2:40 a.m. when I looked up from my journal. I locked the luggage locks on the pack and lay down on the bed with my clothes on. My stomach was still upset despite eating six Pepto Bismol tabs. All my anxieties had funneled into my guts.

As I lay there in my clothes I started thinking about the sendoff I'd gotten at the airport. Peter had pinned a button on my jacket that read Brotherkeeper. He hugged me and said in my ear, "Come back home, brother."

Ten men from my ongoing men's group showed up. Many had to drive over 30 miles to reach the airport. Ron Robbins, my current therapist, came. He and I had been reliving much of Vietnam and my childhood in his basement office. Helise had squeezed my hand, frightened to let me go. It was her steadfast love I'd been drawing on to face my past. Mom had stood in the background, shy of the new people. She'd held back all emotion until I turned to leave. Hearing her muffled cries, I took her in my arms and felt her body shake. I hadn't realized till then it was also her second time.

I was up at 5 to do more unnecessary organizing. I stared at the red numbers on the digital clock, waiting for the time I could leave the room. The previous afternoon, while shopping in a local mall, I'd been walking down a hallway that connected two buildings. I turned to look at some young girls and walked directly into a plate glass door, my face leaving a smudge on the clear glass. Later on I bought a cup of coffee, paid with a $20 bill and walked away without waiting for change. The waitress was nice enough to follow after me and return it.

The People to People delegation was to meet at 8 a.m. in the hotel conference room. I roamed the lobby for an hour. A few minutes after 8 o'clock I stood in front of a table of coffee, donuts and name tags. I found mine and pinned it on, then started looking for David Read Johnson, our group leader. I'd spoken to David several times on the phone but had never met him. A handsome man with a confident manner, dark hair, and erect build was moving around the room greeting people, I thought it must be David. He stuck out his hand and through a set of fine white teeth said, "Hello, Larry, how you doing?" His handshake was solid, and he looked directly into my face.

Glancing at his nametag, I said, "I'm good, Niki. How you doing?"

Niki lifted his arm in a sweeping motion towards the table.

"Help yourself to donuts and coffee. I'm the Peoples to People's guide. If you need anything or have any questions, just ask." Then he bent towards me for a better look at my nametag.

"You're a Jarhead? I'm Army, 68-69. There's five other vets on the trip. Six, including myself. We'll have to talk."

The next hour was filled with meeting people whose names I'd lose as soon as I was introduced. We were briefed on the areas of Vietnam we were going to be visiting as well as on how to behave as a group of US citizens. David Read Johnson and Hadar Lubin were introduced as delegation leaders. David was a head psychologist for the Post Traumatic Stress unit at West Haven VA Hospital in Connecticut. Hadar, his fiancée, was the medical director of that unit. David and

Hadar told us that Niki was to be our Supreme Commander. All decisions concerning the group in Vietnam were his. I felt relief knowing a vet was in charge.

We'd been given room assignments and it took me a while sifting through 26 people before I found Larry Ashley, my roommate. David had kidded me on the phone about the Larry and Larry room. Larry A. was a short, slim man with a long gray beard that disguised a cherubic smile. His voice carried faint music of the South. His eyes darted everywhere, stopping only for brief moments to punctuate a sarcastic comment. Larry A. was also to be my seatmate for the flight. Someone must have figured this was a good way to get to know your roommate. Larry A. was a vet. He'd served with the Army in 66-67. I could tell he'd seen action; he had the 1,000-yard-stare.

After leaving Hong Kong airport en route to Hanoi, I started feeling an upwelling in my guts. Larry A. had stopped talking. As we began our descent into my old enemy's capital, I looked out the window. The ground was covered with tens of thousands of small, perfectly round ponds. It took me a few minutes to realize they were bomb craters filled with water. There'd been no attempt to fill in these scars of war. I caught a reflection of our plane in one of them.

We landed, and as I stood in the aisle gathering my gear from the overhead compartment, an attractive Vietnamese stewardess read my nametag and said, "Winters is also a Vietnamese name." She then pronounced my name in Vietnamese. I thanked her and moved past her toward the exit. When I reached the top of the mobile stairs, a quiver took hold of me. At the bottom of the stairs stood an NVA solider in full uniform: the man I'd spent 13 months trying to kill; the man I'd sung about killing in boot camp; the man I prayed got killed during the nights of mortar attacks. There he was--the man who'd been dancing at the end of a long string of M-60 machinegun fire. Now, right in front of me, stiff and proud, stood a VC in his clean jade green uniform.

Before I reached the bottom of the stairs, reality worked itself into my head. This man was in the cradle the last time I was in Vietnam. He looked about 20; I was 46.

Our small contingent snaked its way to the customs counter. The tropical heat was flowing off of me. There was a young man

277

standing in line who started talking to me. He told me he was a male nurse from Austria and was six weeks into a 12-week vacation with his girlfriend, who stood shyly behind him.

"Why did you come to Vietnam?" he asked.

"To heal from the War."

"I admire your courage."

"Thanks," I mumbled and moved through customs without a hassle.

Twenty-six of us loaded into a bus. We started to Hanoi and it was as if the bus was the head of a large serpent winding its way through throngs of motorbikes, bicycles, animal-drawn carts, lorries, buses, and thousands of pedestrians walking in the road. Headlights were beginning to come on, and Niki asked the driver to turn off the interior lights, making the hootches we were passing more visible. None of them had doors and we could see glowing TV sets with faces of well-known Americans flickering on the screens.

A fishy tang in the air was bringing back memories. I closed my eyes and let myself remember when I was here 30 years before. Then, all Vietnamese were potential killers. I'd seen hatred in their eyes. Now I was riding on a highway with an oozing mass of Vietnamese, wondering if they'd changed. Outside the bus window a sea of black hair bobbed. I looked for the hatred I'd known, only to see my reflection in the glass.

No buildings in sight were higher than two stories. Beyond the borders of the road was farmland with water buffalo barely visible in the fading light. Occasionally a familiar looking old US military structure made of cement or wood appeared.

The bus stopped for something. I looked down at a family of Vietnamese on a motorcycle. Four of them on a tiny bike, the father driving, mother sitting in front of him on the gas tank holding a child who rested his legs across the handlebars. A teenage boy rode on the back with his arm around his dad's waist.

The bus pulled up in front of a white masonry building with a sign in faded blue letters: Saigon Hotel. We'd been told the hotel was first class, but it turned out to be third-rate compared to anything in the States.

Evidence of earlier French wealth was visible in the white marble floors and the elegantly carved mahogany banister that swept up a spiral staircase. The Saigon Hotel was a French jungle flower that had long ago lost its blush. The staff was friendly and rushed to help us settle into our rooms so that we could be seated in time for a dinner of rice and cooked vegetables.

Tired from the trip, Larry A. and I went to our room after we ate.

"It looks a lot different than what I saw the last time," I said.

"Damn right. How many soldiers actually saw Hanoi? Almost none."

"That's not what I meant. I spent almost no time in any cities. I was either flying over the countryside or on base," I said, folding back the sheets on the bed.

"I know what you meant. I was just pulling your leg. It's gonna take you a while to get used to me," Larry A. said, reaching for the pull chain on the lamp.

"Lights Out...Marine."

"Aye Aye, Sir."

Chapter 11

Thunder in Vietnam

I thought I'd slept well until I looked at the knot of sheets tangled around my legs. Looking at my wristwatch I saw that I'd been asleep for only a few hours. My over-wound body clock had reached the open eyes setting. It felt like all time anchors had spun free and my head and body were floating on two different oceans. I'd been dreaming that I was in bed with a King Cobra.

I slipped out of bed trying not to disturb Larry A, sleeping two feet from me. Entering the bathroom, I closed the door and turned on the light then lowered myself into the bathtub. The cool ceramic felt good against my sweating back. The flood of images poured back into my mind:

A large thick female King Cobra wrapped her cool strong body around me. I could feel each of her scales as she pressed her firm flesh into mine. I loved the way it felt as she tightened against me. I didn't fear her. I knew she was feeling the life in my heart. The deep ridges of my spine reached out to her. Her spade shaped head rested lightly on my shoulder. Deep, unflinching reptile eyes held me in unquestioningly.

It took a long while for me to settle from the dream and get back to bed. I was ripped awake by an explosion. Suddenly I was under the bed yelling, "INCOMING!" Every molecule of my body was alive.

"It's only thunder, man," Larry A's calm voice said in the dark. "You OK, man?"

"Yeah, I'm OK," I said, coming out from under the bed.

"It looked like you jumped right off the bed."

"I did. You must have been awake to see it."

"I was, or I'd a been under mine."

We both laughed.

Chapter 12

Are They the Same?

By the morning my senses were supercharged. The thunderstorm had brought back the old rhythms of Vietnam for me. Thirty years before my nerve endings had been jumping to Jimi Hendrix's earsplitting guitar riffs, bass provided by exploding mortars.

On the balcony of the Saigon Hotel, five floors above Hanoi City, I listened to the streets begin to come alive. I quickly recognized that the horn was the most-used piece of equipment on all Vietnamese vehicles. The morning started with the peeping of small motorbike horns, soon to be followed by deep-throated Russian lorry air horns.

The title of our group, People to People, seemed a fitting a description of what Vietnam looked like to me. We were told before we came that there are 72 million people in Vietnam, a country the size of Rhode Island. The only place left to escape in the city was inside yourself, and then the sound followed you like a viper into a hole.

Looking out at the rooftops of Hanoi, I wondered about Uncle Ho's hometown. How had he spent his days in Hanoi? As a GI, Hanoi had been a mythical place. I knew about it when I heard Hanoi Hannah's voice on the radio. She broadcast pro-Communist propaganda aimed at undermining the fragile patriotism of the American troops. So seldom did we hear a women's voice that I had imagined her as beautiful. She told us we were going to die for unjust reasons. She was right. If Hanoi Hannah was still alive, she was an old woman. Maybe she was in one of those ramshackle hootches below me.

At nine that morning we met our Vietnamese tour guide in the lobby. Her name was Hoa.

Her black-silk hair fell upon her red traditional Vietnamese dress, called an ao-dai. She appeared porcelain and, in perfect English told us her name meant Peace in Vietnamese. She went on to say that she was born during the War and her parents named her Hoa in the hope that her birth would bring peace. When asked by someone in the delegation how Vietnamese people feel about the War, she said, "We want to let bygones be bygones. The war's over; it is time that we become friends."

Hoa told us she'd been a guide for several returning American vets. As she spoke I felt my upper teeth sinking into my lower lip. I was fixated on her beauty and at the same time realized that I'd once tried very hard to kill her and her family. I wondered how many of the Vietnamese standing around me in these streets I'd tried to kill, and how many of them had tried to kill me.

Chapter 13

Round Eyes

We left Hanoi and arrived at Da Nang to visit Hoa Khanh Hospital just outside Da Nang in a mint-green, low roofed, cement block building that stood among many ramshackle hootches. Hoa Khanh Veteran's Hospital had been a US Army military headquarters building during the War. One shaggy palm tree grew out of a hole cut in the parking lot, providing the only visible shade. Vietnamese men dressed in what looked like pajamas stood against the tree smoking. As we filed off the delegation bus, a few of the men smiled and bowed their heads in greeting. One man was missing the lower part of his leg; in its place was a round wooden peg with a brass cap at the bottom.

A man in a white lab coat came out of the building and addressed David; then he introduced himself to our delegation as Doctor Sun. Striding out ahead of us, he led us past a series of patient quarters. Several of us stopped and looked into the 15 by 15 rooms that held as many as ten patients. Metal beds were crammed so tight they were almost touching each other. Most of these beds had no mattresses; the patients were lying on the steel springs.

Doctor Sun waved for us to come along and funneled us into a large meeting hall. He pointed to folding chairs arranged on one side of the room, then went over to speak to a female nurse. A few minutes later the nurse came around to each of us, offering bottled water. The cool metal of the chair felt good against my wet shirt. Across the room several heads were crammed through a doorway, craning to see us Americans. Hadar noticed them and asked Doctor Sun if he would allow them to come in to the room. He hesitated and started a quick exchange with the Vietnamese nurse. Doctor Sun appeared to submit, and what looked like staff made their way in carrying their own folding chairs.

Doctor Sun then announced to us that he was the Director of Psychiatry for the hospital. He told us there were seven psychiatrists, 150 in-patients and another 4,000 outpatients. He explained that most of his patients were over 40, reminding us that the War ended 25 ago.

"Hoa Khanh Hospital treats North Vietnamese, South Vietnamese and Viet Cong patients," Doctor Sun said looking at his wristwatch.

Hadar, a psychiatrist herself, led the interview with Doctor Sun. The rest of us listened and took notes. Her first question was, "Is it necessary that you place so many patients in one room?"

"Hoa Khanh Hospital is one of the better-equipped hospitals in Vietnam," Doctor Sun replied.

"How many of your inpatients are veterans of the War?"

Doctor Sun motioned to a woman in a white lab coat who replied to him in

Vietnamese.

"One hundred and six patients are veterans. Out of this number, 86 are men and 20 women," he translated back to us.

Hadar's questioning was interrupted by a blood-curdling scream. A woman in blue pajamas was being brought through the doorway by two attendants. The attendants were struggling to hold her, each man clutching an arm.

"What is she yelling?" Hadar asked.

"Forgive me! Don't hurt me! Don't beat me anymore! I'll tell you everything you want to know," Dr. Sun translated.

Her ponytail whipped back and forth across her face as she shook her head in protest. Cords of muscles knotted in her thin arms. Her face became an exaggerated grimace when the two attendants began dragging her into the room. They forced her down on a metal chair before Doctor Sun. The attendants remained, holding her shoulders. .

It became clear this patient was here to be interviewed. Doctor Sun said he'd be the interpreter. The Vietnamese woman put her chest to her knees and her hands over her eyes. She rocked in the chair, causing the attendants to move with her. Doctor Sun spoke softly urging the women to take her hand from her eyes. She just rocked and made whimpering sounds.

"She was a prisoner of War. Her village of Hoa Qui was once a battlefield near China Beach. The South Vietnamese and Americans captured her and tortured her with electricity. They made her eat soap and hung her from the ceiling to make her talk." Doctor Sun's voice grew sharper. "Her husband was in the South Vietnamese Army, but she'd fought for the North." He explained that they'd been married before the war.

The two attendants reached for the women's arms and forced her hands from her face and held her upright in the chair. The woman began thrashing and screaming hysterically. The attendants tightened their grip. Her wiggling on the chair was forcing her pants off.

"Stop it!" Hadar yelled.

Doctor Sun, surprised, looked at Hadar.

"Leave her alone. We don't need to speak to her. Please let her return to her room."

Doctor Sun nodded to the attendants, and they carried the kicking women out of the room.

Mopping my forehead with my forearm, I tried to focus.

Hadar asked, "What was she screaming again?"

"Forgive me! Don't hurt me! Don't beat me anymore! I'll tell you everything I know!" Doctor Sun said, bowing his head. "She'd been behaving normally for several days. Maybe it's your round eyes and light hair that's frightening her.

I felt ashamed.

On the bus after leaving Hoa Khanh Hospital, I sat next to Mildred. She looked equally shaken. She asked, "Did you see how she was shaking when they took her away? She must have thought we were going to torture her."

"We came to see if there was PTSD in the Vietnamese. I guess we found it."

"I work as a nurse with vets in a VA hospital back in the States. I once had to do a few months of night shift work. My God, some of the

285

screaming that came from those vets at night. The War didn't care who it hurt did it? What branch of the service were you in?"

"Marines, Mildred. There was this guy I met in Nam back in 1969. He told me he and a buddy pulled their jeep up to a Vietnamese riding a bicycle and blew his head off with a 45. Before they fired, they'd bet on how far he'd ride before he fell."

Mildred took in an audible breath and looked at me.

"I guess that means you want me to shut up."

Chapter 14

Doorways to Hell

Red dirt billowed behind the bus when we turned into the entrance of the Chu Chi Tunnels. Just inside sat an olive-drab helicopter with US MARINES painted on its side. Its blades drooped. Further on, at the visitor's center, uniformed NVA soldiers waited to welcome our bus.

Once off the bus we milled around waiting for our NVA tour guide to tell us where we were going. A rifle shot made me flinch and I ducked towards cover. I searched the tree line for where I thought the shot came from. The NVA soldiers started laughing and told us in broken English that the rifle fire was just target practice. They said that for one US dollar we could fire off a round from an AK-47 at a human paper target.

"Fuck You," I whispered under my breath.

Our NVA tour guided stepped up, told us he was going to lead us, and then headed down a narrow path through bamboo. Our shoes kicked up the red dirt of the trail. We ended up at a small clearing and stood in a semi-circle around the soldier while he told us in good English about the tunnels of Cu Chi. His lapels were blood-red, the rest of his uniform a peculiar green. Standing with his arms across his chest he said, "The he Chu Chi Tunnels were first constructed in the 1940s. At that time we were fighting the French. Chu Chi is located 25 miles northeast of Ho Chi Minh City." The soldier went on to describe a vast network of underground facilities including hospitals, command headquarters, storage depots, ordinance factories and living facilities for the NVA.

The soldier continued, "Chu Chi was bombed more than any other place in Vietnam. The US attempted in vain to destroy the tunnel complex." A strange smile came to his face. "Today there is an industry that has arisen out of this historic calamity. Scrap metal reclamation has become a way some Vietnamese make a living. They pick up the pieces of the bombs you dropped."

The NVA soldier removed a flashlight from his pocket and motioned us towards a steep set of wooden stairs leading down into a dark hole in the earth. Several group members followed him. I stayed back, not interested in the earth grave. I rationalized I'd be safer between the limbos' of earth and sky.

Niki, the delegation tour guide, didn't go down either. He told me a about the last group of American tourists he'd brought here. "Several people had gone down into the tunnel. This lady pulls out her camera and snaps a picture of the group. The flash blinds everyone. A few months after we get back home I get this photo in the mail with a note asking me if I could identify the small snake coiled in the corner of the photo."

"Could you?" I asked, glad I'd stayed topside.

"It was a bamboo viper, one of the most deadly snakes in Vietnam."

I watched the group climb out of the hole. By now, everyone had dark blotches growing under their armpits; only the NVA solider looked fresh and clean.

At almost every meeting over the past several days we'd been listening to the horrible stories of the Vietnamese struggle during the war. We were told about the devastation we delivered, and we'd seen the tears of mothers. David suggested that we dispel some of this grief by having a tree planting ceremony in this most-bombed-out place.

"We will plant a sign of new life. It will be a tiny symbol against the thousands of tons of defoliant we dumped on their land."

We all agreed and bought a tree.

We found a large clearing and stood in a circle. David asked the NVA soldier if he could find us a shovel. Looking stunned by the request, he nodded and trundled off. I saw the soldier returning with a shovel and wondered how many shovels and shovelers it had taken to dig the vast network below our feet.

David asked the vets to form an inner circle and handed the shovel to Niki. He shoveled for a few minutes and offered the shovel to Larry A. One at a time we vets dug the hole.

Mario's wife Margie stepped from the outer circle and put her arms around her man. Margie is a lieutenant in the Air Force Reserves. She released him and turned to the group of vets. One at a time she saluted us and then gave each of us a hug, whispering how proud and thankful she was for what we did in the War.

We planted the tree, and the vets found their way back into the larger circle. Mildred then stepped into the circle, unfolding a crumpled piece of paper.

"I want to read a poem that I wrote many years ago to my boyfriend who was getting ready to leave for Vietnam. We had been planning to get married. He was drafted and right out of boot camp got orders to Nam. We spent long nights while he was on leave discussing how he might get out of it. A few days before he was scheduled to leave he told me he'd made up his mind to cut his foot off with a chainsaw. I begged him not to. I told him that the odds were very good he'd not go to the front lines and would be home in a year and we'd get married. I talked him out of hurting himself."

Mildred pulled a tissue from her pocket and wiped her nose.

"Three months after he left for Nam I got a call from his mother telling me he'd stepped on a land mine and was killed."

Mildred slumped over. Margie put her arm around her. Mildred couldn't read the poem, so Margie did.

Mildred's poem seemed to open a door for others to share stories about the war. Some told stories of War protests; some said a prayer; some asked for forgiveness. Vets remembered dead buddies. Then we walked back the narrow path to the parking lot and climbed the three steps up into the bus that would take us away.

Chapter 15

You Who Take Care of My Enemy's Graves

We left the Chu Chi Tunnels and drove down Highway One. Rice paddies and thatch-roofed hootches flashed by the bus windows. We rode in silence. Suddenly, I heard Dave speak to the bus driver.

"Please pull over."

The bus pulled to the side of the road. In front of us was a graveyard.

Larry A., my seatmate, nodded his head. "This is a scheduled stop. It's a Vietnamese War Memorial."

We'd been passing memorials like these from Hanoi to Ho Chi Minh City.

The group unloaded from the bus. I was full of feeling from Chu Chi and moved away from the group to be alone. I strode towards a large monolith at the far end of the cemetery aware that each marker represented someone I'd wanted to kill. Here I was walking over their bones.

I approached a man sweeping leaves at the far edge of the cemetery.

"Come here. I have something for you," I called.

He mumbled.

I called again.

He mumbled again.

I waved for him to come to me.

He looked away and said clearly, "I no come here."

"I want to give you money."

He turned away, both of us knowing it could never be enough.

Chapter 16

Heart of the Enemy

We were closing in on the end of the trip. Tired and sweat soaked we gathered in yet another large room and sat on folding chairs. The meeting was with an organization called the Social Development Program. General Nguyen Nam Diep and Dr. Pham Huy Dung from the Center for Support of Social Development were the speakers. I was exhausted from the trip to Chu Chi the day before so I'd skipped out on our morning trip and now regretted it because I'd missed speaking with VC vets. So now I ignored my fatigue.

General Diep's full head of dark hair and smooth face made him look ageless. Professor Dung interpreted for him, but sometimes he answered questions before the Professor had a chance to translate. Professor Dung was a squat, round-faced man with spectacles. He looked like a "geek", his white shirt threadbare at the elbows with two pens in the breast pocket. He started the session by telling us about the Vietnamese, giving us a detailed analysis of culture, health, technology, and sciences.

When Professor Dung finally stepped from the podium to let General Diep speak, we all felt a sense of relief from his statistical bombardment. The first thing General Diep said was that he'd been encouraging the Vietnam government to adopt a stance of acceptance regarding the US.

"We must forget the past and look to the future. We are seeking to become friends with all people, especially Americans."

His gold stars gleamed under the fluorescent lights as he told us, "The wounds of war are worst for the mothers. A mother I know lost nine of her children in the war. In one province there are 5,000 mothers who have lost more than five children each. There are over 300,000 dead that have not been found." Looking at each one of our delegation one at a time, General Diep finished, "Every family in Vietnam has lost someone."

A silence settled in the room. Professor Dung's eyes were full. When it came time for questions, Niki asked, "General Diep, sir, how do you feel about the men you have known that were killed by Americans?"

Dung translated the question and the General replied, "I'm 68 years old and have been in the military for 50 years. I fought the French, Chinese and Americans. Despite this history, war is not in the hearts of our people."

Larry Ashley was silently weeping. The General noticed.

"I have seen a lot of war, a lot of death. When I was fighting in Cambodia my troops had surrounded 5,000 Chinese soldiers. I had seen so much death at this point, there was no need for more. Instead of killing them or taking them prisoner, I sent a scout, telling them to retreat back to China and I would not follow."

His voice was quavering as he concluded, "The suffering of our enemy contributes to the suffering of us all." A tear dropped from his eye, and professor Dung placed his hand on the General's shoulder.

The meeting ended and Professor Dung told us that the General had invited the veterans of our group to a Vietnamese dinner the next evening.

Chapter 17

Wings of Freedom

At six the next morning in Ho Chi Minh City, I sat in the lobby of the Hotel Rex looking out a large plate glass window at a group of kids playing soccer in the street, the same street that last evening was filled with motor bikes no less than ten abreast, most with young men with their ladies on the back, out for a Friday night drive. I couldn't sleep and left the room so I wouldn't bother Larry A.

I watched an old man peddling a bicycle with loaves of fresh baked bread sticking up in his front basket. A kid tying his shoes sitting in the middle of the street waved to him. The old man pulled out a loaf and handed it to the boy. The scene stirred sadness in me.

Reaching into my pocket, I fingered the Air Crew Wings I brought from home. I ran my thumb over the etched ridges that formed the feathers, feeling the stars designating my combat missions. In the Marines some saw helicopter gunners as heroic.

That evening General Diep sent Professor Dung with a small bus to pick up our six-man veteran group at the hotel. The restaurant was located several miles out of town. As we drove, close-clustered hootches thinned out into farmland. Tree shadows bent long on the plowed red earth. We pulled up to a flat-roofed building that looked like an old gas station. It was made of cement, with a large open eating area. No other customers were in the restaurant. White plastic lawn chairs surrounded matching plastic tables that had been pushed together. Professor Dung and General Diep were seated at the head of the tables. We exchanged hellos and sat down.

It felt good to be with just the veterans. It was clear that at one time in our lives we'd all had a single focus: to kill. Beer was brought to the table and war stories began to flow. The waiters came continually with a variety of Vietnamese dishes, the grand finale a large fried fish decorated as if swimming on its plate. Its gills were extended and mouth open with a pink flower in it. With each course we drank more Vietnamese beer.

Professor Dung raised his hand and said, "General Diep would like to tell a story." The table went silent.

"It happened on the Perfume River, at night, before a large offensive. I was asked by Ho Chi Minh to meet him by a boat at the river's edge. We took the small boat to the middle of the river where no one could hear our conversation." General Diep paused and looked at each of us and raised his arm. "The moon reflected on the water. We made battle plans. Ho Chi Minh asked if he could recite a poem to me. I told him I'd be honored. I listened; then we returned to shore. I tried to sleep that night but was anxious about the upcoming battle, so I got up from bed and wrote a poem about talking on the river with Ho Chi Minh."

In the General's pause I asked, "Could you recite the poem for us, sir?"

He nodded.

What I remember of Professor Dung's translation is:

Voices travel great distances over water.

Starlight in the fish's eye.

A mother's tears drop to the river.

All Vietnam floods.

Everyone told the General how much they liked his poem and the party continued. It was getting late when I finally spoke to Professor Dung, asking him if he would translate what I had to say to the General. He said yes and I started.

"General Diep, Sir, I have brought with me my Crew Wings, the most honorable symbol I have of my war experience. I fired my weapon on your people. I tried hard to kill your people. I am not proud of killing. I want to give you these wings as a gesture of peace between us. Now I give up the hatred for the Vietnamese I have carried for years."

I walked around the table, stood before the general, handed him my wings, and saluted.

"General Diep, I too am a poet and would like to read you a poem I have written for this occasion."

If a man kills a man
He must dig two graves,
One in the earth for the dead man,
One in his heart, for the dead man's spirit,
Or he will not return.

Chapter 18

Ambush

On the last day of our ten-day tour we were to meet with former NVA and Viet Cong military leaders. Our group exited the bus and walked through a stone gateway. There was seriousness in our hushed voices. This was the meeting where we'd truly meet the enemy.

The meeting was chaired by General Vo Nguyen Giap, head of Vietnamese Veteran Affairs. General Giap was a four star General under Ho Chi Minh and served as Commander-in-Chief of the Viet Minh during the Vietnam War. Born in 1912, he had a long history of fighting against Chinese, Japanese and French occupation before US troops landed. In 1954, he made a reputation for brilliant logistics in the siege of Dien Bien Phu by successfully commanding 70,000 soldiers in the final defeat of the French. By 1959, he was in charge of the North Vietnamese guerrillas in the south, called Viet Cong. After the US left in 1975, he returned to Hanoi to become Minister of Defense.

Hoa, our guide, led us toward an official-looking building. Tension was growing in my stomach and sweat was running down the center of my back. Mildred tapped me on the shoulder.

"There's a dark spot on the back of your pants."

Tucking my chin in, I murmured, "Sorry."

She turned away, frightened.

Before we reached the room I slowed, allowing Mildred to catch up. I took her hand. "Mildred, I'm sorry. I'm just a little up tight. Please forgive me?"

She squeezed my hand and nodded her head in acceptance. "It's OK. I understand."

The six vets led the group into a narrow, dimly lit hallway with cracking green paint on the walls. The hallway emptied into a large, well-lit room. Tables had been arranged in a large square. Around the perimeter of the tables were wooden folding chairs. On one side was a red and yellow official placard with printed block letters that read VIETNAM. The communist flag was pinned on the wall. On the opposite side of the table was a hand-lettered cardboard sign that read USA with a tiny American flag. This meeting was different from any we'd been to before. In other meetings we sat together with the Vietnamese, but the boundary line here was absolutely clear.

There were only enough chairs at the table on our side for the six vets and the two delegation leaders. The rest of the delegation sat in chairs behind us. We took our seats. Across from us sat a deep bank of men in dress uniforms. There was only one woman in their group. A television crew occupied the other sides of the table, their extra lighting adding heat to the already stifling hot room. Large TV cables rested on the floor like snakes sleeping in the sun.

A small, tired-looking man stood up and introduced himself as General Giap. His black hair was streaked with gray. He looked to be in his 70's. His dark eyes poked at the American faces before him. He officially welcomed us, telling us that the gathering was to address the effects of chemical warfare on Vietnam's national welfare.

"Agent Orange continues to damage the forests and people of Vietnam," he said.

General Giap droned on about his Agent Orange agenda. Finally, David Read Johnson introduced himself and the veterans sitting at the table.

"We are happy to be here. We have spent ten days in your country. Our delegation is made up of physicians, nurses, psychologists and mental health counselors." David's arm swept up from his side toward us. "These men at this table are Vietnam veterans who fought here in the War.

"We are all here to learn as much as we can today about your country. We are impressed with the strength of your people. We have talked with Vietnamese who say they still carry a heavy burden from the terrible destruction in your country, which is a beautiful country."

David stopped and moved his head from side to side to take in his audience.

"As Americans we also carry a burden. Many of the people before you are still suffering from the War. This opportunity to speak with you is very important. Many people within our group want to help your people with the traumas from the War. We are interested in what you are doing for your war veterans, not only medical treatment for those who suffered from chemical warfare and dioxin, but also the treatment for spiritual trauma, nightmares, depression, sadness, isolation, hearing voices of their dead soldiers and friends. These problems some American veterans still experience. We are interested in your questions. We hope today you will address these issues with the veterans before you. Thank you."

David bowed his head, surrendering the floor.

A thin, gray-haired man stood up. His legs were shaking as he walked up to a tripod where he unfurled a map. He spoke broken English, introducing himself as Dr. Hai Van Trung from the Center for Ecology. Trung told us that chemical warfare continues to wreak a silent havoc, causing birth defects and ruining agriculture. He indicated several regions affected by Agent Orange.

"Defoliation was aimed at depriving our army from protecting themselves." He snapped his pointer against the map, and it made a sound like a round going off. "Over 72,000 tons of Agent Orange were sprayed on Vietnam. Vietnam was once 40% forest; now it is 14% to 29% forest." He reiterated these facts over and over, drilling us with his jittery whine. It felt like he would never stop. Then he flicked a switch on a projector that threw a picture of a child with no legs against the blank wall. For 15 minutes we watched pictures of children with birth defects, crops that wouldn't grow, as well as attempts at replanting trees that could not take root in the poisonous soil.

Our delegation was not prepared to address the issue of Agent Orange. We were mental health professionals. It felt like we'd been ambushed by an old man with too many facts.

We vets looked at David. He raised his eyebrows indicating that now was not an appropriate time to interrupt. Trung finally shut off the projector, and General Giap introduced those at his side of the table. There were several high-ranking men: a colonel who was a medical doctor, a woman who was a doctor in the War and was now a minister in the government, two other colonels who were psychiatrists from a nearby hospital. General Giap told us that all of them had served with either the Viet Cong or NVA Army during the War.

General Giap motioned to Dr. Trung to finish his presentation, but David rose to his feet and bowed.

"General Giap, please excuse me for the interruption but our intention is to discuss the issues of PTSD."

"We think it was good to look at this film," the general replied. "Now you can ask questions."

David sat down. "General Giap, how many veterans are in your veterans' association?"

"Our organization embraces all who fought for independence, in all wars-- the French resistance and the war with the US."

Mario Mercado asked, "How many of your veterans suffer from Agent Orange poisoning?"

"We have 4 to 5 million veterans in our country. There are a higher percentage of birth defects in Vietnamese than in any of the people in surrounding countries. American scientists have come to our country and have found higher levels of dioxin in the blood of our veterans than in American veterans."

The General's eyes seemed to harden on Mario.

"We're learning more and more about the effects of Agent Orange and are happy to provide information to your doctors and scientists," said David.

I stood up and asked, "How do the Vietnam veterans at your table deal with their anger towards American veterans?"

All heads seemed to turn. A loud silence filled the room.

General Giap spoke. "We used to hate Americans but don't worry about these things anymore. Our hatred is of the past. The world is changing, like the goodwill for our people demonstrated by you coming here. We want to achieve friendship between our peoples."

A chair screeched and one of the VC colonels stood. Pointing his finger at me, he said through clenched teeth, "I don't know your name, so I'll address you as Friend. Your question was how we deal with anger towards Americans. Frankly speaking, I hate Americans. I suffer from the War and specifically the chemical war. My wife died because of the Agent Orange you people sprayed. I hate Americans. Anger is still in my heart."

He stopped and took in a deep breath to control his emotions. Then he continued, "Perhaps some of you personally sprayed Agent Orange, and if someone here did spray..," The colonel looked towards General Giap. "...I want these things to be in the past. There was misunderstanding in the past; now there is understanding. Perhaps my anger can become history. I will try to push it aside."

"Thank you for your honesty," David replied. "We appreciate your comments. We do not ask you to give up your anger; however, we are in agreement that we can build friendship. We cannot erase history. Let us create a new history beginning today."

Niki stood. "General Giap sir, an American general once said, 'No one hates war more than the soldier who fights in war.' The fact that, today, we can meet in this conference where before we met on the battlefield, proves people can move beyond war. The purpose of this delegation is to bring people together. It's a privilege for us to be here today, and perhaps in years to come, you can meet with us in the United States."

General Giap nodded.

David spoke. "Many years ago we dropped bombs on you; they did not work. Today we will try poetry." David then motioned to me.

I stood and pointed my finger at the colonel who'd spoken about losing his wife. "I wrote this poem for you, my friend, who just spoke about his hatred for Americans."

I had arranged with Hoa, our interpreter, to translate my poem as I read it.

Viet Cong,

The spirit that I have taken from your heart

From your country

From your land

From your people

From your beauty

From your soul

From your mothers

From your fathers

From your children

I return to you.

I am one man.

I have lived with sadness

Holding your spirit prisoner in my heart.

Forgive me.

The TV camera stopped and stillness filled the room.

In a spontaneous gesture, David said, "Now may we come across the table and meet with you one-on-one?"

We led the way, moving single file towards the Vietnamese. Hands extended, we entered the crowd of green uniforms. Arms encircled shoulders, muffled slaps on backs. Tears squeezed out the corners of the eyes of both sides.

Two old men approached me. One man who had been the interpreter introduced the other man as his friend. They danced from foot to foot in front of me like school children. The interrupter asked if he could have the original of my poem. He explained that he and his friend would share the poem. I handed the poem to them. It was as if

I'd given children candy. They bowed in unison. I placed my hands together before me and bowed to them.

I caught Niki's arm and whispered, "I'm here to report no casualties, no dead, Sir!"

Chapter 19

Home for Good

As I packed to go home, I thought of the man I'd seen on the streets of Ho Chi Minh City who'd lost his legs when he'd stepped on a land mine. He got around using his arms to push what looked like an automotive dolly. When I gave him a $20 bill, his face it looked like he'd struck gold. Twenty bucks could feed a family for a month in Vietnam. A friend in the States gave me the money to give to someone in need. There were so many in need.

In Hong Kong we had our last meal together and exchanged addresses and phone numbers. David and Hadar asked me if I'd come and speak to the vets at West Haven Veterans Hospital; Niki wanted to know if I'd read a travel article he'd written about the trip; Larry Ashley and I said we'd stay in touch and maybe work out some way that we could come to teach at each other's hospitals.

Cathay Pacific Flight #202 lowered its landing gear and blue smoke jetted from the tires as we touched down at 3:30 p.m. Los Angeles time. At the exit gate, we scattered like birds frightened from a tree to various parts of the United States.

My flight to Stewart Airport was not until the next day. The hotel shuttle took me to the Marriott. I was spent and yearned to lie down on a soft bed. On the trip from Hong Kong my large frame was crammed into a middle seat with two equally large men on either side.

The first thing I did when I got to my room was to take a shower. I let the luxurious hot water pound the back of my neck for 20 minutes. Even though we'd stayed in the best accommodations in Vietnam, the hot water dribbled.

I closed the shades, trying to block out the daylight, and rolled back the sheets. When I closed my eyes, a kaleidoscope of pictures started behind my eyelids. I'd taken too much in. Vietnam whirled in my head and I knew only the familiar would help it stop--like Helise's face. I got out of bed and called the airline for an earlier flight. I booked a red-eye, not caring about the extra 50 bucks, or the $150 I'd spent on the hotel room.

By the time I arrived at Stewart all my time anchors had been cut free. I floated between time zones. Helise and Peter met me at the baggage claim. After a warm welcome, I melted into the front seat of the car. Helise started asking questions and I responded as best I could.

"It was great; I think I got what I went back for... No, I didn't get sick... I saw the exact places I was stationed the first time I was in there... The people are so poor; kids were begging everywhere... I spoke to generals... I read a poem to the Viet Cong... I left my passport in the hotel safe and they had to have it sent through Vietnam mail; it was amazing it got there. I was afraid I wouldn't be able to leave without it..."

Then I started with my questions: "How's my Mom...? Did she have to go in the hospital...? Did you speak to Jamie...?"

"Mom's fine, I called her several times... Jamie wasn't home for many of the calls I made. I did speak to him a week ago and he sounded tired, but fine. He asked how you were doing."

Peter was silent as he drove us home. Then, as we got off the Thruway, he asked, "So, brother, did you find him over there?"

"Looked high and low, saw signs, but God's a little like those MIAs that nobody's ever seen."

"You said you left Him over there, so I figured you'd know where to look."

"I'm gonna have to develop the pictures to see if He's in any of them."

I'd once told Pete, "I lost God in Vietnam." I said I'd taken him there with me but came back without him.

As we got out of the car Peter said, "I thought about you a lot. I prayed for you."

"Thanks, brother." We embraced.

Helise and I made our way into the house. I petted the cats, kicked off my shoes and made my way up to the bedroom. Once in bed,

I fell into Helise's arms, letting the weeks of tension and fear come out in a dirge against her chest.

I cried for a long time. She asked no questions.

Chapter 20

Return to Life

The long night's sleep I desperately wanted wasn't in my luggage when I unpacked. I continued to spin the sheets. I was still untangling what I seen in Nam. I'd thought I'd have an epiphany, but instead, new material had been unearthed for me to sort through.

I settled back into my routine of going to work at Four Winds Hospital. I loved working there because I got to see daily how good I had it. Many of the patients I dealt with were suicidal or traumatized in some way. It felt good to be able to help them, and at the same time, they were a great comparison for me to see how good my own life had become.

About a year after I got back from Nam, Helise and I decided to go on a well deserved vacation. We both love to read and started collecting books to bring. I brought Robert McNamara's new book In Retrospect. It almost ruined our vacation. As I lay in the Caribbean sun, I read McNamara's acknowledgment of his catastrophic mistakes during the war. By the time I finished the book I was enraged. He was just an old man singing his swan song. It was more like one last chance on center stage than an apology to the 58,000 dead soldiers.

After I returned home, I wrote a response:

My Response to <u>In Retrospect</u>:

The first line in Robert McNamara's book is "This is a book I planned never to write." I wonder what he planned to do? This reminded me of my father telling me 20 years too late that he never really planned to beat the shit out of me.

Old men are bastards. They act like bastards most of their lives and before they die they tell you they're sorry. Abraham took his boy up the on mountain where he tied him up and held a knife over his head. Then he made up some crap about God

telling him to let the boy go. Robert took 58,000
men up his mountain and 30 years later he tells us
he should have let them go...

After Robert McNamara's book, I started to understand that it
might not be a soldier's job to make reparations, but instead, the job of
the people who sent him.

I'd become fully engaged at work, running 12 groups for Four
Winds Hospital and three outside men's groups. The gift of returning to
Vietnam had finally come: I was sleeping deeper than I had since high
school.

Chapter 21

You're A MF -- In the Good Sense of the Word

It was a warm spring day when I stepped into the courtyard of Main House, the psychiatric unit where I worked at Four Winds. I stopped by a large butterfly bush that had just bloomed. The day before, I'd watched a hummingbird moth gathering pollen from its purple flowers. The courtyard was a place for patients to sit in the sun, smoke or just get out of the building.

I bent to smell one of the pollen-powdered blossoms and noticed a thin line of smoke circling up from behind the bush. As I pushed aside some branches to see what was going on, a voice bounced out at me.

"Chieu Hoi."

"Di di mau," came out of my mouth automatically.

I saw a Black man with his back against the stone wall, smoking a cigarette. He started at my words and was trying to disentangle himself from the bush.

In Vietnamese, Chieu Hoi means Open Arms or I Give Up. My response meant Move Your Ass Out Here Quickly!

"Are you OK?" I asked.

"OK, Sir. Can't stand anyone at my back."

"Are you a Vet?" I waited for an answer, which didn't come. "My name's Larry; I'll see you later."

I left the man standing with his cigarette dangling from his mouth. I was late for an 8:30 a.m. meeting.

I pulled a chair up to a table of nurses, psychiatrists and social workers, who were all listening to a nurse read the morning report. James Davis, a thin, clear-eyed man who'd once worn an earring but had long since exchanged it for a blue suit and short cropped hair, turned towards me.

"Larry, you're a Vietnam vet, aren't you? I got a new patient in last night who's a vet. He presents with PTSD, drug, alcohol abuse, and depression. His medical chart reads like a novel. He's been in enough rehabs and psychiatric hospitals to be able to teach recovery. He's angry one minute, self-deprecating the next. Since you're a vet I though he might listen to you. Could you work with him in your group? He just made faces at me when I told him I'd never been in the service."

"Tell me more, so I know who I'm looking at," I said.

"He's a 52-year-old black male who spent two tours in Nam. He has nightmares about women and children he killed there. He's been drinking and drugging since he came back in 1965. At most he's got one year collective sobriety. Been married four times, and has eight children, two with each wife. He came in intoxicated. From the few stories he told me I think it's a miracle he's alive."

"What branch of the service?"

"He said he was a Jarhead; that's Marines, isn't it?

Knocking my fist against my head, I replied, "I think so."

"He said he wants to forgive the Vietnamese for what they did to him and his buddies."

"I wonder if he doesn't want to be forgiven, himself, for what he did to them. I think I met your man already; he was hiding behind the butterfly bush in the courtyard. What's his name?"

"John."

"I'll have him in my 1:30 group. I'll keep an eye on him and see what I can do."

Patients straggled into the large living room. The first arrivals were several kids with hair cropped at odd lengths angling up off their heads, sporting scared-to-death looks. Then came hardcore heroin addicts with wizened faces and pill popping housewives who blamed their addiction on the generous doctors who filled their prescriptions. All the patients in this group were dual diagnosed with both substance abuse and psychiatric disorders.

John did not show up. I started by introducing myself. I was half way though my spiel when John stuck his head in the door, surveyed the room and then sauntered in. Pulling a chair from a stack, he placed it in the corner and sat.

"John, come join us in the circle," I said, waving my arm.

"Nah, I'll be OK here."

His voice had an edge, so I decided not to push. I started around the group asking each patient to introduce him or her self. Then I launched into my preamble.

"My name is Larry. This group's called DGT, which stands for Directive Group Therapy. I recited the guidelines and presented the final rule:

"If you are here because you are interested in working on your issues and you want help, tell me you're in. If you don't want to be in the hospital and you're here to please someone outside the hospital, or you're here so you won't lose your job or go to jail, you can choose to be out and there will be no penalty, no consequence. Choosing to be out is a courtesy to me and the rest of the group, letting us know you don't want to waste our time. Is everyone with me?"

I started around the group. After asking if they were in or not, I asked each patient to bring an issue to the floor that had to do with why they were in the hospital. I explained that the second time I came around I would look deeper into their issue. John had his head is down; I wasn't sure he was awake. When I got to him he lifted his head.

"I'm out."

He was the only one in the group who'd chosen to be out.

I decided to push him a little.

"What brought you to the hospital, John?"

"I thought you said I didn't have to participate if I said I was out."

"I did say that, but I thought you might at least let us know why you're here. Most people have a good reason for coming."

"Listen man, you made a rule and turned right around and broke it. I'm here because I can't sleep. I hear the screams of the women and children I killed in Nam. You happy now, man? Did you get what you wanted?"

His tone was so angry several patients started fidgeting in their seats.

"Sorry I pushed you. I promise I'll step back. Let me know when you're ready to talk. Could I ask you one last question?"

John rolled his eyes up into his head and pointed his chin to the ceiling.

"What branch of the service were you in?"

"Marines!"

"So was I," I said looking into his eyes. "When were you in country?"

"65-66-67. You?"

"69-70," I said, scanning the group members to see how they were taking this.

I moved on to other patients, knowing if I kept the focus on John too long I'd loose him. I finished the group, and all the patients left the room except for John. He came up to me. Sticking out his hand, and smiling, he asked, "What unit you in?"

"Air Wing. HMM 262 Flying Tigers."

"See action?"

"Flew helicopter gunner."

"No shit! What the Hell you doing here?"

"Helping people."

"Do you dream about Nam?"

"Not as much as I used to. I went back a year ago and put some of it behind me."

"You're shitting me. You went back? Why?"

311

"So I could sleep again."

John had been in several of my groups by mid-week and he was beginning to speak more. A few days of sobriety and some psychiatric medication seemed to calm his anxiety enough that he started coming out of himself. In the last group before the weekend John asked, "Can I use the group to tell some of my Vietnam story?"

I looked around at the patients and tried to assess whether they could handle what I imagined John was going to say.

"Sure, John. Why don't you start?"

He took off his ball cap and picked at his hair. "This is going to take a little time. Can I have extra time?"

I knew he'd been working himself up to do this. His hands were shaking, and his words vibrated with nervousness. His left foot was hopping as if it were connected to someone else's body.

"Take whatever time you need."

"I was walking point with 12 of my buddies behind me. It had been quiet for days. Whenever it was quiet too long, we got edgy. It's funny how no action made us more nervous. It gave us too much time to think about when the shit was gonna hit."

Some patients in the room began to shake as John forced his voice through his clenched teeth.

"I was on my belly moving through elephant grass, checking for trip wires, when the rip of a machinegun tore into the grass just behind me. I turned to see two of my friends twisting on the ground. Then they got loose and slack. Weapons fire opened up everywhere. I got into a crouch and ran for the tree line. Only four of us made it. The VC let me pass right under their noses so they could kill us all. The four of us made our way back through thick jungle to the platoon. I told the captain what happened. He called in an air strike. When the Phantoms finished we made our way back."

Looking at me with tears on his cheeks, he said, "You know Marines never leave their dead."

I nodded, knowing exactly what he meant.

"When we got back into the area we met no resistance, not a fucking shot. Our men were lying in a circle. I knew all their names. They'd been disemboweled. The place stunk of shit. Ribbons of guts were spread all over the grass. Billy Jasper's penis and balls were stuffed in his mouth. My man Johnson had a conical hat jammed on his head and one of his arms contorted into a salute. I went to boot camp with Johnson. I met his mama in Philly. She cried for so long the day Johnson and I left for Nam that she lost her voice. In the end she couldn't say good-bye. She just mouthed the words.

"Then the chopper came to take our dead. We made our way to the nearby village where we figured the VC had gone to hide. Rifle fire broke out from two hootches. It was supposed to be a friendly village. The captain split us into two squads, each taking one side of the village. It was quiet for a little while. Then I heard M-16s unloading on automatic. My squad moved to the center of the village. Dole spotted two VC running out the back of a hootch, and we emptied all we had into them.

"A little child came running out of a hootch; what was left of his arm was flopping. He swung his little piece of arm in the air; blood splattered my uniform. I unloaded my weapon into him. A young woman screamed. She'd been wounded and was crawling out of the hootch toward the child. She yelled so fucking loud I fired into her."

All of us were holding our breaths. John stared at the floor. I was so deep into his story my head was spinning. I'd put faces on the woman and child. The window was open, and the sounds of children squealing in the swimming pool came in.

Time had run out and I had to end the group. I asked John to wait after group so I could speak with him. He made his way up to me after everyone left. Lifting his head he said softly, "I hate those mother-fuckers."

I placed my hand on his shoulder. "You have lived some hard times, my friend. Why do you think these people keep coming to you in your dreams?"

"I don't know man. Maybe it's because I got kids."

"You came to the hospital to work this shit out, didn't you?"

"I want to stop hearing that screaming."

"Maybe you could write a letter of forgiveness to that mother and child?"

"Man, I can't do that!" John looked into my face. "You helped me, man. I never told anyone that story before. You're a motherfucker."

Startled, I squinted at him.

"I mean in the good sense of the word."

John turned and walked out, leaving me to wonder what I'd have done if I were him. It's one thing to be at the stock end of a machinegun firing at a tree line 500 yards away. It's a whole other thing to kill someone whose eyes you look into.

John was discharged over the weekend. When I came to work on Monday, a nurse handed me an envelope a letter inside:

> *Larry,*
>
> *You know you asked if I could write a letter of forgiveness to the mother and child I shot. Last night I had a dream and in the dream I saw the faces of some of my close buddies who got killed over there and I realize that I really don't give a fuck about the VN people who got killed by me and the other Marines. I am sorry that I didn't kill more of the slope head slant eyed bastards. The South VN Army were cowards, I believe half of them were V.C. sympathizers. I hate them for what they did to us. All we were doing was fighting for our lives. I remember places like Duc Pho, Ounag Ni, Phu Bi, Elephant Valley, The Rock Pile, and other places where we fought for our lives. We were not fighting for America, but we were fighting to just stay alive. I remember operations Junction City, Star Light, Oregon, Colorado etc. I remember the Fifth Marines were immobilized with just enough manpower to man the lines at*

314

Duc Phu--150 Marines coming back with 83
men, the rest being dead or wounded. I remember
the cowardliness of the ARVN soldiers and how
they would sell us out when the shit got hot. I hated
them and I hated the war. The truth is I enjoyed
killing them and I am sorry I didn't kill more. I
remember us Marines never leaving our dead and
wounded behind. Those slant eye slope-head
bastards owe us an apology. I remember the Tenth
Marines-- the walking dead--and how we relieved
them at a place called Can Thee Mt. I remember
the look on their faces when they came back from
patrol. I don't give a fuck about any of those gooks
that I killed and who were killed, maimed or
wounded by me or anyone. The South Korean
Army had the right idea and that was that every
single round should be used to kill every
motherfucker in the area that is living. I am sorry
that I didn't kill more of them. Men, women and
children, fuck them. I remember sleeping, eating,
shitting in the rain during the monsoon season. I
hated war, but I loved being with the finest bravest
men I ever met. There has never been anyone in the
world as dedicated and loyal as these fighting men.
I started writing this letter of apology but my head
couldn't think it and my hand wouldn't write it.
Some of the finest bravest Marines gave the
ultimate for their country and the Corps. I thought
about when I went to the memorial and found the
names of the brave men who died for nothing but
honor and Corps. I don't mean to leave out the
Army, Air Force, and Navy. I loved my comrades
in arms and I am not going to disrespect them by
betraying them with the feeling that I did something
wrong. Fuck that Larry, it was the politicians who
fucked up.

Now don't get me wrong Larry. I hate the NVA, but I respect them as warriors. Every infantry 0311 man would have to say that they respected those gooks because they fought their asses off for what they believed in. I salute General Giap for his tactics. He was one smart general. Smarter than Westmoreland and more dedicated. Some people say we lost the war, but if we did, they didn't lose it while I was there. I love my brother Marines who were willing to give their lives in a place we never knew existed before the Vietnam War. I celebrated my 19th birthday on the way there and my 20th in country. I had a kind of survivors guilt but now I know I did my best, it is just that my number didn't come up. I was wounded mentally and physically but I still love my comrades who died in a hopeless, useless war. As far as the VN people were concerned, I will always hate them, but I will always respect them because they stood up to some of the baddest, bravest fighting men in the world. I don't feel sorry for them anymore because in War "SHIT HAPPENS"

Cpl. E-4

John

****

Dear John:

I am sorry you left before I could talk with you. I got your letter and wanted to respond. As you know, I was also a Marine. In our conversation I mentioned I went back to Nam in 1994. What I didn't tell you was that I went back to ask the Vietnamese for "forgiveness" for what I had done in the War. Having read your letter, it feels strange

*to tell you what I did. I gave my Aircrew Wings to
General Diep. I gave him my wings as a symbol of
forgiveness. I explained to the general that I didn't
want to be in Nam killing his people but my
country gave me no choice.*

*Like you, I found myself in a war that I did not
believe in. But my primary goal, like yours, was to
stay alive. What you did in Vietnam was what I
feared I'd have to do. I didn't murder women or
children. I don't have the same pictures behind my
eyes that you do. I can only imagine the pain and
confusion you live with. The truth is, there is still a
part of me that thinks you're a hero, a real
Marine, one who killed the way he was taught.
You lived that War; I flew above it. Your hands
killed; I administered a distant death. I could hear
no screams because every sound was drowned out by
the whopping of the chopper blades.*

*You were courageous. You did not leave your dead
behind, and you will not betray them now. You
have sacrificed your soul for those who sacrificed
their lives. When you were in the hospital, I
wanted you to ask the women and child you killed
for forgiveness. It was wrong of me to think what
was good for me would be good for you. I apologize
for not understanding. Perhaps you deserve your
rage. You earned your hatred honestly. Only God
should stand in judgment of what you did. The
saddest part is that you have become your own
enemy. The drugs, the dreams and the guilt have
become your weapons of self-destruction. Perhaps it
is self-forgiveness you seek.*

*A good friend once told me he thought it was
possible to un-make a Marine. I know now he was
mistaken. I also know it's a damned good idea to
try.*

Semper Fi!

Lawrence J. Winters, U.S.M.C. Cpl E-4

The End

About the Author

Born and raised in New Paltz, NY, Larry Winters entered the United States Marine Corps after high school and served in Vietnam 1969-1970. Twenty-five years later, by then a licensed mental health counselor at Four Winds Hospital in Katonah, he returned to Vietnam with other health care professionals to study P.T.S.D. in the Vietnamese people and to make peace with his past. Larry is a widely published poet, men's group leader and group psychotherapist.

For more information on this writer and poet visit

www.makingandunmaking.com

About The Publisher

The Millrock Writers Collective was formed by a group of writers presently located in New York's Hudson Valley with the intent of publishing the quality poetry, fiction, and non-fiction of its members. The Collective provides an organized means, outside traditional publishing routes, for its writers to gain substantive input into the editing and publishing processes.

The efforts of the MWC are intended to stimulate the interest of the public in work that is compelling and honest, and to act as a springboard for the future success of these works in the marketplace.

www.millrockwirters.com

Links to Larry's favorite websites:

- The Millrock Writers Collective is a group of writers in the New Paltz, NY area interested in publishing high quality work on a small scale.
www.millrockwriters.com

- Steve Lewis, Writer Author, father, grandfather, freelance writer, workshop leader, speaker, mentor and master wordsmith whose gift for insightful critique and unflagging encouragement is unsurpassed. www.SteveLewisWriter.com

- John Lee Online Author and consultant. Books include *The Flying Boy*, *Growing Yourself Back Up*, and *THE MISSING PEACE: Solving The Anger Problem For Alcoholics/Addicts and Those Who Love Them* www.jlcsonline.com

- Bibliodrama, playing with White Fire. Peter Pitzele, Ph.D's role-playing that invites participants to find their voices in the text and the text's voice in themselves. www.bibliodrama.com

- Soldier's Heart, a project of International Humanities Center. Dr. Edward Tick, author of "War and the Soul "and founder of Soldier's Heart

- Sanctuary, a Center for Mentoring the Soul, is committed to creating an effective healing environment for individuals and communities by using modern therapies combined with the wisdom of traditional cultures. www.mentorthesoul.com

- vision4hope "When All Else Fails" by Jeffrey Vreeland
vision4hope.com

- <u>Voices in Wartime Education Project</u>. Healing the Wounds of War, Creating a Less Violent World. <u>www.voicesinwartime.org</u>

- <u>"Strong at the Broken Places: Turning Trauma to Recovery"</u> by <u>Cambridge Documentary Films</u>

- <u>Flying Tigers of HMH 361</u> (Al's Vietnam Home Page) <u>vietnam.northfork.net</u>

- <u>VA National Center for PTSD report</u> on a 1994 delegation to Vietnam entitled "Uncovering PTSD In The Republic Of Vietnam" by David Read Johnson, Ph.D., and Hadar Lubin, M.D.

- <u>Post Traumatic Stress Center</u>   A clinic specializing in the evaluation, treatment, and training for Posttraumatic Stress Disorder New Haven CT <u>www.ptsdcenter.com</u>

Two Poems by Larry Winters

OLD MEN ARE BASTARDS

The first line in Robert McNamara's book is:
"This is a book I planned never to write."
I wonder what he planned to do?
Reminds me of my father telling me 20 years later
he never really planned to beat the shit out of me.

Old men are bastards.
They act like bastards most of your life
and before they die they tell you they're sorry.

Abraham started it when he took his boy up the mountain.
tied him up and held a knife over his head.
Then he made up some crap about God, and let the boy go.

Thanks old man.
This is a poem I planned never to write.
But you wrote your book.
I wish you had found a ram on that mountain you old bastard.

FOOTPRINTS

They came down in their footprints.
Just like they were designed to, said the engineer.
Their gigantic feet squashing six thousand lives.
Six thousand lives, crushed six thousand times on our TVs.
Six thousand stories multiplied by sixty thousand storytellers.

They came down in their footprints.
Our brains and hearts force-fed on terror and grief.
A dreadful mantle lies over our shoulders it has taken our breath.
Tightened our stomachs.

They came down in their footprints.
Their giant footfalls shuddered America.
Our remote controls spread panic like a virus.

They came down in their footprints.
Shivering our land of the free.
We flex muscles like a colossal country bumpkin.
A stumbling giant whose been cut on the face.

They came down in their footprints.
The bar fighter circled with a broken beer bottle.
A Cyclopean stagger.
A Goliath's roar trembled the curtains in a distant land.
Looking to strike we saw only the saloon doors swinging.
Like the last inches of a viper's tail disappearing in the rocks.

They came down in their footprints.
Fists full of empty air.
We listen for the sound of the next footfall.